"A deep dive into the depressing world of grifters, bullsh★t artists, plagiarists and long con experts turbocharged by the Internet—and what, if anything, separates those scammers from some of our most respected captains of industry. Fyre Festival, Bluestone makes clear, may have been a low-water mark so far in the history of empty hype—but the tide, as ever, just keeps rolling out."

ANNA MERLAN, author of *Republic of Lies: American Conspiracy Theorists and Their Surprising Rise to Power*

"*Hype* is the best kind of nonfiction: juicy, sharp, savage and wildly entertaining, with a celebrity behaving badly on every page. What more could you want?"

CAT MARNELL, *New York Times*-bestselling author of *How to Murder Your Life*

"Gabrielle Bluestone is one of the most gifted chroniclers of American culture working today because she is one of the coolest people alive. In *Hype*, she delivers the story of what the f★ck is wrong with us as only she can: with detailed reporting that skewers the subjects who deserve it—and without an ounce of sanctimony—while taking us for a ride so fun that, by the end, it takes you a second to realize that *Hype* may have indicted you, too (she is a lawyer, after all). We may not deserve this book, but we do need it. *Hype* is the most fun, most outrageous, and—most of all—most true book of the year."

OLIVIA NUZZI, author and Washington correspondent, *New York* magazine

"Scams are hot right now, and Bluestone covers the hottest here." *Booklist*

Hype

Hype

How Scammers, Grifters, Con Artists and
Influencers Are Taking Over the Internet –
and Why We're Following

Gabrielle Bluestone

HarperCollins*Publishers*

HarperCollins*Publishers*
1 London Bridge Street
London SE1 9GF

www.harpercollins.co.uk

HarperCollins*Publishers*
1st Floor, Watermarque Building, Ringsend Road
Dublin 4, Ireland

First published in the US by Hanover Square Press 2021
This UK edition published by HarperCollins*Publishers* 2021

1 3 5 7 9 10 8 6 4 2

A catalogue record of this book is
available from the British Library

HB ISBN 978-0-00-838264-3
PB ISBN 978-0-00-843867-8

Printed and bound in Great Britain by
CPI Group (UK) Ltd, Croydon

MIX
Paper from
responsible sources
FSC™ C007454

This book is produced from independently certified FSC™ paper
to ensure responsible forest management.

For more information visit: www.harpercollins.co.uk/green

For my parents, Janet and Andrew Bluestone,
who were right about (almost) everything.

Table of Contents

Introduction

Like most people, my first glimpse of the Fyre Festival was on Instagram. The slick commercial venture exploded onto America's social media feeds in December of 2016, as hundreds of verified influencers—blue-check Instagram celebrities with tens of millions of combined followers—started posting the same ambiguous burnt sienna square, suggesting their fans *#joinme* by purchasing tickets to the mysterious event. The festival organizers who had hired the internet stars to promote the event were promising ticket buyers "two transformative weekends" of fabulous luxury on a private island formerly owned by Pablo Escobar, where they'd be flown in on private jets, pampered by a dedicated wellness team and nourished with meals designed by Starr Catering. A follow-up commercial—a medley of half-naked twenty-something models interspersed with stock footage of other music festivals—subsequently went viral, and *Vogue* immediately deemed it the "supermodel antidote to the winter blues," recommending the festival as a way to "preemptively fix that Coachella

FOMO."[1] (*Vogue* has since edited any references to Fyre from the piece, though it lives on in the URL.)

That was enough for me to know as a consumer that the event wasn't for me, and as a journalist, I probably would have let the whole thing pass me by, had a guy I had gone to high school with not put together his own little Instagram commercial on his private account, flaunting his VIP Artist Pass wristbands and outlining, slide by slide, all the outrageous amenities guaranteed by the festival organizers.

Suddenly I felt anxious. Was I about to miss the party of a lifetime? I clicked the link to find out.

What I found there made no sense. The site was offering $250,000 ticket packages with yachts and private chefs, yet it looked like it had been designed in a high-school coding class. The text promised slick, intoxicating luxury beyond comprehension, but outside of a commercial shoot interspersed with obvious stock footage, there were no photos to back any of up. The headliner for this supposedly exclusive luxury event was Blink-182, a band that peaked when I was in elementary school, which I will just say generally was…quite a long time ago.

Now I was extremely interested, but not for the reasons Fyre Media CEO Billy McFarland and his cohorts were hoping. Quite simply, I smelled a scam. And I wasn't the only one. At least two men—one with connections to the music industry, and one with connections to the Bahamas—had already taken the dramatic step of registering social media accounts and websites to anonymously warn consumers that this thing was never going to happen. It seemed so obvious something was terribly wrong.

The most incredible part of the whole thing was that no one was listening.

Even my editors at *VICE* News, focused as they were on

international stories and war documentaries, were initially dismissive. "A music festival that was overhyped? Not sure that's a *VICE* story," one of them told me. I've joked that getting my initial story on the Fyre Festival published felt a lot like trying to convert to Judaism, but in the end it wasn't that far off base: I had to pitch it three times before the editorial *beit din* saw the now-legendary cheese sandwich photos on social media and decided it was go time. And even then, they only allowed me to cover it in text, rejecting requests to send a *VICE News Tonight* camera crew to the island to capture the disaster in real time. (Luckily, between the Fyre organizers' own cameras and the hundreds of tech savvy millennials stranded in the gravel pit, there was plenty of footage to go around.)

I've often wondered if the breakdown was due to my failure to appropriately describe the story I had stumbled into, or if the adults in the room's failure to recognize it reflected just how normalized pure, substantive-free hype had become. After all, Fyre's influencer blitz had yielded immediate returns on social media, which triggered national press coverage, which gave the whole endeavor a patina of legitimacy. Within hours of the Instagram onslaught, the Fyre Festival name was everywhere—on Facebook, Instagram, and Twitter; on news websites; and even old-fashioned but still-coveted TV segments. Marketers involved in the campaign estimated 95 percent of the festival's tickets were sold in that first week, even though, as the world later discovered, the festival they sold consumers never even came close to existing. As we all know now, that divide between Instagram and reality resulted in the *Lord of the Flies*–esque chaos seen 'round the world, as hundreds of well-heeled millennials were trapped in the Bahamas with not much more than a wet mattress and an

Instagram Story to show for the thousands of dollars they'd invested in the experience.

But as I followed the story past the initial Bahamian disaster into Billy McFarland's felony arrest, surprise felony rearrest, and federal sentencing, it became clear to me that there was something bigger at play: the natural end point of a society primed to trust their own emotions over objective, verifiable facts, in a world that tends to value the signifiers of success over actual achievements.

I saw it as I broke the story of the Fyre Festival implosion for *VICE* News,[2] and it continued as I executive-produced the Emmy-nominated Netflix documentary *Fyre: The Greatest Party That Never Happened*. Along the way, I learned a whole lot about how scams are thriving in the age of social media— and how often we've collectively agreed as a society to treat hype as an indicator that we're playing with the real deal.

These dynamics played out in a number of ways through- out my reporting on Fyre. At first I thought the story had reached its zenith when Billy McFarland, then twenty-five years old, was arrested in the summer of 2017 and charged with wire fraud not for pied pipering a bunch of desperate twenty-somethings to Paradise Lost, but for defrauding his investors about the state of Fyre Media.[3] (He had claimed the company was generating millions of dollars in revenue, which it was not.)

A bonus shock came a year later, long after he had pleaded guilty to the first set of charges. At the time, McFarland had been out on bail pending a sentencing hearing for the charges stemming from the Fyre Festival. Most, including the prosecutors and the class action attorney representing his victims, assumed he had spent that time hiding out in his parents' basement in New Jersey. But I had heard a rumor he was actually back in the city, living large in a Midtown hotel penthouse and bragging about his crimes at nightclubs and upscale strip joints. In any event, he definitely wasn't sitting at home thinking about what he had done wrong. For weeks, I had been getting credible reports that Fyre Festival attendees were being targeted with emails from a new company called NYC VIP Access, which was offering ludicrously expensive tickets to exclusive celebrity events like the Met Gala, the Victoria's Secret Fashion Show, and Burning Man. That someone would be brokering these types of exclusive opportunities wasn't totally implausible—high-price concierge services accounted for an estimated $297 million market in 2017[4]—but something just felt off about these offers, in the same way the Fyre Festival website had felt off when I first clicked through. I started investigating and found, rather quickly, that it just wasn't possible to fulfill the experiences NYC VIP Access had been offering. For example, Met Gala tickets can't be purchased, and anyone with a tenuous connection to the event who plans on trying to buy their way in anyway, like, say, an executive representing one of the brands who sponsor the Gala, has to first be personally approved by Anna Wintour. When I called up an NYC VIP Access sales rep under the guise of an interested customer to ask about an offer for tickets to the Victoria's Secret Fashion Show, the man who answered the phone explained to me (in a rather condescending tone!) that the models confirmed to walk in the show had promised the company their allotted VIP seats. He went on to suggest he might deign to sell me a pair if I filled out and returned a credit card authorization form that same day. But that year's show hadn't even announced its location yet, and the annual casting, which famously guarantees no spot to any model—even if she walked the year before—was still months away. A simple Google search revealed Burning Man had no corporate sponsors to provide NYC VIP with the tickets they assured me had been provided by corporate sponsors, and I was able to confirm that, despite NYC VIP's backstage *Reputation* tour offers, Taylor Swift had stopped selling meet and greets some time ago, due to security concerns.

On June 12, 2018, having debunked almost all of NYC VIP's offers, I published a final article in a series focused on the many connections between this shady new access company and Billy McFarland, who had repeatedly denied any involvement.[5] About six hours after the piece went live, Mc-Farland was rearrested and charged with a pair of felonies related to the ticket-selling scheme. According to the FBI, he had managed to pocket more than $100,000 by scamming his original victims while out on bail.[6] In July, he again pleaded guilty and was sentenced that fall to six years total for both incidents—two counts of wire fraud stemming from the festival and two counts of wire fraud and money laundering related to the NYC VIP Access scam.[7]

Still, the fact that he had turned around and committed two felonies while out on bail for two other felonies ultimately made little difference in his sentencing. In a bizarre turn, the judge actually challenged in open court one of McFarland's psychologist's conclusions that McFarland did not meet the criteria for a diagnosis of antisocial personality disorder, and then turned around and granted him the relatively lenient sentence, to be served in a low-security white-collar prison.[8] It wasn't exactly a bad outcome on charges that could have landed him more than seventy-five years behind bars under the maximum sentencing guidelines before a judge who had just suggested he might be a psychopath.

But by then I had realized, while reporting on McFarland's myriad scams, that the real meat wasn't a recap of his crimes and how he did them but, rather, why they worked so well—and why so many people he had already duped once fell for it again just a few months later. Why were his victims, once burned, willing to take another chance on an offer that seemed way too good to be true? Why did experienced investors repeatedly give millions of dollars to a college dropout with no real product or sales record? Why did serious professionals, with decades in their industries, who knew or should have known that the original festival wasn't going to happen, keep working toward its inevitable implosion? Why was one of them willing to give a Bahamian official a (literal, not figurative) blow job just to ensure McFarland's shipment of Evian water would make it on time[9]—and still be open to visiting him in prison after? Why did thousands of the most image-conscious, web-savvy youths in America eagerly throw their money at an illusion? And why, long after it became clear something was seriously wrong with the event, did hundreds of those young people still jump on hastily chartered last-minute flights to a foreign country? Suddenly I was seeing patterns everywhere, like the John Nash of influencer marketing, with red yarn tying together Billy McFarland and Donald Trump, while Elon Musk and Kris Jenner faced off from opposite ends of my brain conspiracy board.

Con artists and hustlers have presumably been around since prehistoric times. But there was something new here at play, a tech-assisted accelerant, that enabled McFarland to subvert our hyperconnected society, which, given all these technological advancements, should have spotlighted him from miles away. But by filtering his scam through a network of trusted influencers on social media, which caught the attention of legacy news outlets more than happy to cover things superficially from an entertainment angle, McFarland had been able to wash the stench of fraud from his scheme, resulting in a pure hype cycle that bypassed any need for proof of concept. And with a millennial army willing to follow these influential generals from the screen to the literal ends of the earth, McFarland was able to convince a series of experienced investors to keep funding the scam—at least until it all fell apart in real time, where else, but on social media. McFarland may, for a time, have been the most famous, but he is not, by far, the only con artist feasting on hype in the digital age.

It's tempting to chalk all this up to the naivete of young people. But it's not just millennials and Gen Z'ers falling for it—it's their parents too. This impetus to dive blindly into a shallow pool of unverified claims spans generational, socio-economic, and educational levels, from the twenty-eight-year-old North Carolina man who shot up a pizza parlor because he falsely believed it was a front for child sex trafficking, all the way up to ninety-seven-year-old Henry Kissinger, who accepted a seat on the board of directors of Theranos, which turned out to be a company that had attracted millions of dollars in investment for a blood testing product that simply didn't work. At least Kissinger just lost his dignity—the Walton family (which owns Walmart), Rupert Murdoch, and the DeVos family—all of them presumably sophisticated investors and certainly long-term professional rich people—reportedly lost a combined $375 million in Theranos.[10] It's the same mindset that brought us Juicero, the $400 juicing machine that managed to raise 120 million real dollars before a journalist figured out the machine only worked almost as well as squeezing the bags of fruit pulp with your own two hands. It's the millions of people tuning into Newsmax, a television channel that appears to exist solely to cater to people who feel Fox News committed a crime punishable by death for calling the state of Arizona for Joe Biden on Election Night. In retrospect, it's little wonder McFarland thought he could sell a half-brained idea and use someone else's money to try to make it come true. Wishful thinking wrapped up into an aggressive sales pitch and pounded into the public psyche via pop culture and social media until enough people give up resisting the idea is just good business practice.

The result is a curious conundrum of this connected age. We have more tools available to uncover bad actors than ever before, yet we persist in playing along with them. We keep arguing online with bots and ordering products on Amazon from companies that produce counterfeit goods (this happens far more often than you'd think) simply because they were favorably reviewed by someone we don't know. An entirely new currency that doesn't actually exist is thriving in the multibillion-dollar crypto exchange, enabling companies like Burger King Russia and Kodak to goose their stock prices just by announcing plans for their own branded version of fake digital money. We're taking vitamins we don't need and swallowing supplements we can't pronounce and putting jade eggs in our vaginas because we were told to do so by freelance writers whose only health qualifications are working for a site that happens to be owned by the beautiful and famous movie star Gwyneth Paltrow. Is any of it all that different from the thousands of kids who entrusted their physical safety to a twenty-five-year-old scammer simply because the model Bella Hadid accepted north of $300,000 to wink at a camera (for which she apologised in a now-deleted post)?

Public Enemy's "Don't Believe the Hype" dropped in 1988. Thirty-some years later, it would seem we've learned nothing. In fact, for just $250, you can now pay Flavor Flav to make a video saying literally anything you want on the celebrity booking site Cameo.

Whether it's the value of a company, the authenticity of a person we've never met, or the efficacy of face masks during an airborne pandemic, at some point along the road, we as a society tacitly agreed to start trusting our emotions and feelings over verifiable facts—all without ever realizing just how much our social media use is manipulating those judgments in the first place. Scholars call this a *post-truth world*, a concept that arguably originated with Friedrich Nietzsche but which took on particular urgency after it was named Oxford's 2016 word of the year. The phrase is most commonly invoked to refer to Trump's election and Brexit, but I see it playing out everywhere. We've become so confused by the constant barrage of what former Trump advisor Kellyanne Conway famously deemed "alternative facts," that we're desperate for someone to tell us what's right, and there's plenty of evidence for us to gather after the fact, once we've already decided the conclusion.

It all got me thinking one day about writer–director Derrick Borte's first film, *The Joneses*, a dark comedy starring David Duchovny, Demi Moore, and Amber Heard. I'll forgive you if you hadn't heard of it; the movie didn't get a ton of attention after its initial premiere at the 2009 Toronto International Film Festival, and with a limited release the following summer across 217 movie theaters nationwide, it ultimately earned back just $7 million of its $10 million budget.[11] But its 63 percent fresh rating on Rotten Tomatoes and 6.5/10 stars on IMDb seem a bit unfair, especially given that *Avatar* has something like an 82 percent. I mean, storyline aside, *The Joneses* has a cameo from Lauren Hutton! What does Avatar have, besides almost three hours of my life I'll never get back?

But who can blame the critics? Certainly not the writer of a book wide-open to them. And it's only with the benefit of hindsight that a viewer would even notice the funny little thing about the film, which follows a perfect family of four living their perfect lives in a perfect house stocked with enviable brand-name items. Of course, in what an optimist might refer to as a *shocking twist*, it turns out they're not re-

ally a family at all, but a cell of actors—professional lifestylists
the educated viewer might now refer to as *influencers*—hired
by a covert marketing firm to inspire a frenzy of conspicuous consumption in the upper-middle-class neighborhoods
they're sent to infiltrate. Nowadays, of course, the 2009 film's
satire seems almost too subtle, given the Kardashian-Jenner-
West family's tidy conversion of their reality show's Nielson
ratings into hundreds of millions of Instagram followers and
billions of dollars in direct-to-consumer sales, or the existence of a number of gated Los Angeles mansions inhabited
exclusively by teenagers who can afford an entry fee of what
appears to be a minimum of one million TikTok followers.
Or the fact that in 2019, an eight-year-old YouTuber named
Ryan Kaji made $26 million just for opening and reviewing
toys[12] you and I have probably never heard of. (Most of that
money apparently came from a video he made about plastic
eggs?? I don't profess to understand any of it, but I'd be happy
to do a collab if you're reading this, Ryan.)

But I digress. Given the current landscape, I'd argue the
remarkable thing about *The Joneses* is that, despite its now-
familiar pattern of elevating civilians to the roles of celebrity
spokespersons, the film actually predated the rise of Instagram
and the first big wave of YouTube influencers by at least a year,
maybe more, depending on when Borte actually finalized the
plot points of the script, which he began in 2002. YouTube's
mammoth Partner Program, now an $8.5 billion operation[13]
with an algorithm the company simply cannot stop from rewarding and recommending conspiracy theorists and viral
pranksters, was still in its infancy the year *The Joneses* went
into production. And while today's influencers make Borte's
marketing family look archaic in their methods—imagine
using your cell phone to only make phone calls!—they still
work with the same underlying modus operandi.

"You're not selling things anymore. To succeed here, you can't just sell things. You're here to sell a lifestyle. An attitude," Hutton purrs to Duchovny in that aforementioned cameo. "If people want you, they'll want what you've got."

In real life, the street of desire may be more of a two-way road than Hutton lets on, at least if the booming market for sugar babies is any indication. But in the film, her prediction comes true as Duchovny floats through his performative life, with his neighbors cast as an unwitting audience for what amounts to a 24/7 QVC show. Duchovny's character is the platonic ideal of a wealthy man with no clear job, who drives off into the sunset in a gleaming Audi convertible, golfs perfect rounds with his new top-of-the-line clubs, and buys pricey Van Cleef and Arpels jewelry to surprise his wife because, as he intimates to his new neighbour-clients, it's a fun way of guaranteeing copulation. No one in the community is exactly sure of his net worth, or even how he makes his money—in fact, the mystery is a running plot point—but it's clear he has a lot of it, and it's not long before his neighbors decide that they'll have what he's having.

Now, I don't want to speak for society, but I know I've been shopping for thirty years looking for the one thing that's going to change my life forever without ever really questioning the hypothesis. And Duchovny's character's neighbors apparently feel something similar, because soon after his arrival, they're all driving brand-new Audis too, cornering like race car drivers on the winding road to self-fulfillment.

I don't want to shock anyone here, but things do not end well for the influencer-family's neighbors, unaware as they are that their shiny, well-dressed new friends are actually paid spokespeople, blithely strolling through their living rooms flaunting their wares with nary a #ad disclaimer in sight. In the movie, the ramifications of this deceit include Gary Cole's tragic demise in a swimming pool, though I'm relieved to report no harm comes to the brand-new Audi.

But Borte, who—surprise, surprise—worked in advertising before branching into feature films, was certainly well-versed in the advantages of native advertising, a model that played no small part in the movie's financing.

"If you don't leave this movie more aware of the new Audi models, you slept through it," Roger Ebert wrote in his review at the time—a rather dry assessment, given that the film's characters explicitly note the model number and individual attributes of every Audi vehicle that appears on-screen.

That was in part a budgetary decision, Borte told me in a phone interview more than a decade after the film's release, citing the difficulties of indie film financing. But he also considered it a meta commentary, using product placement to do a film about real life product placement. A few of the companies he initially approached said no, but Borte was ultimately able to secure luxury sponsors for just about every spec product in the script except one: an alcoholic beverage that comes in a kid-friendly pouch marketed toward teenagers. And even that was based in part on real-life stories he'd heard.

"I saw a special, I think maybe on *20/20*, that talked about Campari or one of the alcohol companies hiring models to go bar-to-bar in New York, and order their drink, in hopes of spreading the word in that way," Borte said. "And then I heard a few things about one of the camera companies sending someone out with a digital camera to Disney World to pose with their fake family, to get people to take their picture and try to talk about the attributes of the camera. And it just seemed like a natural progression, with, what if it was a whole family and they literally were just planted in a neighborhood, and had products to talk about and soft-sell in whatever way? And it just sort of blew up from there."

The only conservative prediction *The Joneses* made, in my opinion, was assuming that guerilla marketing—stealth product placement embedded into everyday life—was a worst-case scenario for the ad industry. Nowadays, of course, social media influencers are much more transparent about what they're selling, but their audience is just as rapt as the Joneses' neighbors. Which is what's so insane about today's landscape. What was, in 2009, intentionally surreal, now seems almost banal, what with the former Goop employee who staged a sponsored multi-city engagement extravaganza for a live audience of about 5,000 emotionally invested strangers (and lost her day job not long after it went viral for all the wrong reasons),[14] or the TikTok users who caught coronavirus after participating in a viral toilet-seat-licking challenge for clout.[15]

"I think now, with influencer marketing, what was covert has now become overt," Borte said.

For one thing, Audi's costarring role opposite Duchovny in *The Joneses* turned out to be a precipitating event in the car company's rather clichéd move into the arena of life imitating art. In the decade since the movie's release, Audi has moved to the forefront of this new, blended reality of influencer marketing—namely, loaning out free cars to wealthy social media users with tons of followers, whose vibe supposedly "fits the brand," in exchange for their generous, subliminal, and tonally appropriate integration of the Audi logo into their content. A review of the surviving posts featured in one 2016 UK campaign found none that explicitly alerted consumers to the fact that the influencer was advertising for the company.

It's even spawned a new industry that caters to regular people who just want to fool their friends into thinking they're influencers. They're the target audience of The Private Jet Studio, a Russian company that leases out blocks of time aboard a grounded Gulfstream for Instagrammers who can't yet afford a private-jet trip but want their followers to think they can. (Russia also happens to be the home of the Instagram Likes vending machine, though you can find endless bootleg versions of them online promising organic interactions with your account for just a few dollars.) Which is not to suggest this issue is limited to the former Soviet Union: in September, an eagle-eyed TikTok user discovered a number of Los Angeles influencers had been shooting their "private-jet content" inside a decidedly down-to-earth $64-an-hour, 700-square-foot photo studio that's still available on a rental site called Peerspace. At the same time, the sales of used high-end shopping bags on resale sites like Depop and Poshmark have been soaring as wannabe influencers stage shopping spree photos around their favorite brands. Small, used Hermès shopping bags are currently selling for $30 apiece on Etsy. But these things pay off, in their own way. For example, a video of a young woman unboxing the cheapest thing she could find at Hermès—a $23 soap—has racked up close to 80,000 views.[16] A similar video focused on Cartier got more than 250,000.[17]

(It's a unique pressure even Borte has felt affected by, telling me, "The studio that I was working for on this last film sent a plane for me for something recently. And I was so tempted to take a picture on it. And I thought, if you fly on a private jet and you don't post a picture, did you really fly on the private jet at all? Kind of a thought like, if a tree falls in the woods and no one hears it." In the end, he says, he was able to stop himself with a healthy dose of contrarianism. "I resisted. I didn't do it. Because I just felt like not posting it, to me, just sort of made me feel elevated in some way. So as much as I wanted to do it, I didn't do it.")

Meanwhile, a picture might be worth a thousand words… unless those words are a disclaimer. And unfortunately those tend to be few and far between. The Federal Trade Commission (FTC), understandably concerned about the recent explosion in unmarked influencer advertisements, has found itself without a clear enforcement mechanism to use against marketers who decline to clearly identify when they're being paid or talking about gifted items,[18] and the best the agency can do at this time is send a strongly worded letter.

"Influencer marketing is only going to grow," noted marketer Dan Wheeldon in the summary of that 2016 UK Audi Instagram campaign, the one that loaned free cars to influencers in exchange for unlabeled advertisements. "Ad blockers continue to rise, as do savvy audiences who would rather see something inspiring from within their circle than to ingest poorly executed adverts from outside."[19]

Wheeldon was right, of course, but he missed a bigger issue. Forget the old *New Yorker* joke that no one on the internet has to know you're a dog. These days on the internet, no one has to know you're a fraud. With just a few of the right assets—some combination of a well-curated Instagram or Twitter account with a decent following, a professional website, a celebrity spokesperson, and maybe a sprinkling of those Russian-bot likes—it's not hard to get internet users, bloggers, and even the mainstream press to accept an Instagram Story as fact, whether it's a Russian scammer pretending to be an heiress in New York society, a self-described entrepreneur promising to sell you the secrets to success in exchange for three easy payments, or a wannabe influencer paying her college friend to write viral captions underneath her heavily edited photographs in order to trick strangers into thinking her life looks cool.

Still, it's a low-stakes game for most brands and the influencers they rely on, exchanging samples, gifts, and direct deposits for tags, links, and favorable reviews. For most of the companies involved, the worst that can happen is that an in-

fluencer will fail to advertise the goods on their page. (Given
the contractual nature of these agreements, it also gives companies an easy recourse, like the time Snapchat sued the actor
Luka Sabbat for "failing to influence" by allegedly reneging
on a $60,000 deal to do a series of swipe-up stories modeling
the company's line of camera sunglasses called Specs.[20]) But
in general, these companies tend to be pretty chill about the
deals, because just like the Audis and Van Cleefs who advertised with Duchovny's fake family, these brands aren't necessarily looking for clicks—they're looking for credibility.
And it doesn't take much for an influencer to make a product look aspirational. Rationally, of course, the public knows
that much of what we're seeing on social media is fake. But
emotionally, the game influencers and celebrities play—let's
call it something like the Allegory of the Fave—by selectively
revealing brief, staged glimpses into their personal lives, well,
it just hits differently than a banner ad.

But no one's going broke betting on the vapidity of the
social media–using public. Take the Museum of Ice Cream,
for example—not really a museum at all, but a series of
Instagram-tailored ice cream–themed sets, with backdrops
and props that were literally designed for the sole purpose of
taking selfies. After just three years in business, the pop-up
Instagram background just opened its first permanent New
York outpost—and raised $40 million at a $200 million valuation,[21] thanks to the hundreds of thousands of would-be
influencers who willingly paid more than $40 a head to take
pictures in a giant vat of sprinkles.

And it's not like anyone was bothering to pretend they
paid the price of admission in exchange for anything other
than a good social media photo. "If you lie in a pool of rubber sprinkles without a smartphone to capture it, is it like you
never laid in a pool of rubber sprinkles at all?" mused *New*

York magazine's Anna Silman on a recent trip to the exhibit. One of her fellow attendees answered the thought exercise rather succinctly: "Did anyone come without their phone? Why would you pay? What's the point?"

Because for most of us, social media isn't just another messaging program. It's long since morphed into an extension of the physical identity, a digital résumé of one's personality. As Borte recently wondered while flying aboard that private jet, if it's not on the 'gram, did it even really happen? But it's a valid question—just think about it. When we shuffle off this mortal coil, what remains behind, for the vast majority of us, will be our curated digital footprint. I mean, hell, Facebook has been converting social media pages into dedicated in-memoriam pages for more than a decade now. Aren't we all, on some level, aware that we're now the executive producers of our own multimedia in memoriams, digital legacies that will long outlive our mortal forms so long as the Wi-Fi stays connected? But forget the morbidity—who we are online will likely reach more people in our lifetimes than our offline selves ever will. Can anyone really blame you for presenting to the public an idealized version of yourself? Is there any way not to? Are we not all, then, just influencers working for scale? Outside of someone having a legitimate public breakdown, isn't everything we post online ultimately nothing more than our own personal fan edit?

In my opinion, all of this has had a flattening effect, where there's no difference online anymore between a Kardashian and someone we actually know, with all the real-life lines separating them blurred and eroded until we feel like these strangers are sort of our friends, and we like their content and comment below as if we know them.

So is it any wonder then, the outsize role aesthetics have taken in recent years? Researchers tracking the negative relationship between social media use and body image, self-esteem, and overall quality of life say it is not.

But beyond the aesthetics, there's no denying that we, as a people, are heavily influenced by what we're seeing online. It's easy to track these effects because in the digital world everything is quantifiable. Take, for example, the attractive, photogenic orange drink Americans suddenly started knocking back in 2017, in large part because Campari paid JWT New York handsomely to "position the Aperol spritz as the real 'Italian aperitivo' and go-to drink for the Social Striver (a trendy Millenial [sic] that doesn't mind splurging on the new/hot product if it advances their social status), with its bright orange color and easy preparation as the key message," at least according to the agency's case study.[22] To put it in English, Campari mostly just put its product in places where influencers were already taking pictures: out and about in the Hamptons, in front of aesthetically pleasing backdrops at trendy music festivals, and with branded merch distributed at places like Miami's Art Basel. Of course, Campari paired those efforts with a blend of traditional advertising—bus wraps, billboards, magazine ads, and the rest—but they did it all with a narrow focus on well-heeled millennials and their social media audiences. And it was wildly successful.

It's not exactly a new concept—remember, Borte was inspired to write *The Joneses*, fifteen years earlier, after seeing a news story about models being paid to order Campari and sodas at popular bars. But thanks to the internet, Campari no longer had to settle for local results. Plus, the Aperol spritz was perfectly positioned for the Instagram set: new in its rarity, connoted with wealth in its European heritage, and visually distinctive with its Fyre-orange color. It was the kind of cocktail you might take a picture of before drinking. (It's no coincidence that those same qualities were also shared by what was then the reigning status drink Aperol eventually displaced: the millennial-pink rosé.)

As it was, that summer the Aperol spritz hashtag swelled to hundreds of thousands of posts—and scores of headlines. And the orange aperitif has been Campari's biggest seller ever since. With most bars now carrying the once-obscure spirit, it's transcended social media and settled comfortably into real life. And all this, despite the *New York Times*'s stern conclusion that "the Aperol spritz is not a good drink" but rather one that "drinks like a Capri Sun after soccer practice on a hot day."[23] (Ironically enough, an alcoholic Capri Sun was essentially the sole product prototype Borte found himself unable to find a sponsor for on *The Joneses*.)

"For longtime spritz lovers like myself, this news was a jarring wake-up call: No, I am not original in my enjoyment of the Aperol spritz—and neither are you," confessed *Racked* writer Nisha Chittal after studying Campari's targeted Aperol marketing efforts. "We have all unknowingly fallen prey to our corporate overlords, yet again."[24]

Still, that's nothing compared to the sudden rise of White Claw, the hard seltzer that knocked Aperol right out of the hands of the Drink of Summer–voting public last summer. When the spiked beverage first hit shelves in 2016, no one would buy it. But that all changed in July 2019 following the release of a viral video declaring there "ain't no laws when you're drinking Claws."

It was the perfect wedding of viral meme humor and a deeply confused wellness movement that tends to promote the appearance of health over any actual nutritional statistics, part of a larger trend toward describing something you felt like doing anyway as *self-care*, regardless of its actual benefit to one's physical or mental health. Low in carbs and sugar,

White Claw was, more often than not, positioned as a healthy choice for cool kids.

The ad was a hit on social media with the same Gen Z crowd that helped JUUL corner the market, however briefly, as the mango-flavored wellness alternative to cigarettes.

"It's interesting because the younger demographic [of men that] broadly gets defined as 'bro culture' is very active on social media," Sanjiv Gajiwala, the senior vice president of marketing at White Claw, told *Business Insider*. "They're very passionate, and they love sharing things that they think are fun, so I think it's caught the attention of a lot of people."[25]

It certainly did, clawing its way into a whopping 55 percent stronghold over the hard-seltzer market,[26] according to *Brewbound*, citing Nielsen data. It's also part of a growing wave of so-called wellness-oriented products, where the hard-seltzer category as a whole has, pardon my pun, also spiked more than 200 percent[27]. But according to Nielsen, 164.3 percent of that growth occurred in just one month—July 2019—after YouTube star Trevor Wallace released a video "destroying" the typical White Claw drinker with a parody video that also happened to neatly position the product for his million-plus frat-boy audience.[28]

"It's basically just a vegan Four Loko. If you think about it. LaCroix? It's just a virgin White Claw," he drawled, a spiritual sibling of Tom Hanks's youngest son, Chet Haze, an up-and-coming rapper who apparently just decided one day that he could be Jamaican whenever he felt like it. "It's like a Four Loko that went to private school. It's basically just a rich person's Lime-a-Rita."

"Throw a dart at my fraternity composite, and you'll find a guy who's into hard seltzer," a college junior and fraternity member told *Business Insider* at the time, granted anonymity in the interview because he was apparently not yet of drinking age[29]—a perfect advertisement for the brand's audience if there ever was one.

It's the same type of humor billionaire and former New York mayor Michael Bloomberg invested in for his 2020 presidential campaign, sending Instagram and Facebook into brief existential crises about the nightmare of regulating political-influencer endorsements.

"Mike Bloomberg 2020 has teamed up with social creators to collaborate with the campaign, including the meme world," the campaign said in a statement. "While a meme strategy may be new to presidential politics, we're betting it will be an effective component to reach people where they are and compete with President Trump's powerful digital operation."[30]

In other words, the campaign had enlisted as online surrogates a host of influential meme accounts (the largest of which were known professionally as FuckJerry and ShitheadSteve) to spam their tens of millions of combined followers with advertisements for his campaign. It was, in a sense, a natural continuation of the "TransAm Joe" character first invented by The Onion that helped transform President-elect Biden into a relatable guy you might want to have a beer with. (Former Onion writer Joe Garden has since apologized for his role in that humanization, writing in 2019 that "If you've ever thought of Joe Biden as a clueless but lovable clod, a well-meaning klutz who is predictable, friendly, and ultimately electable, I am in small part responsible for that image. And I'm sorry."[31])

Still, the 2020 election couldn't have come at a better time for the team selected to head the Bloomberg influencer campaign, formally titled "Meme 2020." At the helm was Mick Purzycki, the eldest son of Wilmington, Delaware, mayor Mike Purzycki and the current CEO of Jerry Media, the social media and digital marketing company that controls, among other things, the immensely popular FuckJerry meme page, which boasts more than fifteen million followers.

In 2019, however, Jerry's booming marketing business had all but cratered, going from millions of dollars in accounts to almost zero following a widespread protest against the company's apparent aversion to giving credit to artists, led by a coalition of popular and pissed-off comedians and content creators. *#FuckFuckJerry*, a call to unfollow FuckJerry for using other people's jokes and memes without credit or compensation, didn't ultimately have much of an effect on the company's incredibly large Instagram following. But it did, for a time, successfully render the brand toxic to advertisers. At the same time, the company had been fighting off a number of lawsuits and legal threats related to another project, and morale was low. Purzycki and FuckJerry's founder Elliot Tebele were finding themselves increasingly at odds. Overall, the company centered around jokes and memes hadn't been having fun for a long time.

So for Purzycki, a curious contradiction of a thoughtful guy who makes his money off frat-boy humor, the Bloomberg account was the first sign of spring after a very dark winter.

And it wasn't like he didn't have a proven talent for executing incredibly effective social media marketing campaigns.

He had, after all, helped sell out the Fyre Festival.

1

The Cult of Flounder

In the beginning, Billy McFarland seemed average in every way. He was tall, stocky, and, one might say, sort of handsome-adjacent. With his squinting, pinched smile, atheletic build, and preppy style, he certainly blended in physically with the other primarily white, affluent kids at the Pingry School, the coed prep school in Short Hills, New Jersey, from which he was flung into the unsuspecting world in 2010.

Like most of the families who sent their kids to the then-$30,000-a-year private school, the McFarland family lived in suburban comfort. McFarland's parents, Irene and Steve, made their money in the loosely defined arena of real-estate development. They had the requisite shore house, annual vacations to resorts in places like Aruba, and nice cars to drive around town. McFarland and his sister grew up secure in the knowledge that they would be able to attend private colleges without having to take out loans, though McFarland wouldn't end up making it past his freshman year at Bucknell.

But despite his comfortable upbringing, McFarland had a laser focus on making money—and he didn't seem to care whether any of it was aboveboard. In fact, it was almost like he needed to feel like the smartest person in the room before he could even get started on something.

According to McFarland, his first business venture occurred at the tender age of seven, when he apparently realized he had an opportunity to coax some money out of a girl he had his eye on.

"My first combination of technology and marketing happened in second grade," McFarland said in an interview featured in Hulu's *Fyre Fraud*.[32] "I was put next to a girl who I had a crush on, and her crayon broke. I said, 'If you give me a dollar, I'll fix your crayon.'"

Then, for good measure, he claimed, he hacked his teachers.

"I figured out the school's administrator password, and I started messing with them. I changed the password and, like, locked all the teachers out," he continued. "So every time the AlphaSmart was turned on, it would say 'For your broken crayons, basically come and find me.'"

Setting aside his inclination to fleece the girl he liked instead of, say, doing her a favor, McFarland's deep-seated need to start building capital in the second grade set the stage for what was still to come. McFarland made wanting more than what he had his entire personality. Sure, his parents had money, but his family wasn't the flashy kind of New Jersey wealthy. But some of his friends—a number of whom would later work for him—*were* that kind of rich. And McFarland, who friends described as talkative, somewhat "scattered" (though "not in an ADD way"), and always "the life of the party," became a sort of mascot for them.

"Billy always had something going on, even in middle school," explained childhood friend Eric Rubenstein.[33]

In the seventh grade, for example, jealous that they couldn't get on Facebook, which was only open to college students at the time, Rubenstein and McFarland ended up creating their own version. They named it "Your Hot Site," a knockoff of Facebook's original "Hot or Not" page that Rubenstein says they selected in large part because the domain happened to be open.

"We got together with a few of our friends, and they invested in it, and we built it. Me, Billy, and another person were the admins on the page, and it was cool. It was pretty rudimentary. There was a thing where you could rank your friends and be like, 'Who do you like more?'" Rubenstein recalled. "It got really popular after the first week, we had a thousand users after the first couple of days. And I know in today's standards that's not that much, but we were just kids, just fucking around."

Unfortunately, they were forced to shut the site down not long after launching, Rubenstein said, when the school found out and called McFarland's parents in for a meeting.

"I think the worry was that if something bad were to happen as a result of this website, it wouldn't be a good look for the district. So Billy's parents asked him if he could just sell it, and that's what we did. We sold it for $3,000 to a guy in Canada. I want to say his name was Mike, but I can't remember," Rubenstein said.

Rubenstein has tons of memories of hijinks with McFarland, including one bat mitzvah party where they sneaked into an adjacent office area and programmed all the computers so that photographs of women's breasts would pop up every time someone pressed "X." Another time, he recalled, McFarland burned him a bootleg copy of *The 40 Year Old*

Virgin and labeled it as the animated film *Madagascar* so that Rubenstein's mother wouldn't find out and ground him for watching inappropriate movies. The R-rated comedy, however, was positively tame compared to another one of McFarland's schemes: a business he built selling passwords to porn sites to his preteen buddies.

"Billy was always looking for ways to monetize things, and it's completely understandable since he was offering a service that no one else could provide," Rubenstein said. "Billy was a fun kid and he was very funny."

That was the thing—it wasn't just that McFarland had the unique ability to provide special services for his cohort. He also had a way of making it all seem so exciting.

"[Billy] was fun. He was really funny. He was always a big flirt," says another high-school friend who asked to remain anonymous because she would later become a victim of his schemes. "He was a fast talker, he'd go from one thing to the next, and his mind was always bouncing around."

McFarland has been referred to on more than one occasion as a "used-car salesman" kind of personality, which made sense because he did always have some sort of fantastic deal queued up for his friends. During his last year at Pingry, for example, he led his friend group in a series of senior pranks, including one where they faked a wild party, buying a keg of root beer and rolling it into the senior lounge. Another time, they took advantage of the school's honor code and gathered up all the backpacks their classmates had—up to that day, at least—felt comfortable leaving unguarded in the hallways during assemblies. While their unsuspecting classmates sat in the auditorium, Billy and his friends deposited all the bags on the football field, then sprayed the students with water guns when they tried to retrieve them.

It was, looking back, not all that different from the Fyre

Festival, which marked the end of its first (and last) day with a crowd of desperate millennials tearing through a pile of wet, unmarked luggage.

By that point in Billy's young life, other patterns were also beginning to form. Though McFarland later claimed to have started and sold three companies before graduating high school, none of his claims were ever exactly "verifiable." Like the business McFarland says he launched in elementary school, "behind my parents' back when I was 12 years old, getting my friends' parents to invest."[34]

According to McFarland, that business was a web-hosting company he had launched that somehow led him to employ three people working full-time in India.

"When he came to Pingry, he was already running some overseas server operation, renting out server space to various websites, most of which were porn sites," a high-school friend named Aaron Davis told *Death and Taxes*. "He always kind of toed that line of whether it was a scheme or legitimate."

McFarland later called the venture a massive success and often referred to it as evidence of his business acumen, which helped his self-created image as a child genius. "Four days after the website launched, I was forced to sell and subsequently gave each investor a 3x return on their investment," he wrote in a 2011 investor pitch.[35]

In a 2017 interview with the producers of *Fyre Fraud*, however, McFarland repeated the story, though this time to highlight how easy it had been for him to deceive his overseas employees.

"I'm talking to people entirely across the world when my friends are playing kickball at recess. I had, like, the worst fake deep voice on the planet. I would pick up the phone and never say how old I was," McFarland said. "The internet doesn't have parents, doesn't have teachers, doesn't have rules."

That, in particular, was an important realization for Mc-Farland. If there was ever a through-line to all of McFarland's schemes, it's that they occurred primarily over the internet, were valued not by their worth but by his enthusiasm, were targeted at his fellow millennials, and appeared to be designed to acquire as much money and attention in as short of a time period as possible. In that way, Billy was not unlike other start-up founders such as Theranos CEO Elizabeth Holmes or WeWork CEO Adam Neumann, both of whom also rode waves of hype to become rich and famous at the expense of their investors.

But McFarland was a peculiar sort of millennial entrepreneur, one who started out just as Instagram began to gain attention—and with it, the rise of performative wealth among the underage scions who first sparked the *Rich Kids of Instagram* Tumblr page and subsequent reality television show. Like many of his eventual customers, McFarland was a fan of the milieu, which had originated as a fan page following the antics of a group of jet-setting millennials with wealthy, largely absentee parents. What made these kids different from the famous-for-being-famous socialites of yore, however, was that they weren't just content to be outrageously rich. This new breed was dedicated to documenting it with photos, videos, and comments that showed exactly how they were spending it.

Suddenly, almost overnight, "doing it for the 'gram" had become a viable business model. But there was a catch that's still active for most people hoping to make money as an influencer, which is that you had to have money already.

As a college dropout still getting his family's support, Mc-Farland might not have had to worry about paying his credit card bills while he figured things out, but he couldn't compete with the conspicuous consumption playing out every weekend at New York City clubs like Le Bain and 1 Oak—at least not without using his friends' wealth to fill in the gaps.

"I don't think [the McFarlands] were a private-jet family, but there were two other people from our high school who I know were involved in his first company, and they are private-jet families, so I know he was definitely rolling with those kinds of people," a former Pingry School classmate told me.

More importantly, McFarland had figured out that "those kinds of people" might give him even more than he asked for, if he played his cards right. When he got really enthusiastic about a plan, most of the people around him, he was starting to learn, were happy to go along with him for the ride.

"He definitely was a dreamer and he had big ideas and they were good ideas. I think he just would get wrapped up in the scene, and trying to be this big shot in New York City. And we all thought like, 'That's great. We all want to be that,'" the former classmate said. "We all thought if we were part of it, we could probably ride the wave, just like you would do with any start-up or anything like that. I mean it just takes people that you might trust, or they think they know you, and then you ask them for some favors. And if enough people buy into it, then it can get pretty big."

There, the classmate trailed off. "But yeah, I don't know what it was that caused him to just lie constantly... I don't know."

Rubenstein has his own theory, which he pinpoints squarely to their upbringing.

"Growing up in Short Hills, we were basically raised to think that we were invincible, and it shows with him, and it shows with me and my friends, because we would do some really stupid shit and not face any consequences," said Rubenstein, who realized the rest of the world lived a bit differently after moving away to Los Angeles. "Short Hills...I don't know if it's still that way. I only go back for funerals and Millburn Deli. But the culture, I mean, it's a very stereotypical rich place. You can only succeed if you're a doctor, a lawyer, or go to an Ivy league school. There's no accepting mediocrity, and I think that they raise you to have more materialistic values."

Despite the town's values and some of his best efforts, however, Billy had managed to graduate high school without any felony arrests. He matriculated at Pennsylvania's Bucknell University in the fall of 2010, with the intention of studying computer engineering, but by the spring of 2011, he was no longer a student.

Billy's friends remember him framing his decision to drop out as a Mark Zuckerberg–inspired move that would enable him to immediately start squeezing big money out of a start-up he had founded called Spling.

Early pitch decks show that Spling had originally been intended to be a sort of mash-up of Reddit and Pinterest, a site where users could share links with their friends in an "intersection between social networking and microblogging with a scope refined for entertainment."

The interface was both simple and clunky. In its beta form, the home page featured a leaderboard, where registered users could vote and comment on Top Splings, though few did. The posts, archives show, were comprised primarily of YouTube links with headlines like "Hilarious commercial," "Fat kid gets hit by paintballs–funny," and "Bike Trick Landing FAIL."

But something had convinced Billy that the idea was worth pursuing—perhaps the $5,000 Bucknell University Venture Plan Competition prize he won in April 2011 or the $50,000 angel investment he'd collected around the same time from a Philadelphia pharma CFO named Mitchell Blumenfeld.

Whatever it was, he was excited enough about the com-

pany's prospects that he was able to successfully convince three
of his high school friends to drop out alongside him to join
the start-up's executive team.

"As far as our team, Spling abides by the 4–5–3 rule," Mc-
Farland, then nineteen, joked in the 2011 pitch. "Our four
founders have sold more companies (five) than our combined
years of college experience (three)."

"Mac Cordrey, Spling's COO, spent more time in university biology labs as a high schooler than as a college student,"
McFarland went on. "After graduating from Lawrenceville,
Mac was planning on attending Georgetown—until he realized that Spling is much more fun than biology."

Spling's CFO, Nic Meiring, "should have been a sophomore at Duke. But he realized his marketing skills could be
put to better use for Spling than for fraternity parties," Mc-
Farland continued. And lastly, "If you're wondering where the
accent's coming from, that's Henry Clifford, Spling's CTO. I
actually met Henry online six years ago, and we've worked on
projects non-stop ever since. Henry was a rising sophomore
at the Sheffield University in England, until he came over to
America, for the first time this summer, to join us locally."

McFarland claimed as early as April 2011 that Spling's user
numbers were literally off the charts. And they were, in the
sense he was both paying for the activity and massaging the
numbers. The site, one early press release stated, had gener-
ated nearly a million hits with over 5,000 unique visitors and
125,000 page views, "making it one of the fastest growing
social media sites ever to launch."[36]

But while there may have been some activity on the site, it
was nowhere near the kind of growth McFarland was claiming in pitch meetings. And it hadn't been provided so much
by users as by a small army of friends and family members

McFarland had recruited at colleges across the country to se-
cretly fuel the company in exchange for future equity.

One of those recruits was a then–college freshman who
had known Billy growing up and enthusiastically signed on
when she got the email inviting her to join the Spling team.

"It was like, 'You were referred to us by one of our partners. We started a social media networking website and we
want you to join us as a campus intern.' So the idea was that
they got all these friends to promote Spling at all different
schools," she recalled in a recent phone interview. "And they
told us, 'We're going to send you branded sunglasses, bottle
openers, et cetera,' and then, most importantly, it says, 'This
will be a paid position. We'll give you large additional cash
and equity rewards as well as owned shares of Spling to our
top interns, and the top performers will be considered part
owners and asked to join our team full-time.'

"So I thought that was awesome. I was in. I started promoting it," she said. Her marketing work also included recruiting
a number of her own friends to compete for the cash prizes
and challenges McFarland would issue over group emails.

"I reached out to a bunch of people in my network and
everyone was excited about it and they said, 'Start offering
them to get paid based on how many posts they do.' I forget
exactly how much, it was $10 or something per post," recalled
the former campus intern. "So essentially they were promising me money. They were telling me to promise other people
money, and it's just the same exact thing with the Fyre Festival. It just never happened."

None of the merch McFarland had promised to send ever
materialized—and more importantly, neither did most of the
checks.

But the people who thought they were helping to build
something exciting were real. One of them, an intern who

had been recruited in the second wave, was a Colorado teen-ager named Peter Huffman.[37] He was in his senior year of high school when he got looped by a camp friend into what he thought would be "the next iteration of social network-ing." What that really translated into was a sort of rudimen-tary, early version of social media influencing: in exchange for $10 here and $20 there, Spling would pay him to do simple tasks, like signing up all his friends for the site, or generat-ing a certain number of comments under the videos of bike trick landing fails.

Though Huffman was one of the youngest so-called interns on the team (most of the others on his email chain had college .*edu* addresses, he recalls), no one seemed to care about his age—or even if the accounts he had been signing up were real.

"They were offering what seemed like a huge amount of money for a very little amount of work on my side. I think at one point they paid me, like, $100 to get five people to sign up, and then get each of those people to share five links," Huffman said. "I remember thinking, 'This is really strange. They've done very little verification that I'm anybody.' And so that also seemed strange to me that they were incentiviz-ing us to do stuff, but there wasn't really any follow-up or any way to track what we were doing. I'm not sure exactly why they were paying, like, $100 for a bunch of almost fraudu-lent clicks, you know? It wasn't like any of this was organic."

Huffman, who now works in tech and search engine op-timization, says that looking back, it seems clear to him that McFarland had been randomly offering teenagers he'd never met relatively large sums of money for very little work in an effort to game Google's rankings and help him hit certain numbers before investor presentations. The paid challenges Huffman had been completing seemed explicitly designed to trick algorithms into thinking the site was something that it was not.

"I'm guessing what their strategy was, was to have a lot of traffic from other sites to Spling. Google rates sites based on how good Google thinks they are, as far as like actually providing quality content, and it uses links, and the quality of the links to judge how good a site is. So for Facebook, if somebody is googling Facebook, one, the names match, but then there's a lot of links to Facebook from quality sites that make Google think Facebook's a good site," Huffman explained. "So I think what they were trying to do with Spling was get a lot of Spling links all over Facebook, and Reddit, and Twitter, and Tumblr, and stuff like that, so that Google would think, 'Oh, this is a good social network. We're going to have the results from Spling be high up on the search result page.'

"The other thing that stuck out to me was it seemed that there were a lot of deadlines on when they were doing these challenges," Huffman said. "And I'm wondering whether they were trying to have a lot of activity right around when they were doing demos, or something like that."

For example: "On May 24th, I got an email about a new Spling opportunity," Huffman said. "It read, 'Congratulations to everyone who completed the $100 tasks the other day. Checks will be sent out soon to those of you who completed all five. Today, we're starting a new event that will last until midnight Friday. And each person you refer is $3, and you have to friend request them, and if that person has 25 points by midnight Friday, you get $5.'

"That set told me they had some guideline they wanted to get some certain amount of stats by, and they were using us almost as a click farm, although a really, really expensive click farm, to get people to come out," Huffman said.

A videotaped pitch McFarland presented in 2011 seemed
to confirm Huffman's suspicions: "Numbers don't lie," Mc-
Farland claimed, gesturing to a slide with four vague graphs.
"[These] hockey-shaped growth charts prove our product and
execution." In his typical hyperbolic fashion, he even claimed
the numbers would have been even better had the pitch decks
not been due more than a week before the presentation. "Unfortunately, I couldn't add our new data in here, but the curves
would be even more tremendous," he said.

What he didn't mention in the pitch was that those
"hockey-shaped charts" reflected mostly paid teenagers who
had signed on to the site precisely once, never to return again.

"It seemed like this guy was a hustler, and that this seems
strange to me that there was a bankroll here, and they were
trying to figure out how to make a successful social network
without having any concept of what a social network was,"
Huffman said. "And then also just strange that they weren't
really responding to emails, or doing some of the simple things
that I would think would be really important at the early age
of a social network."

Despite hitting all the challenges, neither McFarland's high-
school friend nor Huffman were ever paid all of what they
were owed.

"If I'd done four or five of these challenges to get people
to sign up, I think I got paid for one or two of them," Huffman said. "And they were always like, 'If you haven't heard
from us yet about your check, send us an email with your address.' And I'd follow up and never get a response." McFarland's friend, who estimates she had earned a few thousand
dollars, ultimately got a check for around $1,200—and only
after threatening Spling with a lawsuit. She remembers Mc-
Farland seeming unfazed at the idea of losing both an employee and a friend.

"We just stopped talking. I got really mad at him. I was like, 'Oh, we were friends, how could you do this to me?' I had an unpaid internship that summer, so I was banking on having that money," she said. "I mean he just didn't really seem to have any remorse or care about the friendship. It was just all about himself."

The friend suggests that McFarland's questionable form of user acquisition wasn't the only thing he'd apparently been using investor money to pay for. That summer after he dropped out of college to pursue Spling full-time, McFarland suddenly became a fixture on the New York City party scene, routinely buying expensive bottle service at then-popular clubs like Kiss & Fly and Le Bain.

The former Spling intern recalled the incongruity of watching the boss pay for bottle service every weekend while ignoring her repeated invoices.

"They would keep saying things like, 'We're still waiting to get investors,' or 'Oh, yeah, it's coming next week, we have a big investment coming next week,'" she said. "But in the meantime we'd go to Le Bain and have bottles of Champagne, like Veuve, and I'm like, 'All right…?'"

She had no way of knowing it at the time, but the former intern's hard work had paid off—for McFarland, at least. That fall, after she returned to school vowing never to speak to McFarland again, Spling was accepted into the venture capital accelerator Dreamit in Philadelphia, which gave him an additional $25,000 to build his company.[38] After months of work by dozens of unpaid interns, there still wasn't much to Spling beyond a few thousand dubious registered accounts. But between Spling's hockey-stick growth charts, the connections provided by Billy's wealthy friends serving on the executive board, and the legitimacy bestowed on the start-up by the accelerator, McFarland was somehow able to secure a whopping $400,000 in Series A funding from Deep Fork Capital[39] and a number of angel investors including John Ason, Gianni Martire, as well as a second investment from Blumenfeld.[40] Though McFarland referred to these investors as the "adult supervision" of the company in his presentation, it was clear no one really cared much what he was doing.

In less than a year, McFarland had managed to talk his way into half a million dollars. And incredibly, when he had nothing to show for it at the end of the three-month accelerator program, no one held him accountable. In fact, as McFarland described it, in the aftermath of a bungled pitch at Dreamit's Demo Day, the only response was that "We were urged to explore new versions of our idea."

So he moved to New York and pivoted, turning his sights to internet publishers. He hoped to persuade them into legitimizing his site by placing a *"Spling It"* logo alongside the Facebook and Twitter icons that used to pop up at the bottom of news stories to facilitate social media sharing, Brandon Wenerd, the publisher of BroBible, recalled.[41]

"They were pushing this social button like all those Digg and StumbleUpon buttons that were all the rage back then," Wenerd said. "I don't think anyone ever responded [to his email]. I still have no idea what it was supposed to be."

It wasn't clear McFarland did either, but he was clearly doing what he could to make the site look like it was a functioning business. He began throwing ideas at the wall just to see what stuck—including a Google Circles–style knock-off, called, appropriately enough, Circles. In one interview with *TechCrunch*, he even tried to claim his Circles idea had come first.[42]

"We are new, we are different, and most importantly we capture internet users' thirst for entertainment," McFarland insisted in the interview with *TechCrunch*. Unfortunately, the site concluded, "Spling's core concepts around content-sharing and interest-based networking are not unique or original."

What was original, however, was McFarland's marketing. So original, in fact, that it was pure fiction. To introduce the Series A round of funding, McFarland had told potential investors that Spling had at least two thousand active users. Huffman says that wasn't true at all, given that he'd personally and openly signed up a number of fake email addresses to hit one of McFarland's challenges and suspected others had as well.

"It was more of a pyramid scheme, it didn't seem like they were offering anything from a user perspective," Huffman said. "The only way that I was seeing people interact with this was if there was a financial incentive to log on to it."

"I'm sure other people went along with it for longer than I did," the high-school friend said. "But yeah, I mean I guess every con has to start somewhere."

When Spling finally launched out of beta and into the public in the spring of 2012, the site declared, "The wait is finally over—it's time to see what all of the hype has been about." But the hype, if there was ever any to begin with, fizzled out quickly. By 2013—just two years after McFarland and his friends had dropped out of college with big plans of launching the next global social-networking site—records show Spling had already pivoted away from the pseudo–social network plan to become a "website development company" focused on increasing "brands' media engagement and ad revenue by optimizing their content presentation."

What that mouthful of jargon seemed to mean, at least in practice, was that Billy had started working his connections in New York in exchange for one-off website redesign projects that kept him from having to admit the Spling gambit was a big fat failure. One of those connections happened to be

the society photographer Patrick McMullan, who McFarland
volunteered to throw a birthday party for while he mulled
his next move into the events space. According to multiple
sources who knew both men at the time, McFarland's attempt to redesign McMullan's website project devolved into
a complete and utter disaster—but not before their association helped legitimize McFarland in the monied New York
City private school scene.

"Billy was supposed to do Patrick McMullan's redo of
his website, and he totally kind of fucked it up, and Patrick
wouldn't talk to me anymore," said a former mutual friend
of both men.

"We had to fire Billy because Billy never got it done," another former McMullan associate said. "I'd be yelling at Billy
every day, because he kept on missing the timetables."

But it was a learning experience for Billy, and a valuable
lesson (at least for him) that he took forward into his subsequent ventures. He now knew that all he needed to convince people to give him money was a good story and the
right cultural markers. And if he didn't deliver on his promises, nothing bad would happen. Spling had never turned a
profit, never even become what he promised he had already
built in its beta form, but instead of hanging around his neck
like a debt-ridden albatross warning off future investors, it
had instead become a selling point, highlighting his deep experience relative to his young age.

"When you asked about why people would go along with
all this, he is believable and he is a fun person. He's a lik-
able guy. So it's easier I guess to get conned by people like
that," said his former classmate. "I just try to think of it as a
lesson, always make sure you have a contract going forward,
and always make sure to ask more questions before you just
start working, and definitely don't promise to pay anybody

money until you've seen money yourself. So that's how I try to think about Billy, and hopefully jail will make him think. But I wouldn't be surprised if he gets out of jail and tries to do something else."

It's probably worth noting that McFarland was never criminally charged with anything related to the actual products behind any of his companies.

His crime would ultimately be lying to his investors about his income and leaving another company holding the bag financially as it all fell apart. (And committing a few more felonies while out on bail, but we'll get to that later.)

Looking back, I think that's why a lot of people I talked to while first reporting this story entertained serious doubts about whether McFarland had always been a scammer, or whether he was a good kid who just got in a little over his head. To his sympathizers, McFarland had just been sloppily, perhaps somewhat naively, following a playbook established long before he ever splung his first Spling. If other rule-breaking start-up founders like Elon Musk and former Uber CEO Travis Kalanick were all walking free with billions of dollars to their name, why, they suggested, should McFarland be in prison?

Hadn't Uber recently begun jockeying for an initial public offering (IPO) despite losing billions of dollars a year?[43] Hadn't Theranos founder Elizabeth Holmes faced exactly zero consequences in the wake of her alleged $9 billion blood-test fraud[44] (at least not that year anyway)? Wasn't self-proclaimed reality-TV billionaire Donald Trump elected president without ever having to show a single tax return to prove his claims? So McFarland pretended his company was worth more than it was. The anecdotal evidence suggested he was as equally likely to get elected to the White House as he was to end up in jail.

Beginning with Spling and on through the Fyre Festival debacle, the feds say McFarland took about $28 million of other people's money over the course of his seven years in business,[45] using a not insignificant portion of it to sample all the finest things in life. He spent with so much confidence that most of his Fyre employees falsely believed he was a trust fund kid treating his colleagues to hedonistic nights out on the town out of his own financial largesse. And when the bill finally came due in the most public of ways in the Southern District of New York, McFarland came out with a six-year sentence (out of a possible maximum seventy-five) and $26 million in restitution[46] he'll probably never actually pay. It all kind of sounds like a spring break–themed sequel to *The Wolf of Wall Street*, and it's equally, if not more, pop culturally relevant. After the success of two different documentaries about his colossal failures, there's reportedly at least two more feature films in production, as well as a memoir McFarland has been threatening to write since 2019 and a podcast that got released just a week before the 2020 presidential election.

If you're McFarland, then, "What lesson did you learn?" asks Calvin Wells, a venture capitalist who tried to whistle-blow on the festival and ended up appearing in both documentaries.[47] "You learned that you can take $30 million, blow it on a massive party over the course of a year, do three-and-a-half years in jail or four years in jail, which is what my undergraduate was, and leave with more money and more notoriety and more success than you could have done by working a quiet job at the Sprint store making $60,000 a year plus health care. What was learned? I think the lesson was, 'Maybe college isn't the right call. Maybe I need to set up my own fake festival.'"

Wells, a professionally wealthy thirty-five-year-old venture capitalist from Mississippi, has been so frustrated by the lack of accountability in the start-up industry that he even registered the domain name *Generation Fraud*, though he's still not exactly sure what to do with it. But he has a point. Everywhere you look, bafflingly overvalued companies and their celebrity CEOs have been blithely trampling across state and federal laws, failing to turn a profit, and getting rewarded handsomely in return—both on paper, and in the papers.

Uber is not and has never been a profitable company, for example, losing billions of dollars each quarter even as its valuation continues to grow. Nor has it traditionally abided by any rules and regulations it deems unfavorable to its business, though current CEO Dara Khosrowshahi's entire personality does seem to hinge on not being former CEO Travis Kalanick, who's taken the brunt of the blame for the company's early lawlessness.

But when McFarland was still in business and Kalanick was still at the ride share company's helm, Uber's lawbreaking was seen as such a feature and not a bug of its business that the company had even managed to optimize its anarchic methods. In a process detailed by the nonprofit consumer advocacy group Public Citizen's research director Rick Claypool in a 2016 paper, the company would swoop into a city and set up shop, ignoring local regulations and "insisting on the legality of its business." If officials resisted, the company would mobilize a campaign among their local riders to "save Uber." The laws they couldn't skirt, they'd lobby to change. And they're still doing it: in 2020, Uber and Lyft spent a combined $200 million to pass Prop 22, which exempts them from California's unconscionable expectations that state employers provide their workers with outrageous benefits like health care and basic labor protections.[48]

"There is a pattern to Uber's conflicts with cities," Claypool noted at the time. "Uber usually wins these battles against rules and regulations the company opposes, but when it loses, it keeps fighting. When cities pass laws that Uber opposes, the company commonly seeks to have them preempted with Uber-approved state law or repealed through voter referenda."

Then there's Elon Musk, one of the wealthiest, most cultish figures in the industry—the billionaire inspiration for Robert Downey Jr.'s Tony Stark!—who openly violates federal labor laws and has long maintained one of the worst worker-safety records in the industry. In 2019, for example, The Drive calculated that Tesla had "three times as many OSHA violations as the 10 largest US plants combined,"[49] making a job with Musk more dangerous than working in a slaughterhouse or a sawmill, according to a 2017 *Los Angeles Times* report.[50] A Tesla spokesperson told the *LA Times*, "We may have had some challenges in the past as we were learning how to become a car company, but what matters is the future … With the changes we've made, we now have the lowest injury rate in the industry by far." Nor have Musk's problems been limited to the factory floor: he recently had to pay out $20 million for tweeting that he had secured private funding to take Tesla private at $420 a share, when in fact he had not.[51] This is a guy who sells an $8,000 "self-driving" car software that requires an active driver behind the wheel to operate. And *still* three people have allegedly died from crashes stemming from the software, with at least ten other nonfatal crashes also under investigation by the National Highway Traffic Safety Administration.[52]

Still, it's no coincidence that, alongside a disregard for local laws, the vast majority of wealth created over the last few decades has been concentrated in the tech industry, starting with the rise of Silicon Valley venture capital that set the stage for today's obscene IPOs.

These days venture capital is centered around Sand Hill Road, the main thoroughfare connecting Palo Alto and Menlo Park, which might as well be paved in gold. These investment groups act as a sort of way station for big money with no particular place to be, like pension funds, endowments, and trust funds, even as economic inequality in the US continues to rise to untenable levels. But that's of little concern for the people whose only job is to make money. So in exchange for management fees that usually equal out to about 2 percent of the total fund, these VCs vet out young companies in need of cash and invest their clients' money in the hopes that they'll cash out big in the event of a sale or IPO.

"As a midwife, we raise money from endowments, and foundations and wealthy families and individuals and then we deploy it into people who are inventing the future," Lux Capital cofounder Josh Wolfe recently explained on the *Knowledge Project* podcast. "And then we are basically trying to figure out who's full of shit and not, and who is real and who is faking it."[53]

But the tech world, in particular, encourages its valuations to spiral upward by shrouding the industry in a New Age mysticism that transforms a tunnel-boring company into a futuristic shuttle system, a real-estate company into a state of consciousness, and an artist-booking company into a luxury music festival. Even the "real" founders who aren't full of shit, Wolfe says, tend to be irreverent and arrogant—and he considers those positive qualities. Plus, by definition, most of their products don't exist yet, so it tends to come down to what the investors want to believe.

"The super early stage is a bit more intuitive, you kind of have to feel whether or not this is the right team, and if this is a market that you really believe in, because essentially you're looking out five to ten years into the future, and nobody can predict the future," Marc Weinstein, a start-up founder and investor who was hired to help salvage the Fyre Festival in its final weeks, explained to me. "So what you're investing in

is the person, and the TAM—the total addressable market—
investors ask, is this a massive opportunity? Is it a margin of
opportunity that if they win, this could be a huge business?
And then tying it in with the team, are they the right people to do it?"

Sure, the products are ultimately how these investors and
companies justify the sums of money flowing through their
balance sheets, but a lot of the time they seem frankly irrelevant to the bottom line. What seems to matter more often
is who they're aligned with.

"If an entrepreneur is able to garner the support of credible investors with a strong track record for picking winners,
then other investors will pile in, and it's another element of
pattern matching. So oftentimes you see VC's that lack con-
viction will ask a founder, 'Who else invested?' Or, 'Come
back to me when you find a lead,'" said Weinstein. "I think
Theranos is a great case study of this, where other investors
will pile on without doing…they're almost outsourcing their
diligence to a group that they know is more credible than
they are."

Somewhere along the line, what had started as a niche
way of backing engineers leaving Fairchild (the first company to regularly use silicon in transistors that revolutionized
the world of technology) for the private sector converted into
a phenomenal fortune for a small group of people, none of
whom have been incentivized by the market to pay any of it
forward to the larger world in which they live. These companies are worth however much money people are willing
to put into it, and that seems to be the end of the discussion.

"You'd be amazed in diligencing, how many investors fail
to ask a simple question like, 'Does it work?'" Wolfe said.

Just as sharks risk dying when they stop moving, it seems,
so too do professional rich people.

"The VCs are getting paid on mark to market [the 'fair market value' as opposed to the value on a balance sheet], which is very rarely done in public companies. The only public company of note that did it was Enron," Wells explained. "These guys are very incentivized to deploy large amounts of capital, and the faster they can get it out the door and the faster they can mark it up on paper, the easier it is for them to go raise their next round. And a lot of them are charging three and thirty, and when you think about 3 percent on a billion-dollar fund, that's $30 million a year for a group of twenty-five, thirty people on Sand Hill Road. They're complicit because they don't want to do hard work and blow up any of their investments. Who wants to be the VC firm that calls bullshit on Theranos? You're not incentivized to. The incentivization is to get this thing where it's ready to go public as fast as possible. Take it public and exit."

I'd say it's like gambling but dumber, but with the obscene management fees quietly underwriting ventures like Juicero, the juicer that squeezes less efficiently than your hands, to an app that just texts the word *Yo!*, to Quibi, a streaming app backed by $2 billion that failed to even crack the iTunes Top 100 and shut down ignominiously six months later,[54] Wells says it's really more like getting paid to go to the casino.

"So I raise $100 million dollars and pay myself 2 percent manager fees. So $2 million a year for ten years, right? So it's going to be $20 million over the life of the fund, and the fees will cut off. And if you can do three or four in quick succession of those funds, raising on the success of the paper evaluation, paper gains, at your previous fund, using your pro rata rights to remain in for subsequent fundraising rounds, then you create a great outcome for yourself, even if you don't make a dime," Wells said. "So you go to the casino and you lose money…you still made 2 percent of the management fee for ten years on multiple vintages of the fund.

"And if you make money, then you take 30 percent of the profits and start writing think pieces," he concluded.

It all sort of seems like a Schrödinger's catfish situation to me, where the money coming out of a tech company is just as likely to be real or fake until you do an actual forensic accounting, at which point it'll probably be too late to matter, anyway. So I reached out to University of Texas business professor Robert Prentice to ask where all objective facts went in business. Reached by phone in his campus office, where he heads in to work every day (even in a pandemic), Prentice said the charade goes far beyond the tech industry.

"People of every age seem to be in sort of a post-truth sort of scenario here, where I get to pick my own facts. There are a lot of facts out there, I get to pick the ones that I like, and I can go with those, and nobody can really tell me those aren't the facts because it's my truth. Those are my facts, and don't tell me they're not," Prentice said. "The fact that we're all kind of getting caught up in that, leaves me very worried about the world. We even now get to pick which scientists we want to believe. And so I know that 98 percent of the scientists say this, but I like the guys who are in the 2 percent. I think what they say, they're scientists, after all, so I'm going to go with them. You can't tell me not to because, again, that's my truth."

I spoke with Prentice just as the pandemic was starting to peak in New York, so it took me a few weeks to realize that he had indirectly explained the reasoning behind Musk's prediction on Twitter that there would be "close to zero new cases in US too by end of April."[55]

Musk had been lobbying for California health authorities to reopen Alameda County, where his Teslas are manufactured, and to do that, he had promoted fringe science reports to his forty million Twitter followers, telling them that the coronavirus wasn't serious and that children were essentially immune to it. It was an incredibly careless and dangerous tactic but apparently a risk Musk thought worth taking.

Because although Musk framed his desperation to reopen as part of a larger fight against government encroachment, he also seemed singularly concerned with a man's right to make cars, and one car in particular: the Model Y. He'd been struggling to deliver on the crossover hybrid ever since opening up preorders last year, and production had been threatened by the virus. So when the county refused to oblige his death wish, he took a page from Uber's book, sued Alameda officials, and threatened to relocate to another state if they didn't give in.

"The unelected & ignorant 'Interim Health Officer' of Alameda is acting contrary to the Governor, the President, our Constitutional freedoms & just plain common sense,"[56] Musk tweeted. "Frankly, this is the final straw. Tesla will now move its HQ and future programs to Texas/Nevada immediately."

The county officials finally gave up at the end of May and allowed him to proceed with a modified safety plan after Musk announced he would be reopening with or without permission. It even prompted coronavirus-denier President Trump to celebrate his defiance on Twitter, though unfortunately for both Trump and the county, Musk appeared to endorse Kanye West in the 2020 election. And, just like the scientists predicted, more than one hundred cases of the virus were reported at the Tesla factory over the next few months, according to leaked internal documents. But throughout it all, and even in the absence of proper safety measures like social distancing, the plants kept running. (For what it's worth, Musk tweeted in November that he had tested both positive and negative for the virus, continuing his apparent lifelong dedication to never giving a straight answer.)

It's a specific type of confidence I've noticed before while watching, for example, Musk pretend to invent a special submarine to rescue a group of Thai children stuck in a cave that was actually too big and unwieldy to even fit inside the cave's narrow walls. Or how, when one of the rescuers correctly labeled it a "PR stunt," Musk called the man a "pedo" on Twitter and then tried to get BuzzFeed to run a hit piece falsely accusing the international hero of having sex with children.[57]

And then there was the time Musk promised a group of mayors that Tesla was going to manufacture one thousand lifesaving ventilators and distribute them to beleaguered hospitals.[58] And when the devices started showing up in boxes plastered in Tesla stickers like a press box one of the Kardashians might send out in advance of an exclusive makeup drop, the hospitals began dutifully issuing social media thank-yous.

But Musk's gift was exactly what the doctor didn't order, subsequent investigations revealed. It turns out the $800 bilevel positive airway pressure devices, also known as BPAPs, that he sent weren't even close to replacing the $50,000 machines that hospitals were in desperate need of. And while both machines are technically types of ventilators, scientists have warned that BPAPs might actually help spread the virus faster.[59]

Did Musk, who was intelligent enough to oversee the design of a rocketship that could launch a car into space, not know the difference between the expensive, lifesaving machines in the headlines and the cheap ones he was sourcing, or did he just not care? I'm not sure which is worse, but it was ambiguous enough that no real outrage followed.

"There used to be public shaming, but that seems to have gone away because we're now so partisanly divided that when one person accuses someone else of something, there's going to be a group that automatically endorses and retweets. And then there'll be the direct comments that ratio it out," Wells explained. "And that's kind of now where we've come, which is either thumbs-up or thumbs-down. And so nuance doesn't matter. You've got [only so many] characters to make your pitch."

Meanwhile, Musk's ill-advised tweets have become such a core component of his business that not only did the Securities and Exchange Commission (SEC) start requiring him to run them past a securities lawyer before posting, they've even sparked their own cottage industry of scams. "I'm giving 10,000 Bitcoin (BTC) to all community!" reads the typical message posted in the comments of Musk's tweets. All the user has to do is send "Musk" a small amount of bitcoin first as a verification device, which will of course be returned at a 10x rate. These tweets are posted from verified accounts whose names and photos have been changed to look like Musk's and then promoted to hit as many marks as possible before Twitter shuts the account down. As obvious and dumb as their methods are, these Musk pretenders have reportedly pulled in millions this way, and Twitter has been largely unable to stop it in real time. The platform even briefly, accidentally, blocked the real Elon Musk after he tweeted about Bitcoin in 2018. And in July 2020, the scammers were able to hack a number of notable Twitter accounts, including Musk, Barack Obama, and Joe Biden, to post the messages directly. Authorities say they were able to steal about $120,000 before Twitter could shut it down.[60]

But overt Twitter scams aside, if the most celebrated companies are hemorrhaging money, the most powerful executives are openly bragging about all the laws they're breaking in the name of capitalism, and the richest people are promising things they can't actually execute just for clout, what *exactly* was McFarland's crime?

That's not a rhetorical question. I've struggled, over the years, to pinpoint the defining differences between McFarland and these people held up as titans of industry, and honestly, all I can come up with is Musk had more money and a worse employee-safety track record.

I don't think it's any coincidence that these larger-than-life moneymen seem to live so comfortably in the gap between their promises and the reality. They're good at getting other people to go along with their ideas. They're hailed as visionaries. And they never let the truth stop them from a good marketing campaign.

A recent *BookForum* piece described one of these overhyped men as having "three key traits: he was tall, grandiose, and drank tequila." Incredibly, this line referred to neither McFarland nor Musk, who's been trying to launch an alcohol line called "Teslaquila." (It was WeWork's Adam Neumann.)

But back to Musk. He's considered a genius because he made a bunch of money on PayPal and once shot a car into space. But I'd argue his real talent is marketing and figuring out how to get federal subsidies to keep his companies afloat. Because when you really look hard at his legacy, it's not as impressive as the headlines would have you believe. For one thing, Musk's SpaceX rockets also keep blowing up on the launchpad, including one model that destroyed a $200 million satellite owned by Facebook in the process. And then there's his high-tech Hyperloop plan to revolutionize underground travel, an exciting idea on paper that he's yet to successfully implement in real life. But it has been a great way of marketing his tunnel-boring company.

At least I have to presume that's what led Chicago mayor Rahm Emanuel to sign a deal with Musk in 2018 to create a $1 billion high-speed tunnel system in Chicago. The project was supposed to whisk nineteen hundred people an hour to

O'Hare Airport in less than twelve minutes via sealed pods mounted atop electric sleds.[61] But just a few months later, Musk announced that instead of pods, he would be using modified Teslas instead, a bait and switch that saw a mass-transit project suddenly transformed into an individual one. With Emanuel now out of office and the proposed transit limited to individual cars, the project now seems unlikely to proceed. And overhyped Boring Company hyperloop plans in Nevada, Virginia, and California have hit similar tunnel walls. But to hear Musk tell it, the projects are all moving lightspeed ahead.

It's "kind of a standard rationalization to make that 'Yes, I just have this one little problem I have to overcome and once I overcome that, then I'm going to have it. All we've got to do is get the financial footing that we need and then we can pull it all off,'" Prentice said. "'So I'm justified in telling this little white lie because it is going to lead me to the greater gain that is, after all, in the best interest of everybody.' The human ability to rationalize is just kind of unending, I'm afraid to say."

There's not much that can be said about Donald Trump that hasn't been said already, but it's notable to me that the man is simply unable to separate the truth from his preferred version of truth.

"There's no such thing, unfortunately, anymore as facts," said CNN commentator Scottie Nell Hughes in 2016,[62] just a few weeks after Trump, who lost the popular vote to Hillary Clinton by 2.8 million people, started claiming he had actually won it.

"In addition to winning the Electoral College in a landslide, I won the popular vote if you deduct the millions of people who voted illegally," he claimed—and people really believed him.[63] Despite the fact that a voter-fraud commission he himself set up could find not a scintilla of evidence to support his words, close to 50 percent of Trump voters truly believe he won both the 2016 electoral college and the popular vote, according to a Politico poll conducted in 2017.[64]

It's worth noting that Borte—the writer and director of *The Joneses*—pinpoints the blame for much of where we are today on the 2007 writers' strike.

"Reality programming all of a sudden just blew up because they didn't have to pay writers, and I could feel a sense of impending doom immediately with it," Borte said. "Making celebrities out of people just for allowing cameras to not only follow them around, but also create drama where maybe there wasn't drama, that happened with reality programming in general. And then you've got someone that has this influence because they've been in millions of households for multiple seasons.

"I think that when you see someone on a screen, over a long period of time, the repetition of seeing someone that takes on some kind of level of authority figure, or some kind of aspirational hero quality, I think it gives them the power to be able to do those kinds of things," Borte said.

Donald Trump may well not have been a successful billionaire businessman, for example, but he certainly played one on TV.

"You didn't even need to read *King Lear* [to have seen all this coming], you could've just watched *The Apprentice*. I mean, it was basically his training for becoming the president. It's this obfuscation of what's real and what's staged," said Weinstein. "It created this CEO character that gets to fire people and make the decisions and is opinionated and a strong man."

And after spending years in people's living rooms making up his own plotlines that were then aired under the guise of "reality," why wouldn't Trump continue to do it from the White House? It's not like anyone with the power to stop him was requiring him to do anything as mundane as sticking to the facts.

"In a world in which politicians can challenge the facts *and pay no political price whatsoever*, post-truth is bigger than any one person," Lee McIntyre, the philosopher and author of *Post-Truth* says. "It exists in us as well as our leaders. And the forces behind it have been building up for quite some time."[65]

The result is that we're living now in a world where which side you're on matters more than what the facts say. The official Oxford definition of *post-truth* is "relating to or denoting circumstances in which objective facts are less influential in shaping public opinion than appeals to emotion and personal belief." Unofficially, what that seems to mean is that there are no facts anymore—only gut feelings.

"It is endemic, whether it's Theranos or billion-dollar whales or WeWork or JetSmarter or Canadian cannabis or vegan influencers or Tesla or music or the rest," sighed Wells on a recent phone call from his golf cottage, where he's been riding out the pandemic. "There's a whole lot of promotion that doesn't require any substantiation.

"It just feels like our skeptical eye just has been removed entirely from the financial community and somehow PR has replaced journalism," he said. "You've created a perfect storm for fraudsters, well intentioned or not, to fleece the public and the capital base."

Wells, whose Tod's loafers have trodden almost every known port of the global circuit of under-forty entrepreneurs, from late summers in Mykonos to New Year's Eve in Aspen, suspects people also just really want to believe in something. Wells is the kind of guy that knows everyone, including and especially the famous models and money guys McFarland had tried to use as social camouflage for so many years, so he had a front-row seat to the wreckage of the Fyre Festival.

"The whole reason I got involved in the first place with the Fyre thing was that I had friends that were investors who were saying like, 'Hey, look, we're looking at doing this receivable factoring deal.' And I went through the whole effort of saying, 'This doesn't make sense. Duh, duh, duh, duh.' And one guy listened to me, and the other guy didn't listen to me and lost $5 million bucks," Wells said. "And he's a smart guy. He's a very savvy professional investor with hundreds of millions of dollars under management, and he lost $5 million of his personal wealth because he wanted the aspirational stuff, because it was interesting at dinner parties."

Wells, who often refers to himself as an old man shaking a fist at the sky, had thought the whole Fyre Festival scheme sounded idiotic from the start, so he was surprised and dismayed when his friends started showing interest in attending.

"We're in a yield-starved environment. People want to be part of the zeitgeist. Social media allows you to see other investments that became lifestyles and brands in a way that nobody's going to get excited about picking the stock of an oil and gas company in Oklahoma," Wells said. "Unfortunately, I think what people are finding is the consumer-facing brands are not nearly as economically viable as the very boring oil and gas company in Oklahoma."

Wells has thought a lot about how easy it would be to team up with a journalist to invent a fake product and relax as the checks rolled in without ever leaving home.

"I'd hate to fleece family and friends, investors, but we could almost set it up where we did it in reverse merger into a shell and then hyped it on the Robin Hood apps. I don't know if you're familiar with it at all, but it's a scam too," Wells said. "We could hype something and, purely as a think piece, demonstrate how easy it is to defraud everybody while capturing glowing praise and personally enriching ourselves. It's just so easy. The model is so easy to duplicate that it's really terrifying."

(Eight months later, the SEC concurred, charging Robin Hood with making "misleading statements and omissions in customer communications" that cost its users tens of millions of dollars. The firm has agreed to pay a $65 million penalty without admitting or denying the SEC's findings.)

During McFarland's rise, cautious of allegations of tortious interference, Wells was still optimistic enough to think that if he quietly warned the right people, the festival would sputter out on its own. But he had underestimated McFarland, who, court records show, secured a critical last-minute loan by faking a document that showed he had $2.56 million in personal Facebook shares and also came close to a deal with Comcast that would have kept the whole thing afloat by valuing Fyre at more than $90 million.[66] Even the people who should have known better apparently just wanted to believe.

"There's just something about youth and energy and excitement. It's a story that you want to succeed. I mean, you want them to succeed," Prentice, the University of Texas professor, explained. "They're appealing, and you want to believe it so much that you can talk yourself into it.

"People tend to believe that that could be them," he added. "And again, when that story then gets told to you by a young, smart, appealing, persuasive sort of person, you want to believe it, and so it's easy to do it."

According to the SEC, McFarland ultimately managed to induce more than a hundred investors—old and young, but mostly old—to pour close to $28 million into his harebrained ideas.[67] Not only was he being introduced as a hotshot young founder, the press was backing it up. Thanks to the cover provided by his celebrity connections and wealthy backers, news coverage of him from Spling to Fyre had been almost universally positive.

"I think the parallel between someone like Billy and Elon is, as we've spoken about in the past, just being able to fake it till you make it. There was a moment in time when Elon was launching Tesla, SpaceX, and I think SolarCity at the same time, and all of the companies were basically going to go bankrupt, and he somehow managed to pull financing in," Weinstein said. "I think that Trump, Billy, and Elon are all exceptional at raising capital, though Trump and Billy seem better at losing money."

Wells points to the crash of Jetsmarter, a high-flying app that had promised to be the Uber of private jets that is now the subject of at least thirteen lawsuits and embezzlement allegations—despite effusive press and celebrity endorsements galore.[68] "People in the industry are already calling it the Fyre Festival of aviation," an anonymous source told the *New York Post* in 2019 after its valuation dropped from $1.6 billion to an estimated $20 million.[69] (McFarland loved the mindset behind the business model so much he reportedly briefly hired a man named Matt Morchower as COO of Magnises, who worked there in between founding one private jet startup Marquis Jets, which was sold to Berkshire Hathaway, and another company ClipperJet, which failed to take flight.)

"I think about this all the time. The JetSmarter guys, that business model has demonstrably been proven not to work, and yet somehow, the story line for the past four years is how they got to a billion-dollar valuation, and Jay-Z invested, and this and that," Wells said. "No one's like, 'Hey, look, Net-Jets was purchased by Berkshire, and it's publicly available with what you can do with that.' It doesn't work. Why is the coverage glowing and positive versus, like, 'Hey, this thing's hemorrhaging cash and there's no way it works?'"

That's a question Ja Rule (real name Jeffrey Atkins) has for all the people who now think he should have been able to see past the hype around McFarland.

"When I met Billy, I was introduced to him as this child prodigy. He started his first company when he was thirteen, sold it at fifteen. He's onto his next company. He exited with that one, and now he's onto his next. He was only twenty-five. He was onto his third company and had a smorgasbord of smart investors," Atkins said. "So, here Ja Rule comes along. I'm supposed to be the one who cracked the code?"[70]

Atkins is also tired of people asking him to take responsibility for what happened. He knows now McFarland was defrauding investors. But he's adamant that his intentions were always pure and that the festival itself was never a fraud. He truly believed in it, so how could it have been? As far as Atkins is concerned, the question at issue isn't how closely Fyre's product aligned with its marketing, it's whether the company provided a product at all.

That's the disturbing subtext to the quotes about how the Fyre team "almost pulled it off." What those people don't mean is that the Fyre team came close to providing what they'd falsely advertised. What they mean is the Fyre team almost provided enough of the bare minimum required to keep all the money they'd obtained through false advertising. And not to be cynical, but I honestly believe that had either the more famous influencers shown up or the bands on the Fyre lineup actually performed, people would have pretended to have fun rather than lose face after all that bragging, and McFarland would have been sentenced to a *Forbes* cover instead of prison.

The general public's refusal to accept Atkins's distinction between the marketing of the festival idea and the execution of it has haunted him ever since.

In November 2019, I went to see Atkins speak on a freezing cold weekend at an internet-marketing convention in downtown Raleigh, a gray stretch punctuated by the art deco towers that prop up its business district. Between the single digit temperatures and the searing wind, I found myself wearing two coats and still shivering on the short walk to the convention center, which happened to be located around the corner from two different Marriotts. It was a wonderfully convenient, if not somewhat confusing, place to coordinate drinks, such as I did with Raleigh blogger Seth Crossno and his attorney, Stacy Miller, who had recently won a $5 million verdict on behalf of Crossno and another Fyre attendee.[71] (They've yet to collect but seem cautiously optimistic about the process.)

When we sat down at one of the two Marriotts, however, they were much more curious about what Atkins would have to say himself, now that he was free of the constraints of the class-action suit, in which he had been dropped as a defendant earlier that month.

Atkins's "Fyreside Chat" was a one-off event in the larger, nationwide convention called the Internet Summit, a traveling conference that boasts an impressively deranged list of speakers and experts who all share a passion for helping digital marketers sell more stuff.

With dozens of featured talks each day on topics ranging from "Four Automated Email Series That Get Serious Results" to "Convincing Customers to Swipe Right on Your Brand," the summit was a whirlwind of persuasive tactics for just about every program and device you could think of, whether you were approaching it from a direct-to-consumer or business-to-business background. This particular North

Carolina *Glengarry Glen Ross* cosplay convention also included a keynote address in which a woman most famous for being Mark Zuckerberg's sister performed a parody song about the internet, the Marriott did a thirty-minute ad for its Las Vegas property and called it a talk on FOMO, and I gave up my email address at a kiosk in exchange for a two-dollar bill stamped with the name of an SEO company.

But the interesting thing about Atkins's appearance was that he wasn't being billed as some sort of cautionary tale— he was being presented as a marketing legend.

A few minutes into the scheduled speech, accompanied by one of his own songs, Atkins bounded into the room and up onto Stage 2, where he mounted his defense. He began by outlining the major differences between false advertising and fraud—and explaining why that difference made him innocent.

"Every smart person in this room knows there's a difference between false advertising and fraud, right? I'm gonna give you the difference. False advertisement is what you see every day. Commercials, social media. They call it puffery, and it's completely legal," Atkins said. "Before y'all get to screaming, 'This is a fraud, fraud, fraud,' guys, there's a difference between false advertisement and fraud. False advertising, I can go with that. Those tents is not what the fuck we advertised. I got that. But fraud is a horse of a different color, you understand, and when my name is on the marquee, you're going to stop saying that, so we can get this straight and understand what this is."

In an industry that runs on magical thinking, the delineation between thought and action was eroded long ago. So too has the delineation between truth and fiction. You don't have to intend to be a scammer to scam yourself and everyone around you. You just have to believe in yourself.

"The traditional scammer notion has always been fake it until you make it. But with all the success that so many startups have had in Silicon Valley, you've always got lots of examples you could look at and say to yourself, 'They were a long shot. Nobody thought they would succeed and yet they did,'" Prentice said. "When those people are interviewed on TV, what do they say? 'Well, I believed in myself. I believed I could make it work, and I just kept trying. I just kept trying and then I succeeded.'"

It reminds me of something a commencement speaker for the Baruch College graduating class of 2017 once said about the importance of believing in yourself in a world where the Elon Musk types inevitably end up ahead.

"A lot of people talk about the third wave, the new revolution. They talk about connectivity. They talk about internet. They talk about Hyperloops to connect cities really quickly, and tunnels so we avoid the traffic. That all sounds amazing. But let me tell you something: I don't think that's true."

After waiting for the applause to die out, Adam Neumann, the founder of WeWork, continued his speech.

"We will not stand by, and we will not lend our power to presidents, CEOs, ministers, or anybody—any leader—that does not lead us in the right direction, that lies to us, that does not take care of us. No one is above the law," Neumann said.

Less than three years later, WeWork would be so broke that planned cost-saving layoffs actually had to be postponed because the company couldn't afford to pay out the severance.

"It's very hard, in the early, nascent embryonic stages of a business, to really—and I'm being intellectually honest here— know if somebody is going to be an absolute genius or a total fraud. Because the best storytellers are also the best con men.

Or women, as it was in Theranos," Lux Capital cofounder Josh Wolfe admitted on a recent episode of *The Knowledge Project* podcast.

The flip side of that kind of narcissism, however, is how these overpromising, underperforming leaders are unable to see the true limitations of their own abilities. Convincing a group of investors and employees to believe in you is one thing; actually executing it is another. It's only when things get too untenable to continue—and mind you, Theranos still tried to raise another round of funding even after the *Wall Street Journal* had begun the process of exposing Elizabeth Holmes's alleged fraud—that changes are made. (She denies the charges.)

"It's hard to know whether or not she is just a sociopath or if she really believed in herself so much that the lies that she was telling, they just seemed so persuasive," Prentice said. "I don't know, I really don't, if Elizabeth Holmes knew she was lying all the way along and just didn't care, she so much wanted to be rich and famous that she was willing to tell these lies. Or, if she's just so endowed with the overoptimism that a lot of us have—but probably not to the degree that she does—and the overconfidence that she had. 'I really can do this. I really can change the world. I'm really meant to change the world.'"

Weinstein, the start-up investor and advisor who worked on the Fyre Festival in its last few weeks, offered his own take on why the cult of founder is so powerful.

"I think folks, they want role models, and for many reasons, successful entrepreneurs are great role models because they've created value and they've built something out of nothing, especially startup founders, right?" he asked me rhetorically over the phone one day during the pandemic. "They take an idea and they make it a reality. And so that's an admirable quality. It's a creative capacity that, I think, is to be admired."

The problems start, he says, "When we start to objectify the other, when we start to put people on pedestals—we lose sight of the fact that they're just people, and people have flaws, no matter how great they are. And I think that Elon Musk is an example of that; Steve Jobs is an example of that, in the way that it sounds like he was a really challenging person to work for, and a bit of a monster. And there are other examples of those types of charismatic characters who do great things, but also turn out to be a little bit of monsters.

"I think a corollary to that is this guru worship," Weinstein said, pointing to recent coverage of the Indian guru Bhagwan Shree Rajneesh, the subject of the recent Netflix documentary *Wild Wild Country*, and the hot yoga founder Bikram Choudhury, who was the subject of the recent Netflix documentary *Bikram: Yogi, Guru, Predator*. (Choudhury has denied the allegations.)

"It's just strange that so much beauty and good can come out of people. If you look at what Bikram created, thousands, and potentially hundreds of thousands, of people have learned about the yoga traditions through entering a fitness class at a Bikram studio, and gone deeper into that practice. It's had a profound impact on their lives," he said. "But then you also had this character who was at times a monster. I don't know, it's fascinating just how we objectify the other on this pedestal."

There have been a lot of studies and commentary on the cult workplaces created by larger-than-life company founders, but McFarland in particular presents a rare case where we can attempt to understand what was going on in his mind, because he actually hired two different mental health experts to analyze him during the sentencing portion of his trial.

"In my opinion, at the time of the instant offenses, Mr. McFarland's mental state was compromised by a combination of factors. He was experiencing symptoms of mania or hypo-mania due to an untreated Unspecified Bipolar and Related Disorder," Dr. Cheryl Paradis wrote in a document submit-ted to the court.[72] "He was not sleeping and felt exhausted and overwhelmed. He had a diminished capacity to foresee the consequences of his actions."

Another mental health expert hired by McFarland's defense team, Columbia University professor and forensic psychia-trist Dr. Andrew Levin, concluded McFarland suffers from both ADHD and Other Specified Bipolar and Related Dis-order that "resulted in his pattern of undertaking on multiple projects accompanied by unrealistic appraisals of success." Dr. Levin ultimately concluded in his report that McFarland "did not feel that what he did was wrong."[73]

"His success reinforced his grandiosity and distorted sense that there were 'no boundaries.' It was in this context that he developed the unrealistic plans for the festival. Despite input from others that he could not accomplish what he proposed, he clung to his grandiose plan until the end. His misrepre-sentation to investors grew out of an unrealistic belief that the festival would succeed and a fear of letting down those who had already invested," Levin wrote. "Following arrest, he had a brief period of lower mood and then reverted to his grandiose, unrealistic ventures... These patterns derive from his ADHD and mood disorder."

But again, whatever his reasons, McFarland wasn't color-ing that far outside the lines of the tech world. So he had used doctored financial statements and pretended he had deals to land investments. Wasn't he just thinking like a CEO?

"People screw up mostly, not because they're just intentional frauds, at least in their own minds, but because they will tell themselves a story that makes them feel like they're one of the good guys, even as they do bad things," Prentice said. "When they're charming and energetic and persuasive, they can take a lot of people along with them, unfortunately."

Just ask Neumann, who turned his real-estate venture into a $47 billion lifestyle brand,[74] partied his way to fame and fortune, and sailed off into the sunset under a billion-dollar golden parachute while his precious WeWork burned behind him.

Like McFarland and Musk, Neumann hadn't always been that way. Raised on a kibbutz, Neumann had tried his hand at respectable professions, like manufacturing shoes with collapsible heels and baby onesies with built-in kneepads. (Their slogan: "Just because they don't tell you, doesn't mean they don't hurt.") Incredibly, neither took off.

But in 2008, he and a friend cofounded Green Desk and went to work subleasing office space.

In Wells' opinion, he scammed his way to the top.

"His first deals at Green Desk, he screwed over two of his partners, and then they screwed over one of his equity partners and the guy that was fronting the building," Wells said. "He sold that company, exited, took that cash, and then individually restarted WeWork the next day. And then he owned 100 percent of the cap table. And then just can fly around the world on a G650 espousing platitudes without really doing anything and creating anything."

Neumann's real business was convincing the world that WeWork was a game-changing idea.

Tall, affable, and celebrity-adjacent (his wife happens to be Gwyneth Paltrow's cousin), Neumann could have been Billy McFarland's older brother. With his dark looks and confident air, he traveled everywhere by private jet (memorably leaving a cereal box stuffed with weed behind on one flight), rode around the city in Maybachs, and threw lavish, mandatory company parties in remote locations with celebrities like Lorde, the Red Hot Chili Peppers, and Ashton Kutcher.

Like McFarland, Neumann's brand was jet-setting, partying, and making his own rules. Sometimes he didn't wear shoes in the office; sometimes he skateboarded through it instead. His wife, Rebekah Neumann, would sometimes fire employees she barely knew for having the "wrong energy." A former yoga teacher, she also helped imbue a boring real-estate company with a spiritual mission that apparently accounted for much of its valuation. But she also knew what was up the moment she met him, Neumann told the Baruch graduating class of 2017.[75]

"Rebekah went on the first date with me, and within five minutes—I say five minutes to be nice, but it truly took ten seconds—she looked me straight in the eye, and she said, 'You, my friend, are full of shit,'" Neumann said. "She then said, 'Every single word that comes out of your mouth is fake. You talk about business, but you have no passion. You talk about money, but I know you're broke… And worst of all, everything you do, it's without meaning.'"

Rebekah might have seen through him, but when Neumann talked about office subleasing as a calling to higher community consciousness, the people working for him heard a revolution. And because he framed his business as a tech company, with planned housing developments, schools, and even a WeWork on Mars (where Musk plans on landing by 2026), his valuations soared.

And his devoted employees probably would have followed him there too. After closing a deal on the top thirty floors of the Woolworth Building in 2013, Neumann reportedly brought a group of drunk employees to the top for a tour, encouraged them to walk out on a ledge with no guardrails or safety gear, and dared them all to drink out of an old beer bottle he'd found on the ground. Two out of the three We-Work employees took sips, the third told the *New York Times*.[76]

But perhaps Neumann's greatest trick of all was his preternatural ability to profit personally from WeWork. Using his own private funds, he'd buy buildings and then lease them to his company. In 2019, he personally trademarked the word *We* and then sold it to WeWork for almost $6 million, although he later returned the money after a public outcry.[77] He didn't even try to pretend any of the money was linked to WeWork's proprietary tech or real-estate holdings, which were intentionally slim—most of WeWork's branded properties were actually just subleases, an untenable business plan. Instead, he explained in 2017, WeWork's "valuation and size today are much more based on our energy and spirituality than it is on a multiple of revenue."

"That business never made sense," Wells said. "It's been done twenty times before, and it works really well in a growth cycle and very, very poorly in a down growth cycle, the subleasing of rent. There was nothing innovative about what the business model was, and yet it had a tech element to it, and he owned none of his real estate and somehow was going to make money subleasing all this stuff."

In fact, WeWork's valuation and size were almost entirely due to a different man entirely: the Japanese billionaire Masayoshi Son, the CEO of SoftBank who also happens to back Uber. He's probably done more to inflate the Silicon Valley bubble than anyone else, but after losing a fortune twice and gaining it back three times, he's still making big bets that any company he takes a shine to can end up owning a sector thanks to the sheer amount of cash he pumps into it. Even so, it turns out he's also using other people's money to achieve great wealth. These days, most of Son's investing is done through the Vision Fund, a $100 billion technology-focused venture capital fund that derives a large percentage of its capital from Saudi Arabia.

"If a founder asked the Vision Fund for $40 million, Mr. Son might ask, 'What would you do with $400 million?'" the *New York Times* reported.[78] A senior executive reportedly told the paper, "Masa has his own style and others might choke, but Adam would be like, '$400 million? How about $4 billion, and I can do this for you.'"

It was actually about $4.4 billion, when all was said and done. At the end of day, Son had spent less than fifteen minutes at Neumann's office, but it was enough to set off a deleterious domino effect.

"What he did was he reset the market price for valuations because he had more cash to deploy than anybody else. But everyone calls the Vision Fund $100 billion fund. It's not a $100 billion fund. It's $40 billion worth of equity, $60 billion worth of debt, and then $60 billion worth of debt as a 7 percent interest rate. It's a $30 billion fund that could run for eight years based on the interest cost and only repay the equity portion of the fund that was raised," Wells said. "Does that make sense? It's completely insane, this model that he did, and of course he was trying to go raise the second Vision Fund off of the strength of the markup and valuations at WeWork that he was providing in order for a justification to go raise another fund. It was never going to work."

The coronavirus ultimately gave Son a chance to claw back some of Neumann's parachute. But it also revealed the weaknesses in his portfolio, which had become worth less than the cost of its investments in early May 2020.

According to the *New York Times*, Son held an earnings call where he compared himself to Jesus and the Beatles and spoke of a brighter future by referencing a graphic of two unicorns falling into a hole in the ground.

"Our unicorns are facing serious challenges against the background of the coronavirus outbreak, but I believe that some of them will fly over the Valley of Coronavirus and go beyond and fly high," he said.

It could have been Billy McFarland talking to his team as he shut down Spling and turned to his next scheme.

2

Fake It Till You Make It

With Spling all but dead, McFarland needed something new, and fast.

A light bulb went off late one night in 2013 while he was out to dinner with his friends. Though the group was splitting the check evenly, he noticed that the people at his table paying their shares with heavy, metal AmEx cards seemed a bit...elevated, socially, above the plebes who were paying with plastic debit cards. More importantly, he noticed that other people were noticing it too. McFarland, well on his way to becoming an expert at identifying and exploiting social markers, thought there might be a business there.

"I was like, 'Wow, what if I could make these cooler?'" McFarland later described it. "So I went and ordered a sheet of metal from China, and, like, magnetic tape. I had this, like, giant sheet that was super thin, and I found a way to copy my debit card onto this sheet of metal. And I did it, and it worked. And I, like, went down to the deli, and went and, like, bought something with this, like, stupid card, and I was like, 'Shit, it works. I can go to the store and buy stuff with this.' And that was the genesis of the Magnises card."[79]

(Sourcing supplies from China was also something he apparently did from time to time. A former employee tells me McFarland once sourced an order of hoverboards at the height of their popularity and confidently presold them to his members only to see the shipment get turned away at customs.)

The name of his new card, Magnises, was "Latin for absolutely nothing," McFarland admitted in 2014. And so was the business model.

The venture had started with an $11,000 a month loft space that McFarland rented on the sixth floor of a Wooster Street apartment building. He'd provide open bars, bottle service, and professional photography for his guests, many of whom were recent New York City private-school grads. The special metal card and concierge service provided a business excuse to keep the party going.

At the beginning, there was plenty of company money and bright-eyed millennials happy to spend it, dazzling the deep-pocketed middle-aged men in the room, like Deep Fork Capital's Tim Komada, McFarland's old backer from Spling, who was photographed hanging out, conspicuously corporate, at one loft party packed with dozens of young women and the rapper Wale.

According to Page Six, Anna Delvey, the notorious Soho grifter now serving four to twelve years for fraud, even allegedly moved into the loft space, uninvited, for around four months.[80]

"Anna knew people on Billy's team," a so-called insider told the gossip rag. "She just asked to stay for a few days... then she wouldn't leave."

At that point in his career, however, McFarland was too nonconfrontational to directly evict her, the paper claimed. "He hinted, the staff hinted. She had Balenciaga bags and clothes everywhere. The company wound up moving into a town house. That's the only way they got her out! She had been there for four months!"

But it turned out that McFarland had been ready to move out, anyway. In his first year of business, he had managed to pull in $1.5 million in seed funding for Magnises from Deep Fork and Great Oaks Venture Capital. Former Def Jam president Kevin Liles, former MasterCard International chairman Lance Weaver, and the socialite Dori Cooperman, who would later work with him on Fyre, also came on as advisers.

Along the way, he had also gained the patronage of Aubrey McClendon, the then–CEO of Chesapeake Energy and a part owner of the Oklahoma City Thunder. According to someone who knew both men, McClendon appeared to be under the impression McFarland was some kind of millennial whisperer.

"I remember [McClendon] just being totally mesmerized by Billy. They'd invested a lot of money in Magnises originally. So he had a real charisma and a real, great big vision that those tech people and those tech investors get very mesmerized by it," said the mutual friend, who wishes to remain anonymous. "I mean, he was like twenty-two when I first met him, and he was already on his third tech company. His other company had made money, like paid back investors. He was a very charismatic, big thinker. It seems like he had these delusions of grandeur that led to disastrous consequences, which I guess is the flip side of great vision and great inspiration."

Whatever it was about McFarland that ultimately drew McClendon in, his involvement with Magnises bolstered McFarland's reputation almost as much as it did its coffers. And the financier had a personal interest in helping McFarland's venture succeed: McClendon's daughter, Callie Katt, also happened to be an early employee at Magnises, serving first as the vice president of operations and membership and later as chief financial officer.

With his team set up and the company funded, McFarland set out to make a name for himself in the press. It didn't prove too difficult: almost overnight, his face was suddenly everywhere in the media alongside headlines declaring him the next big thing.

As *Fortune* reported: "When McFarland wasn't pitching insiders, he was pitching the public.He went on Fox Business, CNBC, and Bloomberg TV. His company was also profiled by the *New York Times*. Sometimes appearing alongside Ja Rule, McFarland was continuously puffing up his product, using the same talking points almost verbatim. He speaks with a rapid staccato, with every phrase ending abruptly as he hopscotches from one marketing buzzword to the next."

The writer Jack Crosbie noticed a similar detail about the legend surrounding Elon Musk while working as a journalist at an unnamed tech blog. Neither his boss nor the audience he was writing for seemed to care about whether the information they were reading was true, they just wanted a fun, shareable story about a cool tech dude.

"The site largely focused on the kind of stuff that would hit big with the content-hungry crowds of Facebook users interested in pages like 'I Fucking Love Science,' Star Wars, and the Marvel and DC comic book universes. Above all, our readers fucking loved, and I mean LOVED, Elon Musk," Crosbie recalled in a 2020 essay for *Discourse Blog*.[81] "The top-performing social headlines we ran, for the most part, were ones that praised something Musk was doing. In 2016 (and, to a large extent, still), a not-insignificant part of Musk's business relied on coverage like this—his companies enjoyed almost overwhelmingly positive coverage, allowing Musk to repeatedly brag about Tesla's advertising-free business model. His companies didn't actually make any money, of course, forcing him to consolidate Tesla and Solar City into one electric vehicles/clean energy conglomerate, but his pop-culture exposure as a 'real-life Tony Stark' was at its absolute zenith. He sent rockets into space and loved *Rick and Morty*. He played Overwatch in his spare time: the most exciting inventor in the world was a gamer too! His sleek, lightning fast electric cars went "ludicrous speed" and played the nyan cat meme."

Crosbie, who was then twenty-five and making $45,000 a year, didn't go into the job with the intention of shilling for Musk, but found himself trapped in that role anyway.

"As any reporter covering this beat can tell you, almost all of this stuff was complete and utter horseshit. The problem was, our readers did not want to hear that. They wanted to believe," Crosbie said. "And because there were over a million of them following on our Facebook page that we depended on for clicks, the readers got their way. Critical or 'snarky' coverage of the tech world was deemed 'uncurious' (their word), as our metrics showed that our Musk-loving readers responded better to positive stories about big tech."

Crosbie, who was laid off from the site in 2017, eventually ended up at Splinter, part of the Gawker network of websites that tech billionaire Peter Thiel semi-successfully sued out of existence in 2016, the culmination of a Count of Monte Cristo–style revenge plan that apparently stemmed from his deep-seated grudge over the site's critical coverage of his business ventures, including one article which outed him as gay. (Thiel, who referred to the website's writers as "terrorists", claimed to have spent around $10million of his own money secretly financing lawsuits against the company in order to "defend journalism.") After Splinter finally folded in 2019, Crosbie and his coworkers launched *Discourse*, which is entirely worker-owned and currently thriving on Substack. Watching Musk's self-implosion these last few years has just been an added bonus.

"One consolation, to me, has been watching Musk reveal himself to the world at large," Crosbie wrote. "Though there does seem to be some rhyme and reason to his erratic and often illegal tweets, Musk's public persona has transitioned from quirky Tony Stark to Howard Hughes pissing in milk jars faster than you can say 'Azealia Banks' Instagram Story.' He's shot himself in the dick on Twitter repeatedly over the past few years in a frankly embarrassing chain of events involving multiple SEC inquiries and a defamation lawsuit from a cave diver," who Musk infamously referred to as a "pedo guy". "He still has a legion of fans that defend him at every possible opportunity, but the breathless puff parade of free advertising has largely ended. There are a few media outlets still doing it for him, but fortunately, I don't write for any of them anymore."

While McFarland was making the publicity rounds, he had left his new company to figure things out on their own. It was only by hiring experts at the last minute that anything got done, recalls one such expert hired at the last minute to save Magnises's launch.

It was like Fyre, "but without the dire consequences," said the source, a publicist who requested anonymity.

"A friend from New York that's very connected knew Billy's partner at that time's mother, and the mother called him in a panic, knowing that he was very connected in New York, saying her son and his friend were starting a company and they had their launch party in two days, but it was super chaotic, and could he help?" said the publicist. "So he stepped in, he got me to start their PR, he got a celebrity to host it, and found a venue—the Rivington Penthouse, and Rosario Dawson to host. We put it together in two days. When you asked, I just remembered, wow, well, [McFarland] is kind of reckless and sucks. Maybe he is a psychopath or a sociopath."

The Yellow Fever Fashion event, which was featured in *People* magazine, helped put McFarland on the map. Meanwhile, no one on the outside ever knew how close they'd come to failing. And on the inside, even the publicist still thought the kid had a vision.

"I remember just meeting him and just thinking, 'Wow, this guy is fantastic, and so cute and so wide-eyed.' When I first met him, I just set my terms and like, 'Okay, we're gonna fix this. We're gonna get it. Let's get started.' And we did. It kind of turned into a thing," the publicist said. "He has a knack for turning things into things. He has that vision where people kind of drink the Kool-Aid."

In March of 2014, Magnises moved from the loft into a rented $13,000-a-month West Village town house. For one of its very first events, Magnises threw a party for One Management, a modeling agency. The actor Norman Reedus and a handful of models, including Terese Pagh, were in attendance, party photos show. So was Morgan O'Connor, a dreadlocked former Polo model with a long domestic assault rap sheet. (President Trump once said he'd pay "millions" for his hair, though he hasn't indicated any intention of pardoning any of O'Connor's various assault arrests.)

Within a few months, Magnises, at least in reputation, had become a hit, thanks in large part to the effusive press coverage of McFarland. *Bloomberg News*, *Billboard*, glossy magazines, and local TV programs all welcomed him in. Even the normally sardonic *New York Post* feted his new company, alongside a photograph of Billy in a suit, stretched out across the laps of six young women, under the headline *The college dropout behind NYC's most exclusive credit card.*

"You've never heard of this 22-year-old college dropout, but he's cooler than you. (Just ask him.) The Short Hills, NJ, native—the son of two real-estate developers—launched his first startup (a service that matched websites and designers) at 13, and skipped out on Bucknell University during his freshman year to launch a content-sharing site called Spling," the paper reported. "From there, it was a short leap to starting his own credit-card company—and only letting in members whom he and his staff of 11 deem cool enough."

The exclusive-membership pitch had been snatched straight out of the Bernie Madoff playbook, including the persnickety detail that almost none of it was true. Like he had done with Spling years before, McFarland had been employing some big-time magical thinking. Despite his claims of a long waitlist, the truth was anyone who applied to Magnises got a card. The much-hyped special offers were limited in scope and largely dropped off after that first year. And though he initially claimed more than twelve hundred cardholders had been paying the annual $250 fee, that number also included cards he had sent out for free to investors, influencers, athletes, and rappers he admired, like Ja Rule, Wale, and Rick Ross.

The marketing, of course, was a rousing success. But it was never totally clear if Magnises was generating much money— or how. McFarland's estimate of how many members were actively paying the annual fee tended to vary wildly. In 2014, he claimed twelve hundred; in September 2016, he said thirty thousand; and two months later, he told a Portugal audience one hundred thousand.[82] Months later, in a January 2017 interview with *Business Insider*, McFarland revised the number down to forty thousand members.

Depending on who you asked, the company's profit driver was either membership dues or branded content. (For what it's worth, the SEC concluded in 2018 that Magnises derived income "primarily from periodic membership dues."[83]) But ultimately there wasn't much of either form of revenue. Though some early branded events had come off without a hitch—including a Tesla test-drive event that Tesla has since denied paying for—there weren't enough to sustain a company, much less cover the town house rent.

Magnises's paying cardholders, on the other hand, were not celebrities, despite what he and his partners claimed. They were the people who couldn't afford the lifestyle but wanted to look like they did—an early prototype for the Fyre audience.

"[We like] smart people from great schools, so they have the family background and education," said Emir Bahadir, then twenty-one years old, an NYU student, and an adviser to Magnises.[84] The offspring of a wealthy real-estate family in Turkey, Bahadir is perhaps better known for his Instagram page, where he routinely poses in photographs modeling his designer wardrobe and traveling around the world aboard yachts, helicopters, and private jets for his 1.3 million followers.

In fact, a cursory review of Bahadir's 2014 aesthetic looks... well...familiar, what with all the images of him traveling to the Bahamas by private jet, and photos of the mythical swimming pigs one might recognize from the Fyre marketing reel, mixed among pictures of himself at the Magnises town house. In fact, Magnises used a number of Bahadir's photos in its early Instagram collection.

Magnises is also where McFarland (Magnises member #2) met Ja Rule (Magnises member #3), and Grant Margolin (Magnises member #5628), both of whom would go on to become big players in the Fyre scandal. Future Fyre investor Carola Jain, the wife of billionaire Bob Jain, former Credit

Suisse Global Head of Asset Management, also started coming out to Magnises parties around the same time. The Fyre team was starting to assemble.

McFarland and Ja Rule, real name Jeffrey Atkins, first met when Atkins was hired as a performer for Magnises's summer party at Gurney's, a beachside resort in the Montauk. Photos show they traveled to the venue by helicopter, McFarland with a personal bottle of Champagne in hand. Andy King, who would later become famous for his willingness to procure Evian water for the Fyre Festival, was also in attendance.

Meanwhile, Margolin was a short, nerdy Long Island kid who looked and sounded not unlike the Jonah Hill character from *The Wolf of Wall Street*, who had graduated from Syracuse and moved to the city on the hunt for his big break. He'd earned a marketing position as McFarland's number two at Magnises in 2014 after cold emailing Billy an overly detailed business plan of all the things he thought Magnises had been doing wrong, and ended up serving as the vice president of marketing and branding for the company for two years before negotiating his way to become Fyre's CMO.

Margolin seemed to envision himself as the Tim Cook to Billy's Steve Jobs. But when they got together, critics say, it was more like Dwight Schrute and Michael Scott from *The Office*.

"I was very surprised he ended up with Billy because he's kind of the one that brought Magnises more down-market," the publicist said. "Billy's whole thing was his bling, and he wanted it to be very trendsetting and then [with Margolin] he got more down to business, you know, he wanted to get just a lot of people joining, and that's when it really changed."

In the summer of 2014, for example, McFarland booked the rapper Jim Jones for a summer party aboard *Mariner III*, a 122-foot yacht at which he arrived aboard a smaller yacht called *Pipe Dream* with McFarland. Everyone on board had their own personal bottle of Champagne. At another party at the Williamsburg venue, Villain (which was later purchased by Vice Media and used to host the company's 2018 holiday party), Rick Ross entertained a room full of white New York City private-school kids and models—for twenty minutes at most. According to the *New York Post*, he then dipped out, leaving the bemused party without any entertainment—until Ja Rule saved the day by performing an unscheduled set.[85]

"I think it started out with somebody that could overpromise and kind of deliver, and I think they got caught into the fraud thing. It became too big for them to handle," said the publicist. "Billy always wanted to be, like, a Rick Ross, or a Ja Rule, like he's the blackest white boy that you've ever known, you know? He's just bonded that whole bling rap thing with…that was his thing, you know?"

(Eric Rubenstein, McFarland's middle school friend, says that despite their affinity for rap growing up, McFarland's association with Ja Rule actually came as a big surprise: "Ironically, we used to talk shit about Ja Rule because we were diehard 50 Cent fans," he told me, laughing. "G-Unit over Murder Inc. all day.")

But if there was any Venn diagram to be made of the offers McFarland began to put together for his Magnises customers after the first year, it was with his own personal interests in luxury goods and that lifestyle.

"He used to do that kind of stuff. It was always when he was going out to the Hamptons and stuff, he rented big houses, a lot of SUVs, he had the Maserati," the publicist said. "Very prone to excess."

Though McFarland had always been preppy, it was around that time, the publicist said, "The gold watches got bigger."

Meanwhile, Magnises clients got not only the imitation Black Card and access to Billy's town house, but also the promise of access to a concierge service in possession of exclusive events, tickets, and experiences. Unfortunately most of the experiences didn't exist, largely because McFarland had lied about the extent of his industry connections during his investor presentations. And tickets weren't selling out to the events he was able to throw, like a September 2014 party featuring Rick Ross at the Williamsburg Savings Bank for $175 a head, or a disastrous sports-package option that left him in major debt to the Brooklyn Nets.

Not long after Magnises's triumphant launch, the company disappeared from the news. And so did the exclusive offers. And then, so did the company.

In a 2015 lawsuit, the landlord for the Magnises town house sued McFarland, saying that he had "damaged and destroyed several windows and virtually all the kitchen appliances," leaving things "in a state of total disrepair, rubble, and disarray."[86] By then, the company had relocated to a new clubhouse at the Hotel on Rivington, with office space for employees at a nearby WeWork. Although McFarland denied the allegations and the case eventually settled, by this point he had all but checked out for his new venture, Fyre.

"[Billy] was rarely in the Magnises office at all, but the general feeling was that we wanted him to take ownership and provide some kind of company leadership, which he was too busy with Fyre to do," the former Magnises employee said.

Meanwhile, Magnises's events got shoddier and shoddier.

In May 2015, Magnises launched in Washington, DC, giving our nation's capital a taste of what was soon to hit the Bahamas. Despite promising a free Ja Rule concert to his new mid-Atlantic cardholders, the company canceled the performance hours before it was scheduled to begin. According to Rachel Kurzius, a reporter for DCist, Magnises used the same language Fyre would later use, blaming *unforeseen circum-*

stances.[87] But not all was lost: the rapper Wale, a cardholder who had performed at the Magnises clubhouse for a reported "ten minutes" in 2013 (an attendee told the *New York Daily News*, "The mic didn't work for the first couple," which was just as well since the party was shut down by the NYPD not long after), stepped in and performed in Ja Rule's place.[88]

The DC launch wasn't a total bust, but by July of that summer, McFarland was still desperate enough for new members to resort to his old Spling tricks.

"Want a free Apple Watch?" one Facebook post read. "Magnises is giving away a free Apple Watch to each member who successfully refers 5 new members by July 7th. Refer away!"[89]

By August, the company fully pivoted from an event-and-membership club to a lifestyle blog in the vein of *Guest of a Guest*, with the dubious bonus of a concierge app. Not long after, the company gave up on the membership-club aspect altogether. Less than a year later, Magnises had all but given up on hosting events, records show.

"After about two weeks of working there full-time, you could figure out that [Billy] didn't know how to plan anything, and he was more of a big talker than someone who actually went and got very much done, especially things done efficiently. He wasn't really receptive to criticism at all or any suggestions as to how we should do something better or stop doing something," a former Magnises employee said.

Internally, things were a mess. Employees were getting paid irregularly, by wire transfer and cash, if at all.

By December, documents show, Magnises's payroll accounts and health-insurance policies, which were hosted by TriNet, were put into collections over an unpaid debt of more than $68,000. The Magnises employees weren't aware their health-care plans had lapsed "until one of the girls broke her arm, went to the hospital, and then found out she wasn't covered by insurance anymore," one former employee said. (The company eventually switched to a new payroll provider, and the plans were reinstated.)[90]

"[McFarland] is kind of like a car salesman, but you don't realize the car you bought is a piece of shit until you drive away with it," said the former Magnises employee.

Some of the problems seemed to line up with the shocking death of McClendon, who smashed his speeding car into a concrete highway wall on March 2, 2016—just one day after a federal grand jury indicted him on conspiracy charges related to oil bid rigging.

But McFarland had a solution for the company's cratering numbers. He told his employees he had a source at Live Nation who could get him exclusive seats to events for below-market rates.

Starting in 2016, they began spamming Magnises members' inboxes with offers to hot-ticket shows like *Hamilton*, Kanye West, Beyoncé, and Adele. McFarland even rolled up his sleeves and jumped in, creating a fake persona and email account for a concierge host named Blake Wilde, who still has an active LinkedIn page today.

As a short-term cash grab, it was a smart idea. McFarland's members were exactly the kind of people who would want to purchase those tickets. His incredible deals ensured they would act fast. And sure enough, the money started rolling in. But it didn't stay long.

Unfortunately, McFarland had been lying about his Live Nation connections. Though he'd started the private club with good enough intentions, by 2016 Magnises had turned into an elaborate shell game that centered around an elaborate scheme of bait and switch. Far from reflecting actual holdings, McFarland's email offers had just been him throwing ideas out into the void to see what people might be interested in paying for.

Because it was all an elaborate thought exercise, when Magnises members did buy his supposedly discounted tickets, McFarland would either cancel the reservations at the last minute and postpone them into eternity, or he'd fulfill the orders by buying the tickets himself, last minute, from third-party brokers like StubHub and Ticketmaster, at a steep markup.

To pay for it, he used a corporate Fyre AmEx credit card registered in another employee's name.

The employee, Fyre developer MDavid Low, had been hired to work on the artist-booking app in 2016 and had little to do with the festival, which hadn't even been conceived of at the time he signed on. But he was still on the hook for the American Express bill, a $200,000 balance for which he was sued by AmEx, destroying his credit.

As a company, Fyre was still in its infancy at that point, but it was already essential to keeping Magnises afloat. Records show that Gold American Express business cards linked to Fyre Media's $100,000 line of credit were issued to at least nine employees, including Low, cofounder Ja Rule, and the festival's head of marketing, Grant Margolin. The charges incurred by those employees appear reasonably related to the Fyre Media business. But between September 2016 and February 2017, the card issued in McFarland's name was used for more than $1.1 million worth of purchases from sites like StubHub, Ticketmaster, and Vivid Seats.[91]

And most of the charges clearly corresponded with events that had been advertised by Magnises. McFarland had purchased most, if not all, of the tickets on the same day the events were scheduled to take place, ensuring he'd pay the maximum price.

Take, for example, a series of Vivid Seats charges totaling almost $30,000 and labeled *Hamilton*.

The transactions, which were spread across multiple purchases that add up to $28,892.02, were all billed as *Vivid Seats Hamilton*Vivid Seats*, and secured using McFarland's Fyre credit card on January 6. The cheapest ticket or set of tickets in the bunch was $1,401.30. The former Magnises employee says the *Hamilton* tickets were sold to Magnises members for a mere $250 apiece, estimating that McFarland probably took a loss of at least $1,200 a ticket on each *Hamilton* reservation that wasn't canceled.

The same thing happened with Kanye West after McFarland sent out a blast email in June 2016 offering members floor-level tickets for West's Madison Square Garden shows for $275 each. In June, *Forbes* reported the median resale ticket was listed at $375—$100 more than McFarland was charging his members. The Fyre American Express records show that on September 5—the date of the first show—McFarland used the card to purchase more than $10,000 worth of Kanye West tickets in nine separate Ticketmaster transactions ranging from $602.35 to $2,068.00.

But it wasn't until Adele's sold-out run of shows at Madison Square Garden that McFarland's employees realized they were being lied to.

"What happened with Adele was that we found out that Billy wasn't going through a source in Live Nation at all, because for that concert, there were no e-tickets available, the whole thing was all ticket stubs," the former employee said. "We had to go and meet with these brokers who act as third-party buyers around MSG. And we're spending the whole time running around the city trying to get them together and figure out how many they have and who's going to go in which section."

In 2016, Adele put on a series of six shows at Madison Square Garden, performing live on September 19, 20, 22, 23, 25, and 26. The shows went on sale in December 2015 and sold out in minutes. Records show McFarland's Fyre credit card was used to pay for more than one hundred orders on sites like StubHub, Vivid Seats, Fan Exchange, and MyTicketTracker that totaled more than $150,000. The orders were spread across a series of dates including September 19, 20, 22, 23, 25, and 26—the days Adele performed. The records show no tickets were charged to the card on September 21 and 24—the days when she did not perform.

The hundred-odd orders left Magnises employees scrambling across the city, picking up tickets, and delivering them to members just hours—and sometimes minutes—before the shows.

"It was a shitshow, but we were able to get most of these people to their Adele concert," the former employee said. "Not everyone got the seats they were promised, because they were all promised front-row floor section, and obviously for this concert there were not many of those left, so Billy ended up buying just a bunch of 100-levels and then saying, 'Hey, this is the best we can do, blah, blah, blah.'"

But despite the ticketing disaster, McFarland continued offering luxury items for sale, apparently just to see what people would bite at—just as he would going forward into the Fyre Festival. There were Hamptons getaways, Lamborghini races, white truffle dinners, warehouse parties, celebrity meet-and-greets, themed Soulcycle classes and more.

But it was the last offer Magnises provided its followers on Facebook with that made me do a double take. It was a private-jet flight to the Bahamas in 2016, posted just as his Fyre preparations began, part of an all-expenses-paid trip to Norman's Cay in the Bahamas for $3,500.

Punctuated with images taken from Google, McFarland was offering his Magnises customers the chance to spend a weekend on a private island in the Bahamas, transported there by a private jet, and tended to by a personal chef.

"We'll island hop on our planes, swim with the pigs, play with the sharks, dive in the plane wrecks, catch lobsters, and more," he promised, and I suppose to his credit, at least the stolen pictures in that particular email accurately depicted the real places he was describing. But the offer itself wasn't real—internal records show someone actually did book that vacation, only to see it canceled at the last minute.

The Fyre Festival was taking shape.

It may have been his third or fourth time launching a company, but despite all the experience, McFarland still didn't know the first thing about running a business. He had, however, learned how to make it look like he did, picking up a handful of habits that would set him on a direct collision course with the Bahamas.

And he'd found a reliable customer base in his peers, who he'd figured out might be willing to spend a little money in real life if it would look like a lot more online. That was the real selling point behind what *GQ* deemed in 2014 a "bizarro douche cult." But it turns out McFarland wasn't just the president of the Magnises club for douchebags—he was a client too.

It's not that McFarland's early customers were scammers, but Magnises did launch during a heyday of performative conspicuous consumption, a time when people first started to say, "Doing it for the 'gram" and, unfortunately, mean it. And McFarland came early to the trend.

There had always been pressure to overshare and keep up with appearances on sites like Facebook, but it took the ubiquity and ease of the Instagram app to turn sharing a photo of your lunch into a monetizable activity. Filled with people pretending to be brands and brands pretending to be people, social media, now easily accessible by smartphone, had become by the mid-2010s a showcase in performative signaling.

Magnises, both in terms of its corporate identity and its services, knew its role in this grand experiment in personal branding.

So the people who gravitated to Magnises had already internalized what the markers of social success looked like, and they were willing to pay a monthly fee if it meant appearing on trend. The dirty secret of McFarland's so-called exclusive-membership club was that his audience was really the "bridge and tunnel crowd" from Long Island and New Jersey who wanted to live that lifestyle but didn't know how or couldn't really afford it. (McFarland would later use the same phrase to derisively describe his typical Fyre customer, even though he rolled into New York via the New Jersey Turnpike just like the rest of them.) But it made sense for his business model, which was essentially offering his customers access to things they might want to brag about on social media.

All the social jockeying made me think about McFarland's onetime uninvited houseguest, the Soho grifter also known as Anna Delvey, who's currently serving four to twelve years in prison after scamming her way through the city, stealing an estimated $275,000 from friends and local businesses.

Though her lawyer had tried to frame her dishonesty as just trying to make it à la Frank Sinatra in "New York, New York," the court ultimately had a slightly different song in mind.

"I heard Bruce Springsteen's 'Blinded by the Light,'" the sentencing judge ruled. "She was blinded by the glitter and glamour of New York City."[92]

Born Anna Sorokin in Russia, Delvey had created a new identity for herself as a louche German heiress who wanted to use her trust fund to launch a sort of Soho House–style private club for artists. Though no one was quite sure where she had come from, everyone knew where she was going: the wealthy international social circuit with stops in New York, Miami, LA, Aspen, London, Paris, and beyond.

"She was at all the best parties," marketing director Tommy Saleh told *New York* magazine, recalling how she was seemingly pals with a number of fixtures on the list of "the 200 or so people you see everywhere."

So it wasn't long before they became friends too.[93] Her story didn't make a lot of sense to the outside observer—though she was a citizen of the world, Delvey didn't appear to be a resident of any particular country or state, bouncing around from hotel to hotel and occasionally crashing on someone's couch. But it all seemed to make sense in the crowd she'd taken up with who didn't think much of it when her credit card occasionally declined, leaving them to pick up the check. It was only when she failed to pay them back that they thought to ask questions.

"There are so many trust-fund kids running around," Saleh explained. "Everyone is your best friend, and you don't know a thing about anyone."

For a while, Delvey was able to maintain a base of operations in New York at 11 Howard, the chic hotel that had recently opened in Soho, also home to a nightclub called The Blond, popular with the Wall Street crowd, and Le Coucou, then an exclusive new restaurant. It was, in fact, because the whole operation was so new that the front desk had agreed to accept a wire transfer from her in lieu of a credit card.

By the time they realized their error a few months later, Delvey's tab had swelled to a reported $30,000. Though she was able to pay it off at the last minute, her promised credit card to secure future charges never materialized, and she was finally locked out of her room for good. When she finally came to collect her things, a front desk clerk told *New York* magazine, she peeled off into the night in a silver Tesla.

In the same way McFarland had his unwitting lawyers draw up papers showing a sale of stock that never actually happened, Delvey also knew how easy it was to make things look official. She reportedly used her high-ranking attorney to introduce her to different banks as an heiress, which enabled her to obtain a $100,000 line of credit for the private members club, which she had then instead used to pay for the first portion of her 11 Howard hotel stay.

And like McFarland and Atkins, Delvey was insistent that although she'd made some criminal missteps, she really had intended to create a private art club. It sounded a lot like Ja Rule defending his vision at the Internet Summit.

"She seemed most interested in expressing that her plans to create the Anna Delvey Foundation were real," *New York* magazine reported. "She'd had all of those conversations and meetings and sent all of those emails and commissioned those materials because she thought it was actually going to happen. 'I had what I thought was a great team around me, and I was having fun,' she said. Sure, she said, she might have done a few things wrong. 'But that doesn't diminish the hundred things I did right.'"

One of the things she definitely did right was nail the attitude of a trust funder, says Nimrod Kamer, a gonzo journalist and professional social climber who aspires to be one of the first Israelis featured in *Tatler*.

"I met many people who are like her, like an heiress lady [who] would act like Anna Delvey. No charisma, the shouting, being rude to waiters and tipping them in a large way. So, she really played the part. I think she got to observe. I'm pretty sure she's done what I've done, which is sneaking in," Kamer said by phone from his home in London. "And once she got in, she learned how to act like a real lady that inherited money."

Kamer, the author of *The Social Climber's Handbook: A Shameless Guide*, was even moved enough by Delvey's story to spend a night at 11 Howard after her arrest in a sort of dual forensic investigation and séance.

"I stayed one night at 11 Howard just to see how she felt going to the sauna and bumping into the concierge. I have an audio recording with a manager talking to him about how it was when she was there," Kamer told me. "I think also what I've learned from her, which I've done—or maybe she learned from me, maybe she read my book—is going to venues that are just launching, 11 Howard was launching, or, like, stuff that is not fully set up. And then you take advantage of the soft launch and they're willing to extend your credit sometimes, or just give you freebies."

Though Kamer doesn't advocate taking things as far as Delvey did, he's not adverse to using some trickery to bust into traditionally closed social circles, like the time he smuggled a woman into a private men's club in the UK by wheeling her in inside a piece of luggage, or the time he cornered then–Prime Minister Theresa May at a magazine party to ask her about his immigration status.

The first rule to infiltrating elite society, he says, is to build up your social media following and ask for free stuff. When we checked in by phone mid–COVID-19 outbreak, for example, he told me he was practically swimming in free Click and Grows, machines that help you grow your own lettuce indoors. He's also gotten hotel stays, pet food, mattresses, laptops, and even a rent-free apartment in this way.

"I once moved into a sample flat. I told them I might want to feature the new building. So I lived there for a few days and nothing really worked," Kamer said. "Like a sample coffee machine was defective."

(Kamer is nothing if not an ethical scammer, so when it came time for him to decide whether to feature the sample flat on his social media, he apologized and declined, telling the management company, "I can't write about you because you gave it to me for free. So I won't be honest in my review site if I write about it.")

His second rule is never to take no for an answer. Just like a burglar creating his own doors and windows to get into an otherwise-locked building, Kamer knows there's always another way into the party than getting on the actual invite list.

"Pretend, for example, you owe money at the door and you want to get in to pay what you owe them from the night before. You have an open tab in the hotel, or you have something in the cloakroom you haven't taken. There's many ways to get in. I'll even show an email that someone sent you, even a rejection email from the PR," Kamer said.

While Kamer freely admits he, McFarland, and Delvey have all dipped into the same bag of tricks, he says he tries to keep his business activities at least somewhat aboveboard and aimed toward the greater good: enriching himself by pitching inane ideas to people with more money than sense.

"Just by being there and observing the elites, it's like getting money for yourself. Just by being there yourself. I'm, in a way, doing class war because I never bought a ticket. Sneaking in is not a crime, as opposed to maybe scamming and getting money like Anna Delvey," Kamer said. "So sneaking in is the first step, which many of the scammers have done, and that's not illegal. And then, once you're in there, it's a lot easier to get a job or to get someone to hire you because they assume you're part of that group."

That knowledge came in handy in 2012, when he decided to see how far the right-wing media was willing to take its obsession with Barack Obama's birthplace by filming an obviously fake Kenya birth video and distributing it online.

"I paid for half the production, *VICE* paid for the other half. The initial idea was to shoot in Kogelo, Kenya, but *VICE* couldn't afford it," Kamer wrote on Medium.[94] He and the team found what appeared to be a twenty-five-pound baby actor on Craigslist and used an 8mm iPad app to make the footage look more vintage. Then he uploaded the footage to Vimeo and gave a print interview to *VICE* under the guise of a Romanian cotton-based import-export businessman who had stumbled across the footage and had handy explanations for all of the more suspicious elements of the film. ("That baby is massive. It looks like it's at least a year old," the interviewer noted. "Babies are born heavy all the time; I see no issue with that. And I assure you, most of the general public has *no* idea how big infants are in Kenya," Kamer replied. "You might think the US is a fat society, but in Kenya they are born big and then they become light.")

It seemed clear from the jump that the whole thing was an elaborate prank, and indeed, it was generally covered that way in the press.

"The most amazingly, entertainingly fake video of a fake Barack Obama being born—featuring a baby that is all cleaned up and looks about three months old—to a fake Ann Dunham in a fake Kenyan hospital has been leaked to *VICE* because, wait for it, the leaker couldn't get in touch with Donald Trump," *The Atlantic* reported at the time. "It is so fake it makes you wonder if it was made not by birthers, but by liberals mocking birthers."[95]

But we see what we want to see, and apparently Donald Trump saw impeachment on the horizon. The day before

Kamer was set to reveal how he had arranged the prank in
the *New York Observer,* he got a call from Michael Cohen,
Trump's former fixer, whose time in federal prison would
later briefly overlap with Billy McFarland's.

"I asked to speak to Mr. Trump. Cohen said he'll personally wire me $10,000 for exclusive rights and a downloadable
file, as well as any other material I may have from Kenya. I'll
need to sign an NDA. Mr. Trump always wanted to have this
kind of proof, he proclaimed. I asked whether Mr. Trump
watched the video himself. Cohen confirmed that they did. I
said I'll get back to him," Kamer wrote on Medium. Though
he did film a reveal video that was initially posted on *VICE*'s
website, it's since been pulled down, for reasons unknown
to Kamer.

Generally, Kamer sees himself as a sort of Robin Hood,
using his social knowledge for good to help regular people
get behind the velvet rope and exposing the malfeasance he
sees lurking behind it in the dark, smoky rooms where power
tends to congregate.

"I see it as class warfare, where people from Caroline Calloway to Anna Delvey are at the front. They're, like, fighting the elites essentially, and equalizing things," said Kamer.

Those same scammers were the source of inspiration for
artists Karen Knox and J. Stevens when they needed to shoot
a luxurious-looking video short on a pauper's budget. Their
solution? To fake an engagement. For the location, Knox
called up a hotel and asked permission to bring a videogra-
pher to her "proposal." The hotel not only agreed but also
upgraded her room, giving her a half-off discount. For their
wardrobe, Knox and Stevens purchased thousands of dollars
of Gucci clothes, which they then returned the next day for
full credit. Hair and makeup came gratis from Sephora. And
when Stevens finally dropped down on one knee, the whole

lobby started cheering them on—essentially giving their shoot a room full of free extras.

"Everyone got caught up in the fantasy, including us," Knox told reporters, as patrons at the bar started buying them drinks, including an $800 bottle of Champagne.[96]

But gonzo engagements aside, getting long-term access to these deep-pocketed fools generally means making them feel comfortable with you first, which means you've got to show your face over and over at events like Art Basel, where the superrich feel safe and ensconced enough to engage with their peers. That's where Knox says she's headed for her next stealth shoot, and it's also where Kamer got himself written up in the *Daily Mail* as a French businessman named Nimrod-Frederic Kamer after he approached the model Kelly Brook mid-photoshoot with a checkbook, offering her €1 million to go on a date with him and let him touch her knee.

Even vacations have to be strategized if you want to convince the right people you're legit, Kamer said. Take, for example, the $1000-a-night chain of wellness hotels that operate under the Aman brand.

"The Aman hotel is like a network. The key is not whether you can go, it's when you can afford to go, because the interesting people will be there in certain times of the year, and mostly you could not book a room on those dates. So you need to find out an arrangement just to be there in the lounge or by the bar," Kamer said. "It's when you can go, I think, that shows your social power, not where, because usually you could find cheap dates for even Aman hotels as well."

For the less aspirational, a picture-perfect vacation is only a short drive away. YouTuber Natalia Taylor managed to shoot an entire Bali trip from inside a California IKEA. She even left some IKEA tags visible in the shots just to see who would notice them; no one did. "The point of this video was to show people how easy it is to trick people into thinking you're someone you're not," she explained.[97] ("Maybe she is tricking us into thinking that she was in Ikea when she was really in Bali...we can't trust anything on the internet," one of her followers mind-bendingly replied.)

Another popular stop on the international money train is the annual Foundation for AIDS Research (amfAR) auction, which is timed to the annual influx of wealth at the Cannes Film Festival. An international bazaar for fame, wealth, and upward mobility, it draws everyone from Russian oligarchs to American celebrities and everyone in between. A few years ago, for example, I was fascinated to watch the abrupt appearance and even more abrupt disappearance of a mysterious Ukrainian billionaire who openly bought her way to friendships with Kim Kardashian and Pierce Brosnan and launched a music career before suddenly vanishing from view.

Her name was Marina Acton, and she first made headlines after spending $1 million to buy an original piece of artwork created by the actor Pierce Brosnan, whom I had the pleasure of profiling for *Esquire* in the summer of 2018.

During our interview, he mentioned that the painting had briefly been lost in the lead-up to the auction, and that, despite his excitement to put his art out there, he had felt briefly relieved.

Eventually the painting was located, "And then the night was the night," he concluded, in what seemed to me a rather unemotional way of describing an auction price that put him on par with some of the most famous painters in the world.

But when I started looking into the woman who bought the painting—who had later been photographed having lunch with his family in Malibu—I understood the detachment. Before buying his art, Acton had been most famous for paying an overmarked $17.8 million for a home Kim Kardashian had bought a few years prior for only $9 million. (In a funny twist of fate, the Kardashians would also later rent the same $125 million Malibu home where I interviewed Brosnan to film a birthday special for Kim during the pandemic.)

"Was there a *must be my best friend* clause when Marina Acton purchased Kim Kardashian and Kanye West's mansion?" Yahoo asked after the two women were photographed together.[98]

As it turns out, there allegedly was.

"We're told as part of the actual contract for the deal sale, Kim agreed to promote Marina's budding career on her own social media and even hung out with her in public and at industry events. The deal also included a certain amount of public appearances, which Kim appeared to fulfill since the sale. One specific deal point included that she would attend Acton's single release party of her ostensible new friend for her song 'Fantasize.' The two were also seen going out to dinner and parading in front of the paparazzi at Craig's in Los Angeles," The Blast reported.

In a move that reminded me a bit of how her sister Kendall would promote the Fyre Festival a few months later, Kardashian helped promote Acton's music and even dutifully tweeted out a photo of the two with the caption "Happy Birthday my beautiful friend Marina!"[99]

According to a press release, Acton's music, which, to my own admittedly untrained ears, wasn't exactly what I would call *good*, had been produced by a Grammy-nominated music-production team with credits including Fifth Harmony, Ne-Yo, Mary J. Blige, Pitbull, Justin Bieber, and Bruno Mars. The Hot Felon (Jeremy Meeks, whose smoldering mugshot went viral on Twitter in 2014 after he was arrested for gang-related activities) even starred in the video for her single "Fantasize," an auto-tuned pop synth song. Sadly, the YouTube page where her music videos used to live has now been made private and the songs have been pulled from Spotify. But she abruptly reappeared on Instagram in September 2020 with a series of posts about the New York amfAR gala, which she claims to have sponsored through a jewelry company called Merry Belle, which has no public owner and appears to have lifted most of its website's text directly from Wikipedia. (The company's address is registered to a UPS store in Los Altos where other companies linked to Acton are also registered.)

Who Acton really is offline is frankly anyone's guess; various press releases claim Acton is a Silicon Valley venture capitalist, and one former assistant says she once invested $1 million into an email-encryption service. Her music has disappeared, her foundation website is defunct, and she deleted the Instagram where she used to document all her celebrity encounters.

According to a lawsuit filed in Los Angeles civil court, the former Kardashian house ultimately did not make a happy home, though it did serve as the basis for an outrageous lawsuit claiming Acton had allowed her assistant and stylist, Deeona Capital, and her husband to move in before trashing them online, shutting off their gas and water, tampering with their mail, and even hiring private security officers to harass them. (Though the judge acknowledged Acton had shut off the gas, the case was eventually dismissed.)[100]

It's a funny detail to me, though, that this all went down in the former Kardashian house, after Acton made all these efforts and spent tens of millions of dollars aligning herself with the Kardashian brand. Because as it turns out, not even the Kardashians are immune to the pressures of conspicuous consumption.

The *Forbes* 400 has long been a hallowed list among the nouveau riche, a sort of Blue Book that doesn't care where you were born, so much as where you can afford to live now.

Launched in 1982, the list purports to document the four hundred richest people in the United States. But its accounting has long been—shall we say—imprecise, leaving it vulnerable to the sort of people who want the world to think of them as wealthy. (Or not—in 2014, the model Gisele told a Brazilian news outlet that she had been audited by the IRS after *Forbes* erroneously inflated her net worth. "I do ok, I earn plenty, but not as much as they say. I've already been audited by the IRS because of this list and truthfully, whether I'm on this list or not, it doesn't interest me," she said.)[101] But if money talks and wealth whispers, the people scrambling to get on the annual *Forbes* list are screaming at the top of their lungs.

Not all of them are yelling the truth, though, as a series of alleged long-game scams prove. Take Kylie Jenner, who was touted as "the planet's youngest self-made billionaire" in 2018 thanks to the runaway success of her makeup company, Kylie Cosmetics. The young entrepreneur was also given a businesswoman cover to match, with her hair slicked back, wearing a power suit with sharp shoulder pads and a bemused expression on her face.

In 2020, however, the magazine realized it had egg on its own face: according to a subsequent internal investigation, *Forbes* had been had by the Jenner family, which, it revealed, had "spent years fighting *Forbes* for higher spots on our annual wealth and celebrity earnings listings."[102]

To secure the youngest Jenner sister her spot on the list, the magazine says, the family launched an intensive PR campaign with an audience of one, "inviting *Forbes* into their mansions and CPA's offices, and even creating tax returns that were likely forged." (Jenner, for her part, has vehemently denied forging any documents, tweeting, "what am i even waking up to. i thought this was a reputable site.. all i see are a number of inaccurate statements and unproven assumptions lol. i've never asked for any title or tried to lie my way there EVER. period," and later adding, "but okay, i am blessed beyond my years, i have a beautiful daughter, and a successful business and i'm doing perfectly fine. i can name a list of 100 things more important right now than fixating on how much money i have.")[103]

According to *Forbes*, when Jenner's publicists first shared the tax returns in question, the magazine resisted taking them at face value, "since the story they told, of e-commerce brand Kylie Cosmetics growing from nothing to $300 million in sales in a single year, was hard to believe."

Forbes might have been skeptical, but they weren't the only mag in town, and the numbers didn't stay in the background for long. Just two months later, *Women's Wear Daily* bit, publishing the same stats *Forbes* had rejected. Jenner's self-reported revenues went wide, cited in a wide range of major news outlets as fact. Within a few months, the *Forbes* journalists note, everyone in the industry seemed convinced the revenues made sense. Less than a year after Jenner appeared on the cover as the 27th richest woman in the world, and the youngest self-made billionaire ever, the cosmetics giant Coty bought a 51 percent stake at a valuation of $1.2 billion.

It turns out Coty's shareholders also believe that valuation was inflated: in September 2020, they filed a class-action suit alleging Coty had been behind "a fraudulent scheme and course of business that operated [to deceive] purchasers of Coty shares by disseminating materially false and/or misleading statements and/or concealing material adverse facts... about Coty's business, operations, and prospects."[104] The lawsuit is still ongoing.

It shouldn't surprise anyone to learn that Kylie wasn't the only one accused of using *Forbes* to launder the message that she was richer than she really was. *Forbes* says it caught both

Donald Trump and his longtime friend and onetime secretary of commerce Wilbur Ross Jr. allegedly faking documents in a desperate attempt to scam their way onto the annual wealth list.

It was 1984 when Jonathan Greenberg, a former *Forbes* writer, got a call from someone who claimed to be a member of the Trump Organization and said his name was John Barron. Greenberg had determined that Trump was worth around $200 million, which "Barron" disputed. He told Greenberg that Trump actually owned around 90 percent of his father's real-estate holdings, instead of the 50 percent confirmed on paper. As a result, the spokesperson claimed, Trump should be listed as a billionaire.[105]

The call struck Greenberg as bizarre at the time, but he wouldn't realize just how thoroughly he'd been duped until he went back and listened to the recordings more than thirty years later.

"When I recently rediscovered and listened, for the first time since that year, to the tapes I made of this and other phone calls, I was amazed that I didn't see through the ruse: although Trump altered some cadences and affected a slightly stronger New York accent, it was clearly him," Greenberg wrote.

It wasn't the first time Trump had lied to the magazine, Greenberg realized.

"Over time, I have learned that he should not have been on the first three *Forbes* 400 lists at all" he wrote. Though Trump had been included on the first list with a net worth of $100 million, Greenberg estimates he was actually worth only about $5 million.

According to Greenberg, Trump lied about what he owned, how much it was worth, and even where it was located. The inaugural list had valued Trump at $100 million based on his claim to own most of his father's twenty-two thousand apartments, debt-free, located in up-and-coming neighborhoods in Brooklyn, Queens, and Staten Island. Trump seemed to be throwing out numbers just to see what stuck, telling Greenberg they were worth $40,000 apiece. (When Greenberg questioned it, Trump reportedly said, "Okay, $20,000." Greenberg estimated they were worth more like $9,000.) And according to Greenberg, he lied about where they were located to make them sound more exclusive.

Each year, Trump and his attorney Roy Cohn would call Greenberg with outrageous claims of wealth, referencing tax documents and bank statements they refused to produce and lying about the terms of deals Trump had been associated with. In one instance, Greenberg recalled, Trump pretended to decline a $100 million offer for a property he said he'd just bought for $13 million—and then demanded the net worth be adjusted by $87 million to reflect its true value. (Greenberg says he declined, but accepted the $13 million figure. It turned out Trump had purchased it for $65 million, $50 million of which he owed to creditors.)

And so, little by little, Greenberg and his colleagues at *Forbes* began to begrudgingly inflate Trump's reported net worth. It wasn't until years later that they realized how badly they'd been duped.

Greenberg thought that by tempering some of Trump's more "outrageous claims," he'd gotten closer to the truth. Instead, he realized later, what he had assumed were merely "vain embellishments" were actually "outright fabrications."

According to Greenberg, Trump should have never been on the list at all. The twenty-two thousand apartments were really more like eight thousand, and they all belonged to his father, not him. That first year the list came out, all Trump really owned was about $1 million from a trust fund his father had given him, $400,000 in checking accounts, and a 1977 Mercedes.

"Trump was so competent in conning me that, until thirty-five years later, I did not know I'd been conned. Instead, I have gone through my career in national media with a misinformed sense of satisfaction that, as a perceptive young journalist, I called Trump on his lies and gave *Forbes* readers who used the Rich List as a barometer of private wealth a more accurate picture of his finances than the one he was selling," Greenberg wrote. "The joke was on me—and everyone else. Trump's fabrications provided the basis for a vastly inflated wealth assessment for the *Forbes* 400 that would give him cachet for decades as a triumphant businessman." The White House declined to comment for this story. The Trump Organization did not respond to a request for comment.

And Trump's close friend and associate Wilbur Ross Jr., who served as commerce secretary for the Trump Administration, also lied to *Forbes* for years about his net worth. And he probably would have gotten away with it too, if that pesky Trump hadn't nominated him for the cabinet position.

Ross, who had long maintained that he was worth more than $3 billion, was caught red-handed in 2017 after submitting federal filings that revealed he was really worth closer to $700 million. When he learned *Forbes* intended to knock him off the list, the eighty-year-old spent his Sunday on the phone with the magazine allegedly lying his ass off. The bulk of his money was in private trusts, he said, which he claimed he had created sometime between "the election and the nomination."

"So began the mystery of Wilbur Ross' missing $2 billion," *Forbes* reporter Dan Alexander wrote.[106]

"After one month of digging, *Forbes* is confident it has found the answer: That money never existed. It seems clear that Ross lied to us, the latest in an apparent sequence of fibs, exaggerations, omissions, fabrications and whoppers that have been going on with *Forbes* since 2004," Alexander concluded.

It had all started off innocently enough, after a private-equity fund led by Ross took away a cool billion dollars following a 2003 IPO by a steel company he'd rescued out of bankruptcy. Under the mistaken impression that Ross (as opposed to his investors) had been the main beneficiary of the IPO and subsequent sale, a *Forbes* reporter called him up to discuss inclusion on the list. Ross, who had really walked away with a respectable (though not *Forbes*-worthy) $260 million, largely earned from managerial fees, declined to correct the reporter of the assumption.

"I just spoke to Ross," the reporter reportedly wrote after the meeting. "He's one of the easiest new guys I've put on [the *Forbes* 400] in a while. Very low-key, said he didn't really want to be on, but at the same time wasn't going to fight success. He says he doesn't want to juice up his numbers at all."

But privately Ross, who colleagues told *Forbes* had always desired more recognition, had been allegedly juicing everything. He'd recently remarried, to a Palm Beach socialite, and had started dressing better, buying expensive art, and flying around the country on private jets. By the 2010s, he'd begun emailing *Forbes* to complain that their respective estimates of his net worth at $2.7 billion and $3.1 billion were "a bit low, but I understand why you'd want to be conservative." At no point was he worth more than about $400 million, the magazine now says.[107]

I'd argue that $400 million is more than enough money for anyone, but it wasn't for Wilbur Ross. The presumption that he was worth seven to eight times that made a huge difference not for what he could buy but for who he could convince to pay him attention—at work and at home. The wealthier he seemed, sources told the magazine, the more money inves-

tors were willing to give him and the more positive attention he got in society.

"Really, for us, it was a bet on him," explained Sam Green,
who shepherded $300 million from the Oregon Public Em-
ployees Retirement Fund into Ross's fund in part because of
his high net worth.

That's why, when it all started to unravel, Ross's biggest
concern was what people would think. When he was told he
wouldn't be on the list in 2018, he reportedly replied, "What
I don't want is for people to suddenly think that I've lost a lot
of money when it's not true."

As it was, even the money Ross did have may not have
been his to spend. In a subsequent investigation, *Forbes* identified twenty-one business associates who detailed at least
$123 million in claims against Ross—as well as a troubling
pattern of behavior.

Like Trump, Ross stood accused of routinely stealing from
the little guys, and not because he couldn't afford to pay them,
as well as the big guys, even though he was making plenty of
his own money. To many around him, Ross was just lying
for the sake of it, which the people accusing him were careful to distinguish as well beyond the pale of the more socially
acceptable types of fraudulent behavior in his industry.

"Everybody does some cheating, everybody does some
lying. Not everybody steals from their employees," a former
colleague told *Forbes*.

"There are all sorts of fee issues," another investor reportedly told the mag. "But it was just the most egregious that
I've seen."[108]

Ross's alleged penchant for cheating bordered on pathological and could have come straight out of Trump's playbook.
Forbes reported that two former colleagues had accused him
of stealing Sweet'N Low packets from a restaurant near his

office so he wouldn't have to buy them; another two alleged that he'd once pledged $1 million to charity—and then just didn't pay it. Contractors reportedly called the office after he stiffed them on a job at his Hamptons estate.

"He'll push the edge of truthfulness and use whatever power he has to grab assets," financier Asher Edelman told the magazine.[109]

Still, if it's easy to make people think you're rich and famous by convincing a journalist to report it as fact, it's even easier to make them think you have a good product by infiltrating respected online platforms by yourself.

Take London's top-rated restaurant, which was, for a glorious moment in 2017, located inside a garden shed owned by an industrious *VICE* journalist named Oobah Butler.

For about six months, The Shed at Dulwich was the UK's toughest reservation. All Butler had to do was get a phone number, make a website, and list his own address, where the shed was located.

Butler had previously worked writing fake Tripadvisor reviews, and he was curious to see what would happen if he applied the same principles to a different platform.

"We served ready meals, which were, like, I guess, it'd be like a sixty-cent microwavable meal. And we dressed it up like it was fancy food. But I had people in the restaurant who were actors pretending that they're having an amazing time as well," Butler told NPR.[110] "I wanted to recreate that same psychological space as Tripadvisor—you know, the whole thing of like—if enough people around you saying, 'This is delicious,' will you go, 'Yeah, it's delicious, I guess—maybe?' I was really nervous about the way that they'd react. And when they left, they loved it."

As the restaurant started climbing the rankings, Butler says people started to lose their minds, applying for jobs, offering to stock food items, and even trying to step in as PR reps.

After filling one night of reservations, The Shed at Dulwich shut down forever. But the new rise of ghost kitchens makes Butler's marketing operation look rather quaint. These commercial kitchens, which are not open to the public, are generally VC-backed, delivery-only, and might as well not exist outside of the Uber Eats and Postmates platforms.

But online, they're indistinguishable from the other, real restaurant listings, which are, among other things, centered in brick-and-mortar stores and regulated by health authorities. Ghost kitchens, on the other hand, can be located anywhere, cost less money to operate since there's no front of house staff, and are often referred to as *virtual brands*.

As democratic as it sounds, the sleight of hand allows the VCs who have descended on the sector—including Uber's former CEO, Travis Kalanick, the new founder of Cloud-Kitchens—to shortstop business that might otherwise go to real, established restaurants fighting to hold on to their slice of the industry. And the ghost-kitchen business is so lucrative that there's even a sort of WeWork for ghost chefs now—Creating Culinary Communities—which matches the virtual brands with vacant spaces.

But you don't need venture capital to make innocent diners think you're a legit restaurant. In 2020, it took YouTuber Eric Decker (aka airrack) less than a week to start his own Uber Eats business—ten minutes to set up an account using a rap-name generator and then another seven days to wait for the official Uber Eats tablet to arrive in the mail. Using a stock pizza menu he found online, populated with pizza descriptions from Olive Garden, Sweet Pablo's was officially in business.

For the experiment, Decker bought up a stack of $6 Publix pizzas and a box of Bagel Bites and then dropped about $150 on Uber Eats ads to start bringing in the orders. Other than that, he didn't do much else to disguise the prank, other than crossing out the brand name on the pizza boxes with a Sharpie.

After exhausting his small inventory, he shut the restaurant down on his own, satisfied in his short-term success.

The owners of AJ's NY Pizzeria in Kansas, on the other hand, weren't pleased at all to see how easily their restaurant popped up on DoorDash, another start-up funded by We-Work's main benefactor, SoftBank. AJ's, which didn't offer delivery, was initially confused by a series of calls from customers complaining about cold orders. Who was doing this subpar delivery service? When they finally looked it up, they found DoorDash had scraped their menu from the restaurant's website without their knowledge and was placing orders on its customers' behalf. But DoorDash had gotten some of the information wrong, including the price of pizza, which was $24 in the store but listed on the app as $16.

When the owner of AJ's reached out to his friend Ranjan Roy, a consultant who blogs about tech, to ask about Door-Dash, Roy saw an arbitrage opportunity.[111] So they ordered ten pizzas without cheese or toppings to keep their costs low, and immediately pocketed what they calculated as $75.

"If you did this a few times a night, you could start to see thousands in top-line growth with hundreds in pure profit, and maybe you could do this for days on end," Roy wrote. "I was genuinely curious if DoorDash would catch on but they didn't. I had visions of building a network of restauranteurs all executing this strategy in tandem, all drinking from the SoftBank teat before the money ran dry, but went back to work doing content strategy stuff."

Roy made another interesting point, which is that food delivery companies like DoorDash, Uber Eats, and Grubhub are all sort of scams themselves.

"Uber Eats lost $461 million in Q4 2019 off of revenue of $734 million. Sometimes I need to write this out to remind myself. Uber Eats spent $1.2 billion to make $734 million. In one quarter," Roy wrote.

Incredibly, that is currently Uber's most profitable division, and they seem prepared to double down on it by purchasing Postmates.

But these apps aren't just unprofitable for their own investors—they're also eating up the restaurants' profits too, not that those margins were ever that good to begin with. Still, the tech world seems determined to clean their plates. Starting in 2019, for example, Google began adding "Order Online" buttons to restaurant listings. It should have been an added convenience for everyone involved, but Google deliberately cut the restaurants out, partnering with companies like GrubHub, Door-Dash, and Postmates to bypass individual, restaurant-owned delivery platforms. It's been incredibly lucrative for Google, which gets a reported 10 percent cut of orders placed through the button, and incredibly frustrating for restaurant owners, who say there's no easy way to opt out of a cut-rate service they never even signed up for. The affected restaurants can either sit back and watch up to 40 percent of their profits get eaten up in delivery platform fees or essentially stop offering takeout altogether. Even if they're still offering to-go meals, the sad truth is that they might as well not exist if they're not indexed on Google. And that's if they even can get themselves delisted—once Google assigns an "Order Now" button, it washes its hands of responsibility and directs restaurant complaints to the delivery platforms instead.

It's not just restaurants getting affected by the increasingly digital nature of commerce. When the public is forced to rely on anonymous reviews, every industry is affected. Before creating The Shed, for example, Oobah Butler used to get paid about $13 to write favorable reviews of places on Tripadvisor, which is actually quite a generous fee, given the fact that many companies expect their employees to do the same thing for free. Take, for example, the skincare brand Sunday Riley.

From all appearances, Sunday Riley has long been beloved by the Instagram set. With its "shelfie"-friendly packaging, its playfully titled product lines like Good Genes, Martian Mattifying Melting Water-Gel Toner, and C.E.O. Protect + Repair Moisturizer, and scientific bona fides (the owner of the eponymous line notes she is a cosmetic chemist and product formulator), the brand has been a bestseller on sites like Sephora and Ulta Beauty for close to a decade.

But a closer look would suggest that Sunday Riley isn't selling anything all that different than its other competitors in the $135 billion skincare space—it's just better at marketing.

Take, for example, a 2017 *Allure* write-up that differentiated the product not by its ingredients but by its packaging: "The bottle is as far as you can get from the sometimes fugly, superfunctional packaging of certain skin-care products. The font, minimalist and sophisticated. The name, whimsical."[112]

Which makes sense when you consider that the brand began selling to Barneys in 2009 before there was even a product to sell. "We went in, presented a concept, and they took it," Riley told *Allure* in the same article.

Things came to a head almost a full decade later, in 2018, when a former Sunday Riley employee logged on to Reddit and wrote her own review of the company.

"This is a throwaway account because Sunday Riley is majorly vindictive. I'm sharing this because I'm no longer an employee there and they are one of the most awful places to work, but especially for the people who shop us at Sephora, because a lot of the really great reviews you read are fake," the user wrote. "We were forced to write fake reviews for our products on an ongoing basis, which came direct from Sunday Riley herself and her Head of Sales. I saved one of those emails to share here."

Attached to the post was a leaked internal email, purportedly written by a Sunday Riley exec, which instructed employees to create at least three fake accounts to review their new products with. The exec also advised them to review other brands first "to build a profile history" and explained how to log on to the internet using a VPN and a fake Gmail account so that companies like Sephora would be unable to trace the fake reviews back to the company. The employees were further advised to "mix and match your identities" with different ages and locations and required to screenshot their fake reviews before submitting so the company could sign off on them. Like The Shed at Dulwich, Sunday Riley's runaway success suddenly looked questionable.

"It helps to make yourself seem relatable—like you know how hard acne is and you've tried everything, and this one actually works or mention things like yes, it's a little more expensive, but works incredibly well compared to the cheaper masks out there," the exec wrote.[113] "If you need any help with things to come up with to say, feel free to ask myself, Sunday or Addison [Cain, Sunday Riley's Communications Manager]."

The document also instructed the employees to use their fake accounts to respond directly to real reviews.

Despite the irony of a throwaway Reddit account exposing the use of fake accounts, the FTC took notice.[114]

Almost a year later, the company settled with the FTC without admitting any wrongdoing.

It turned out the skincare line wasn't the only Sunday Riley with fake credentials; despite Riley's marketing claims about a scientific background, the University of Texas later confirmed she had never graduated.

Between the packaging and the power of influencer marketing, however, Sunday Riley remains a bestseller at Sephora,
and *Forbes*, of all places, recently declared it the "shortcut to
dewy, glowing skin."

3

Under the Influencer

"We're selling a pipe dream to your average losers," McFarland announced suddenly one late December evening. It was in fact, a perfect summing up of his life's work, but McFarland's mind wasn't on strategy that particular winter day in 2016.[115] In fact, it was a wonder that he was even upright at all. Earlier in the day, he'd passed out on a Bahamian beach, fully clothed, with a half-full bottle of beer still clasped in one hand in the middle of a work event. Not that he was alone in that exhaustion—all the boys (everyone on the Fyre executive team was male, and all but one, the rapper Ja Rule, were white) had been celebrating.

Also present that night were ten of IMG's top-earning models, an elite group that included Hailey Bieber (née Baldwin), Bella Hadid, Shanina Shaik, Chanel Iman, Elsa Hosk, and Alessandra Ambrosio. It wasn't exactly clear if they were still on the clock or not after a full-day photoshoot, but there were still cameras running all around, muddying the otherwise crystal clear waters around them. By that point in the shoot, the Fyre team was already $120,000 in the hole with MATTE Projects, who had been shooting footage for a concert documentary they planned to pitch to YouTube Red, and spending hundreds of thousands a month on the regular use of a Dassault Falcon 7X jet, a $20,000-a-week Dolce Vita villa on Staniel Cay, and nightly parties at the nearby MacDuff's Restaurant and Grille.

Grant Margolin, now Fyre's head of marketing, had officially joined the team from his former role at Magnises in early November 2016. Although he had never attended a music festival before, he had still managed to negotiate a $175,000 salary with added perks that included a driver and access to the Fyre American Express card. The self-produced documentary had been his idea, and he'd even thrown together an incredibly detailed, nonsensical pitch deck for how he thought it might look.[116]

"Welcome to Fyre; a remote island festival packed with 10,000 guests primed for an exotic adventure. The catch? It's about to be planned, organized, and pulled off by a wild assortment of characters that have little experience in throwing music festivals, but a glowing track record in creating successful business," Margolin's pitch read. "WHO? The Fyre core ensemble working to build the festival from NYC / LA / Fyre Cay. WHEN? June 2017 WHY? Why the fuck not? WHAT? A five-part documentary series that corresponds to a different location for each iteration of the festival and it's [sic] corresponding locations around the world i.e. EARTH, WATER, FIRE, AIR."

McFarland, on the other hand, was far more focused on the models than any production—and focused in particular on the twenty-six-year-old model Chanel Iman. He'd been courting her for months with offers of vacations on private islands, trips aboard chartered jets, and catered Nets game suites, much of it arranged by Margolin at McFarland's request and paid for as a Fyre business expense.

So that was the scene in which McFarland frankly expressed his intentions for the festival—not as an honest admission, but as a way to pressure Iman into getting in the water with him despite her obvious lack of interest. Now the Fyre Festival CEO was implying to the group that a shot of them jumping into the dark ocean was compulsory under their contracts, for which he'd paid dearly.[117]

Not that he was alone in that feeling of entitlement.

"Get in the fucking water, Chanel," Ja Rule barked.

Iman grew visibly uncomfortable.

"You want *us* to go swimming with *you*?" Hosk asked in disbelief.

That's what prompted McFarland to make the statement about selling the festival to the average loser. He was envisioning himself, in the water with the supermodels, standing in for that customer.

Under the soothing trap beats of DRAM's "Broccoli," tensions rose sharply that night as Fyre's chief talent officer, Ian Browne, put up a rare challenge to McFarland's demands. What good would an unlit video of McFarland running into a dark ocean with Atkins and a squad of unwilling models do for the festival? he asked incredulously. But McFarland and Atkins were adamant: they were going swimming, and the girls were coming with them.

Finally the group arrived at a compromise: the girls would dance, as it turned out, rather joylessly, while ankle-deep in the dark surf. The moment was captured by MATTE's cameras, all the way down to the smile that slipped off Iman's face, settling into a grimace.

But the Fyre boys were on an unstoppable high that night, essentially living out their fantasies under the auspices of a business expense. Never mind the convoluted arrangement, which saw the bulk of the company's investments to date poured into a single advertisement for a music festival—itself justified only as an advertisement for Fyre's actual product, an app called Fyre Media. As Fyre Media employees, first and foremost, the guys had already spent months building out the app, a talent-booking platform on which even the so-called average losers could supposedly buy time with their favorite celebrities. Now they were on a deserted island with the hottest models in the world—and they were getting paid to do it.

They didn't know it then, but it was the beginning of the end.

"If we hadn't succeeded so big at the beginning, we wouldn't have failed so spectacularly at the end," McFarland would moan later in a post-festival interview.[118]

In that, even the experts agree. "Although it seems clear that the festival was doomed from the beginning due to poor planning, inadequate experience, and suspect financing, the combination of hype, sold tickets, and baseless, overconfident enthusiasm created a momentum that made it impossible for Billy and those around him to tell the truth, which was: 'This concert is not going to happen,'" said University of Texas business professor Robert Prentice.[119]

In theory, the festival was supposed to supplement, not detract, from the app.

But no one paid any mind to the fact that none of the models there that weekend had been or, in fact, would ever be signed to said platform. (Neither would the musical acts—in one email, Liaison Artists booking agent Ryan Smith even explicitly demanded his artists weren't "in any way going to be promoting or used to promote the Fyre app, correct?" He was assured they would not.)

Nor did anyone question what justified shooting a commercial that, between the $1,214,976 they'd spent booking the IMG models, the additional $299,000 to book DNA Models' Emily Ratajkowski, the $100,000-plus they'd spent on private-jet charters in December alone, the captained yacht rentals, the Jet Skis, the hotel suites, the $50,000 hair and makeup expenses from the Wall Group (plus an additional $14,000 for a photo op from the celebrity hairstylist Frankie Foye), the styling, and the tens of thousands of dollars in catering, cost more than $2 million.[120]

And that's to say nothing of the high-end production crew, the marketing teams, and the media buyers Fyre had been paying $15,000 a month to distribute the footage alongside paid ads on Facebook and Google.

Without anything to show for it—and I mean that literally—MATTE Projects had started filming for their self-produced Fyre documentary that October, with a directive, according to the emails, from Margolin to focus in particular, on "what is required for promotional materials," like "necessary B roll (i.e. underwater footage, boat footage cruising through the islands, planes landing, models on private jet) which will allow us to further maximize productivity."

Everything else remotely relevant, like footage of the actual festival site or the sleeping arrangements, for example, Margolin unilaterally decided they would use stock footage for.

(After the festival, the photo licensing site Shutterstock, just to show they could, actually did throw together a stock footage version of the Fyre Festival ad for about $5,000, which included eighteen clips and the music licensing. It was nearly indistinguishable from Margolin's vision, minus, of course, the Instagram-influencer cameos, though nowadays those too can also be purchased, for far less money than Fyre paid, through the website Cameo.)

McFarland suddenly had a lot more money at his fingertips than he'd ever had with Spling or Magnises, but his planning skills hadn't improved any. And as it turned out, the infamous shoot almost didn't happen at all.

With just a day to go before their planned December filming trip, MATTE still hadn't been paid the $20,000 deposit they required to follow Fyre's employees around the island— an island, it would turn out, they didn't even have the rights to feature and would have to edit references to out of later marketing materials.

After a long day of radio silence in response to about a dozen-odd emails, McFarland finally provided MATTE with two credit card numbers. Unfortunately both of them were promptly declined. McFarland was ultimately able to save the trip a few hours later, when, records show, he successfully wired them the requisite $20,000.

Later, when McFarland owed the company closer to $300,000, he would attempt to cut down on his debt by handling a visa problem for one of the MATTE producers by enlisting the help of New York Senator Chuck Schumer's press secretary, Angelo Roefaro. Roefaro, who consulted un-officially on a number of Fyre problems in the lead-up to the event, would continue to advise McFarland well after he was arrested on felony wire-fraud charges stemming from the festival, and even featured in the background of footage showing McFarland committing a second set of felonies. (Roefaro has never been accused of any criminal activity.)

There have been reports that McFarland, who decided to throw a music festival with less than six months' runway, had never even been to a music festival before. I am told by one of his high-school friends this is not true—he had attended,

I truly kid you not, the three-day 2011 Bamboozle festival
in New Jersey.

Despite the lack of attention to important elements and incredible focus on irrelevant details that came to characterize
Margolin's role as the head of marketing of the festival, he
was undeniably laser focused when it came to how MATTE
would be filming. In one October 2016 email, for example,
he detailed his dream-shot list, indicating that the $2 million
dollar shoot still wouldn't cover his vision. Trying to film
something essential to the event, like what a concert stage
or tents might look like on the island, "wouldn't be the best
use of time," he wrote, noting that "we anticipate also using
animations and sketches to augment the piece."

Outside of Margolin's ambitious shooting schedule, the
Fyre team was deeply unprepared in every other way, and
from almost the very outset. When media outlets began covering the lavish Bahamian vacation photos posted by the models in November and December, for example, no one on the
team initially thought to instruct their million-dollar spokespeople to link them to the festival.

"We need them to be tagging us!" Browne finally ex-
claimed from his perch on the back of a speedboat during the
December IMG shoot, thumbing through the *Daily Mail* articles with a combination of excitement and dismay.[121]

Meanwhile, Margolin and McFarland were again pooling
their brainpower, with dubious results.

"We will aim to play of [sic] these five key drivers of ticket
sales: Attractive females, Scarcity, Treasure, Talent and Friend
Groups," Margolin wrote in one team-wide meeting recap.

"The marketing plan is perfect," McFarland immediately
replied to all. "Let's put this into a deck. Pumped for what
we came up with."

The business plan that the two had dreamed up together

was similarly chaotic, with clear roots in Billy's early Spling challenges. Their five-phase plan had directions for the now-infamous *Fyrestarter* influencer team, but in this early iteration, they comprised three hundred to five hundred artists, models, athletes, and influencers whom Fyre would gift "one (1) complimentary ticket for themselves and six (6) tickets each [sic] which they need to sell within 72 hours." One of the six tickets the influencers would be required to sell would be labeled as a "golden" ticket [name subject to change, the boys made sure to note] which would come with a clue for a $1 million treasure hunt to take place somewhere in the islands.

"Tickets are purchasable via a hidden URL (i.e. Fyre Festival.com/breadboygetmoney) for this 72 hour period. After the 72-hour period has expired, the tickets will no longer be available," they decided.

Another phase McFarland and Margolin put together included an unnecessarily complicated Friends and Family sale.

"We will use various cohort groups (i.e. Magnises, Tablelist, Samsung, Neuhaus, etc.), giving them early access to the fyre festival via a private link. This link will only be active for 72 hours. Tickets will be slightly discounted. Similar to these cohort groups, we will strategically partner with other StartUps [sic] (i.e. CYC, JuicePress [sic], Sky), and nightlife organizations (i.e. Tao Group, JoonBug [sic], Tablelist, AIM, EMM Group), giving 1-2 free tickets in exchange for a dedicated email blast (we need to hold these tickets in extreme scarcity and will not give commissions as it will devalue our collective brand)."

Meanwhile, no one was giving any thought at all to the fact that the music festival on which they had been spending all their time, money, and energy promoting, was supposed to kick off in less than four months and didn't have any musical acts, a venue, housing, or any staff locked down. Hell, they didn't even have toilets.

And they were already running out of cash.

So where did the money go? There was the expensive commercial, of course, but they were also hemorrhaging cash flying down to the Bahamas every weekend on private jets. And they were bringing a lot of guests on these supposed work trips.

On November 19, 2016, for example, McFarland flew out a team of Fyre employees and investors, including Browne, Samuel Krost, Margolin, and investor John Bryant, to the Bahamas. Joining them aboard the private jet, tail number N827TV, with a minifridge full of specially requested frozen Snickers bars, were the former football player Jason Bell, and the models Alyssah Ali, Chanel Iman, Nadine Leopold, Daniela Lopez and Shanina Shaik. The trip was memorialized in an infamous Mannequin Challenge video Shaik posted on Instagram.

"They would fly to the Bahamas every single weekend in private planes with models. Every weekend that I was trying to get in, he was like, 'Sorry, I've been to the Bahamas, we flew out,'" a former publicist recalled. "They were bringing girls and bling and renting yachts for at least six months doing all that promo."

"Meanwhile you've got Billy McFarland, who has rented this massive, 10,000-square-foot house that cost $50,000 a week, and he's chartered a plane that's going back and forth from Miami so that he can hook up with influencers," whisstleblower Calvin Wells added.

The shoot had actually cost quite a bit more than $2 million, given all the sunken costs. For example, before the IMG models were confirmed for the infamous commercial, the Fyre team had booked a group of less-known women from a trio of second-tier agencies to appear as spokespeople. But no sooner had those models landed in the Bahamas than they learned their services were no longer required.

"They shuttled off all those girls to a neighboring island, where they felt very unsafe and totally ignored, and they wined and dined all the super A-list models that they got. And then they didn't pay the modeling agency," said a source with knowledge of the shoot. "They felt extremely betrayed by Billy, because he treated the girls so badly, you know? It was kind of a personal relationship, and he just very quickly forgot about that and then concentrated on the big girls. They were shuttled off to a neighboring island where accommodations were really bad. They said that there were no locks on the doors. They had nothing to do, and they heard that the other girls were being entertained on the big yachts, you know, the whole thing, and they were nothing."

Another Fyre employee disputed some of the details, saying that while they weren't ultimately used to promote the festival, most of the lesser-known models ended up having fun on the aborted shoot.

"A couple of models, one girl got offended, one cried and went home," he said. "But the other two or three said, 'This is the best time I've ever had, not really having to do work and coast in paradise.' And they got paid."

It was true—Fyre did eventually pay out their fees, even though they hadn't been required to film, but only months after the contracted shoot, and only after the *Wall Street Journal* published an article questioning the festival's financial situation in early April 2017, according to a source familiar with the transaction.

The lower-tier models weren't the only contracted talent for that shoot who found themselves cast aside without warning—nor were they the only ones behind the scenes demanding payment on a signed contract with the threat of a lawsuit. Re-cords show the Fyre team had also offered the DJ and You-Tube personality Chantel Jeffries $50,000 to participate in the same shoot, only to cancel her at the last minute because the IMG models apparently refused to work with talent of what they considered lesser renown, a category that apparently in-cluded Insta-famous vloggers.

"People choose people, models, influencers in a vacuum without understanding the intricacies of the modeling world, because models apparently have reputational risk…they were concerned about being involved in anything to do with some random music festival," said a source who observed the con-tract breakdown. "And they were concerned for their higher-end IMG models' images to be associated with, let's just call her…a market DJ. She wasn't like a high-fashion model. She was more like, whatever. For whatever the reason it was, they didn't want it mixed."

At that point, and despite their signed contract, Fyre also decided to rescind their booking of Jeffries as a festival head-liner, apparently for the same reputational reasons. In an act of generosity, however, they had at least canceled Jeffries's contract well before she boarded a plane.

"Two days before the shoot I called Chantel's agent and informed her that we had to cancel her involvement. I had been working with IMG and had executed contracts with eight of their biggest models from Alessandra Ambrosio to Bella Hadid," Browne, the festival's head of talent, recapped in one email to McFarland's lawyer. "Accordingly, when I told the team at IMG that Chantel Jeffries would be joining the shoot, they unequivocally said that Chantel could not be part of the shoot since it would hurt all the other girls' brands and was not a proper fit at all. Chantel is known as an Insta-gram model and is not at the same level as the Victoria Secret

Models [sic]. I conveyed this to the agent and offered $10K as a breakup fee."

In a subsequent email to Jeffries's management, however, McFarland described the cancelation as being "due to contractual reasons" and offered to throw in another $5,000 toward her fee.

"We would love to work together again in the future, and certainly have Chantelle [sic] and your team attend as complimentary VIPs to the event this spring," he emailed her team. "We're happy to offer $15,000 as an apology, and would ask Chantelle [sic] post the announcement Monday on social media."

When his offer was rejected, Fyre offered to instead pay her half her fee to DJ an after-party and promote the festival on social media—despite having just offered her a headlining gig only a week prior.

Her team was duly unimpressed with Fyre's counteroffer.

"With all due respect, your client did not terminate due to reasons outside of its control. Fyre specifically chose not to move forward with Chantel for creative reasons. It wanted to replace Chantel with other talent. That very reason is why 'pay or play' provisions exist. If a studio decides to replace an actor in a picture with another talent for no reason other than pursuing a new direction, it pays out the actor," her legal team responded. "With respect to the duty to mitigate, we have email documentation wherein Ian specifically instructed Chantel's agent to turn down a conflicting opportunity days before we received the actual contract from Fyre. That opportunity was long gone once Fyre decided to terminate (approximately one day before Chantel was set to travel for the shoot)."

Ultimately, after weighing the costs of attorneys' fees that might arise in litigation, the Fyre team decided to settle with

Jeffries for $45,000 in exchange for her doing…nothing. She never even posted about the festival.

"If you think about it, most of these people, high-fashion models, like Bella, they do, like, millions of dollars on these high-elevated brands. The point is, with Chantel, nobody had any knowledge of any backstory, that there would be any problem with mixing and matching people. Everybody was concerned about their own brand risk," a source with knowledge of the agreement explained. "So this whole Chantel thing, this is just an example of these people as brands, and people didn't want, let's say, don't put in, let's say, a Lamborghini with their perception of somebody who's more of a BMW."

If that sounds a bit chauvinistic, sources say that's because it absolutely was. Not only was there a constant stream of misogynistic invective inside the Fyre offices, McFarland cared so little about the women in his employ that he would routinely urinate with the office bathroom door wide-open—much to the consternation of his female employees.

"The amount of times they were talking about 'fucking bitches' in conference meetings was insane to me. It's a boys' club. They laughed about it. The girls felt uncomfortable. They cried a lot," said former Fyre Media employee Nyla Coffie, who left the company well before its implosion.

But the boys had their minds on other things. The Fyre Festival Orange Tile campaign kicked off on December 12, 2016. One by one, the four hundred influencers selected and vetted by Fyre started to upload the ambiguous orange square to their Instagram feeds. Though the festival would falsely claim tickets sold out in under forty-eight hours, they did in fact see a respectable number sold in the immediate aftermath of the social media event—about 95 percent, according to *Forbes*. They might not have been buying the $250,000 yacht packages, but thousands of kids were really shelling out thousands of dollars—solely on the strength of their faith in these influencers. And of course, the bragging rights that came with a confirmation email and special wristbands—just like the ones posted by my former high school classmate that first drew my attention to the festival.

"While traditional advertising is at a remove from everyday life, a personal photo stream in which every shot is carefully curated has an 'integrity' that broader branding can't reach," the Guardian's Emma Brockes wrote in an essay looking back at the festival. "In this scenario, the enjoyment of an experience is secondary to that of selling of it down the chain to one's own followers, with the subsequent admiration and envy it's hoped to cause."[122]

Brockes nailed it, but it's worth noting that it wasn't just the people who followed influencers that were feeling that envy. Once the anointed list of influencers began posting the orange tiles on that fateful December afternoon, other influencers tried to get in on the deal—for free. Jerry Media, which had been charged with managing the Fyre Instagram account's inbox, found itself fending off hordes of influencers who were streaming in, offering to post in exchange for a single wristband—private jet and agency fees be damned. At the same time, a large number of lesser-known influencers, still waiting on a reply to their DM that would never come, went ahead and posted the square anyway—simply to trick their followers into thinking they'd been part of it.

Few, if any, of the paid influencers or models—with the notable exception of Ratajkowski—labeled their posts as ads. And why would they? It looked better for them too if the post seemed organic.

"Billy's paying people in cash," Wells explained. "It's like, 'Fuck it, you know what? Just send me a G5 to New York and pay me $10,000 in cash and put me up in an exotic, you know, cabana for four days while I frolic on the island.' Like, 'Fuck it, I'll post an Instagram of it.'"

But that ambiguity also served to cover up Fyre's ongoing efforts to misrepresent the models' role in the festival. With no confirmed acts or venue in place to advertise, all the team had to show for their efforts was a series of paid celebrity endorsements.

But as we all know now, that was more than enough.

There's a reason Billy McFarland spent $250,000 on a single Instagram post from one of the Kardashians. A nod from the family can make a brand (or break one, given the $1.3 billion Snapchat lost almost overnight after Kylie Jenner tweeted, rather nonchalantly, that she hadn't been using the app much lately.[123]) Between their long-running reality show, hundreds of millions of followers and wall-to-wall press coverage, the Kardashians sit atop a pyramid of online influencers who act as walking advertisements for the fashion and lifestyle industry.

One of the key selling points of using the Kardashian family for endorsements is that you don't have to explain who they are or why they're important, so instead I'll illustrate their marketing power with an example given to me by the fashion influencer Danielle Bernstein. The twenty-eight-year-old is no stranger to influencer marketing power herself, as the founder of WeWoreWhat, an Instagram page with more than 2.5 million followers that's spawned countless licensing deals and stand-alone fashion lines over the last decade.

The same January weekend that the dueling Fyre documentaries were released, a photo of Kylie Jenner also happened to go viral. Jenner had uploaded the image of herself, draped across the net of a Bahamian catamaran wearing a western cow-print belted swimsuit, to her Instagram page. The suit she was wearing happened to be "the Danielle," a design that came out of a deal Bernstein had done with an influencer-friendly swim brand called Onia, which the company refers to in marketing materials as *collaborations*.

Though Jenner declined to tag or identify the brand she was wearing in the photo, Bernstein claims an enterprising portion of Jenner's 202 million followers still managed to track it down and purchase an incredible $60,000 worth of Onia merchandise in a single hour. It might have been a one-off, but luckily for Bernstein, the media didn't let it drop. After the suit sold out online, Onia relaunched the style a few months later, which I know thanks to both Yahoo News and *InStyle*, which blasted out articles with links to the June presale as well as a host of similar styles in a variety of price ranges. And a year later, when Jenner wore another Bernstein-licensed Onia suit to Coachella, *Glamour* magazine was on the case, announcing that "Kylie Jenner Wore a Bandana Bikini on Instagram—and It's Available on Amazon." In the spirit of service journalism, they too provided affiliate links. (The writer Brian Feldman astutely noted in a recent newsletter that "E-commerce writing is this 'no haters' type of thing where the only two verdicts are 'this is good' or 'maybe this is right for you.' My attitude is that if you're gonna do e-commerce stuff, you might as well just go into writing ad copy (which is fine!).")[124]

For Bernstein, however, it was a revelation.

"I myself was shocked. I don't know why I was shocked by it, because I know the kind of sales that I could produce for a brand. But it was very cool to see, like, 'Wow, she didn't even tag me and you don't get much bigger than Kylie Jenner.' You don't. I actually literally think you don't get much bigger than her," Bernstein told me. "So for her to wear my bathing suit, post it, and not even call out what it is, and we still see those sales, it just kind of validated what I do in my career."

Generally it's a great racket for everyone involved. The Kardashians get sent literal tons of free stuff (and the occasional payment to induce them to show it off in public), the fashion sites get a cut of sales by identifying and linking to the brands the celebrities wear for regular people to imitate, the regular people get to dress like the celebrities they follow on social media, and the designers get to rake in the attention and the profits. Everyone wins.

That includes Bernstein, a Long Island native who turned a bare-bones fashion blog about her going-out outfits into an Instagram empire and now makes a (comparatively paltry) $15,000 a post to advertise for other fashion, beauty, and health-care brands as an influencer for hire.[125] She was able to parlay that collaboration with Onia into a licensing deal for her own stand-alone brand, Shop WeWoreWhat, which launched in 2018 and claims to have sold millions of dollars in WeWoreWhat and Danielle Bernstein Collection merch.[126]

But the cycle is also a precarious one, which relies on dedicated followers willing to open their wallets for the notion of authenticity, no matter how obviously performative it may appear, explains Robert Prentice, the professor from the McCombs School of Business at the University of Texas at Austin.

"You know, I think there's part of a follower's brain that probably doesn't realize something is sponsored, and there's part of their brain that realizes 'This is just an advertisement and I really shouldn't trust it,' and yet, you kind of get swept up in being part of the crowd," Prentice says. "All my friends follow what this influencer says. All my friends think this influencer is cool. And I think the conformity bias that we're all sort of a part of could be a big part of that."

That's something Weinstein says he sees a lot in the start-up world as well.

"Imagine if you were a caveman and you were walking with your tribe through the fields and the jungle, and everybody started running, you would start running instinctively because you didn't have time to figure out if there was actually a tiger chasing you or not. And so that herd mentality is what drives people to make decisions and not do their proper diligence or take responsibility for the decisions that they make," he explained. "It helps save much-needed mental energy on choosing for yourself."

As humans, we're deeply motivated to accept what the people around us say is true, even when it obviously isn't. We've known about this problem for a while, though that doesn't seem to have helped us resist it any. In a series of experiments conducted in the 1950s by the psychologist Solomon Asch, subjects confirmed time and time again that all it takes to convince us to think something is a sense that everyone else thinks it. In one experiment, for example, he showed subjects a series of three lines and asked them to identify the one that matched the length of a fourth line. His subjects had no problem picking out the correct line—until they were put in a room of actors who deliberately chose one of the incorrect answers. About 75 percent of the subjects chose the obviously incorrect line at least once, all thanks to peer pressure. And the pressure gets worse when the liars are our friends or people we'd like to be friends with.

"This bias to conform is much greater, of course, when the others in the group are not strangers, but coemployees or friends, or when the correct answer is not right there in black and white as it was in the Asch study, but is instead a subjective question like an ethical issue," Prentice notes.

I'm guessing that's what led *InStyle* to predict that "Onia's

instantly recognizable cow print [would] absolutely dominate this season." They may have been dead wrong about the
general public's desire to swathe itself in the hide of a span-
dex cow, but that didn't much matter to the designer or the
influencers driving the attention.

I ended up in contact with Bernstein around the same time
her suits and the two Fyre documentaries went viral. She had
posted on her Instagram page about the Fyre Festival, and I
was looking for sources in order to write about what the influencer lifestyle was like from the inside. So I proposed an
interview for a long-form piece that would eventually turn
into this book, which she immediately accepted. As it turned
out, Bernstein had run in similar circles with Billy McFarland over the years, and I was curious what had made her
decide to decline his offer to promote Fyre—and, she mentioned, a similar offer years before to promote his membership card Magnises.

Her answer appeared to involve a bit of integrity and a
bit of business strategy. When she was approached the first
time, Bernstein says she was already a member of the private
club Soho House, so the decidedly down-market Magnises's
take on a private-members club held little appeal to her personally and, more importantly, offered no advantage to her
personal, upwardly mobile brand. And she says that after back-
channeling with the wife of Kaskade, a famous DJ who, at
the time, had been rumored to be involved in the festival, she
found the Fyre deal to be similarly unappealing.

"First I was asked to be involved in Magnises, and I went to
the Magnises town house, and I just remember leaving there
very confused. I was like, 'What is happening? What is this?
What does he even do?' I was just kind of like, 'I'm just not
sold on this, and I don't really want to be involved.' I was a
member of Soho House at the time, which I'm not now. But

I was like, this is not ever going to replace Soho House for me, so in that sense it really doesn't matter," Bernstein said. "Then they reached out to my agent about having me promote Fyre Festival and be a part of that, and she reached out to Naomi, Kaskade's wife, and said, 'What's the deal with this?' And basically she was like, 'Kaskade's not performing, this is definitely bullshit.' And so that's when I decided not to be involved."

(Though Bernstein assures me she sussed out how shady the festival was in advance, she apparently wasn't averse to the free tickets themselves—according to internal Fyre records, she had been confirmed as a guest for the second weekend.)

When she's not busy influencing, Bernstein also runs a podcast called *WeHeardWhat?!*, and although she had wanted no official part of the festival itself, she apparently didn't mind piggybacking on the popularity of the documentaries. And I, a profiler of celebrities, wasn't opposed to seeing what she was like unfiltered, both figuratively and literally. So when she invited me to come by her apartment to do a broadcasted chat about the festival for her podcast, meant to supplement the interview I had already proposed for my own piece, I eagerly accepted.

It felt just like walking into a real live Instagram post. Upon arriving at Bernstein's chic, mid-century modern Soho two-bedroom apartment, I was immediately greeted by two young assistants who welcomed me in before returning to their laptop stations atop Bernstein's $2,700 Kathy Kuo Home marble dining table. Then they offered me a bottle of designer water while I waited for Bernstein to finish production on a video she needed to post to her Instagram Story before we could officially begin.

A few minutes later, I found myself sitting on the white-carpeted floor of Bernstein's living room as her five-year-old

French bulldog (who at the time had more than twenty-four thousand Instagram followers) humped my leg. And I was powerless to stop it.

As my shin and ankle were pulled tighter and tighter into Bleecker the Frenchie's furry embrace, Bernstein and I spoke into a pair of high-end microphones she had propped up on her $4,000 vintage Milo Baughman coffee table. Rather than ruin the interview, I resigned myself to leaning back against her $6,500 white Timothy Oulton couch and thinking of England until one of her assistants recognized what was happening (apparently the dog is deeply horny and does this sort of thing to her visitors on the regular) and finally stepped in to coitus-interruptus Bleecker.

(Ostensibly, I could have spoken up about the canine sex act happening on my side of the solid rosewood cube anchoring the living room—the podcast wasn't live—but before we started recording, Bernstein told me she prefers not to have to edit the episodes. She would, in fact, upload the recording to Apple within seconds of us finishing our conversation, without removing a single second.)

It was a trippy experience, overall, going from Instagram to IRL with Bernstein. Just from following the WeWoreWhat Instagram page, for example, I knew her coffee table was one of Bernstein's first designer-furniture purchases, that it was recommended to her by her "friend Maggie from Claude Home," an Instagram-based home-decor brand, and that she would soon release a $195 deep brown wood-print suit as part of a swim line, again for Onia, "inspired by pieces in my home."

Before I even got there, I knew more about her apartment than I did about where my closest friends lived, and that's kind of the point. "It seems like influencers are your friends. And you're more likely to buy products on the recommendations

of your friends," writes Chris Stokel-Walker, a British journalist and the author of *YouTubers: How YouTube Shook Up TV
and Created a New Generation of Stars.*

She was also surprisingly forthright, at least to me, about
how connected she was to the major players in the festival.
Before our interview, for example, Bernstein admitted that a
lot of people had been asking her about FuckJerry's involvement in the documentary, and she expressed conflicting emotions about including them in the talk due to her involvement
with a tequila brand they had recently launched.

"I'm in with them on JAJA Tequila so I don't want to make
them look bad at all," Bernstein said, though, to her credit,
she added, "But I want people to know the truth."

During our talk, Bernstein assured me that she, her agent,
and her team thoroughly vetted brands based on whether they
had worked with them before, wanted to work with them,
or had seen other people work with them. And like the artists who demanded multiples of their normal fees up front
before signing on to Fyre, Bernstein said she would probably
require payment in full or at least half before agreeing to work
with a new brand she hadn't heard of before. But primarily,
she said, "I try and only work with companies that I actually
believe in, I actually use, I've actually experienced, whether
it's a hotel that I'm promoting or a new sunscreen. Whatever
it may be, I always test out a product first or will only work
with it if I actually like the brand.

"I'm trying to think of what I would have done if they
were like, 'Okay, we want to pay you $10,000 to post this or-
ange square on your feed.' I would have been like, okay, but
what is it for? And then they would have been like, 'It's for
this Fyre guy.' So I said, 'But I have never been and I'm not
really sure if I'm going to go. So why would I promote it?' I
just wouldn't have. And it's shocking to me that some people

did. But do I think they should be responsible? Yes. To some extent, I think that they should be. And I think that as influencers, we should all be responsible for what we promote and what we put out there," Bernstein said. "I would never tell someone to go to IMD Spa and get a lymphatic drainage massage if I didn't try it out myself, know that I liked it, know that it worked, and know that it wasn't going to harm them. You know what I mean? Even when I give diet advice, I have so many people in my life that I am talking to whether it's Melissa [Wood, Bernstein's health coach and the wife of nightlife impresario Noah Tepperberg] or a doctor about, 'Should I tell my followers that they should get colonics? Is this healthy if I tell them to drink celery juice every morning?' I always do my research. And I just think a lot of influencers involved in this project didn't do their research, and that was, I think, the most upsetting thing about it."

(I actually did do a little research into Bernstein's touting of the supposed health benefits of celery juice, including claims that it cures inflammation, cleared acne-prone skin and ended migraine headaches, all of which reputable nutritionists dispute. It appears the claims about the life-saving benefits of celery actually come not from a doctor but from Anthony Williams, a medical medium who communes with ghosts to get the best undead health advice this side of the River Styx. Williams, it may not surprise you to learn, is also a contributor to Gwyneth Paltrow's wellness retail company, GOOP.)

But I digress. When we had concluded our talk and the podcast was safely uploaded, Bernstein promoted it on social media with a heavily filtered Instagram Story post, in which she graciously tagged me. (Still, despite her 2.5 million followers, my following saw no real bump.) Then Bernstein sent me on my way with promises of doing the originally scheduled interview about social media influence when she had more time. So I let it go—after all, she had already confirmed her participation in writing.

The second interview would never occur.

"Hey babe, so I've been working on a book of my own right now and my team doesn't think I should be involved in any others at this time. Sorry about this and best of luck!" she replied when I inquired about dates.

Six months later, she popped up in my inbox again. She had completed her book and was wondering, "Hey babe how are you?! Not sure if you saw—but I'm releasing a book this Spring—about my life, making it in NYC, and becoming a boss entrepreneur. We're currently exploring TV options and I wanted to reach out to see if you had any thoughts for me!"

Reader, I did not.

The book, which was cowritten with a woman named Emily Seigel, was eventually released through a self-publishing company called Vertel and did not, at least to my knowledge, ever end up on TV. It did, however, technically make the *New York Times* bestseller list—albeit with the tell-tale dagger signifying a bulk order typically made to game the author onto the list in the first place. Whatever happened there to justify the literary asterisk, it's a dubious honor she now shares with other luminaries like Donald Trump and Donald Trump Jr.

Bernstein gets—and often deserves—credit for being among the more "real" influencers on Instagram today. But that's all a relative designation. As it turned out, a year after we first sat down, Bernstein got in trouble for running a similar bait and switch on a secondhand clothing seller who hit the jackpot after Bernstein's assistant accidentally dropped off samples from her own upcoming swim line to a Goodwill store. The woman, a Poshmark seller named Jade Myers, recognized the Onia brand, purchased the items, and immediately posted them for resale on her online store.[127]

Not long after, Bernstein saw the listing and reached out privately to Myers, according to screenshots of their conversation that were later posted on Instagram.

"Hi!! Can you please take my Swim off your site?! How did you get it? I will buy all of it. Those are unreleased samples. Omg please take it down!!!! How did you get that?" Bernstein wrote in the leaked emails.

Records show Myers offered to sell Bernstein the entire lot for the prices she had already posted on Poshmark, allowing Bernstein to ensure none of the pieces would get out to the public, and Bernstein quickly agreed. But after Myers pulled the listings, Bernstein appeared to balk at paying the full price, and demanded that Myers either sell her back the items for what she had paid for them at Goodwill or face a lawsuit. Records show Myers tried to explain the cost and time that went into photographing the items and creating the listings—to no avail. In response, Bernstein also threatened to use her personal connections to destroy the girl's livelihood.

"I am in contact with the Poshmark CEO and can get your entire store pulled if you put them back up," Bernstein wrote after Myers rejected her lowball offer.[128]

But Bernstein's tune changed dramatically once Myers went public with the allegations. Once the story had been picked up by the media, Bernstein immediately agreed to pay the full price and posted a video of herself crying about the things people had been saying about her online.

By the end of the week, Bernstein had posted a photo of herself with Myers on Instagram, explaining that they had worked out their differences and that Bernstein had even proposed that they work together in the future. As far as I can tell, no collaboration ever came of it. A shocker, I know.

Not that it was the first time Bernstein had taken advantage of someone publicly by flexing her influencer status—

nor would it be the last. In 2018, for example, a number of pieces from her debut costume-jewelry line had to be dropped from Nordstrom after the founder of a fine-jewelry company called Foundrae accused Bernstein of requesting samples as an influencer and then knocking them down to the smallest details as a designer.

"This is not Foundrae," company founder Beth Bugdaycay wrote in one Instagram post. "This is a costume line that #daniellebernstein of @weworewhat made for Nordstrom with the help of @lulu_dk. All complete copies. Tonight I feel crushed. Danielle came to my house over a year ago to see our jewelry and we let her borrow pieces several times. How is it not personal when you let a person into your home, let them wear your pieces, and then she knocks it off?? It's an abuse of privilege, taking advantage of access. The buyers of Nordstrom also have a responsibility to protect design integrity and their PR team is creating consumer confusion by endorsing her as the designer which is not the truth. Honestly, I want to turn the other cheek but I need to call out when wrong is wrong."

When the media started picking up on the story, Bernstein responded with—what else—a video of herself crying about the things people were saying about her online. She denied the allegations and claimed that she had personally decided to pull the offending pieces herself, though Nordstrom suggested otherwise in a statement, saying, "We take situations like this seriously and partnered with Lulu DK and Danielle Bernstein to remove each of the pieces in question. We're excited to offer our customers the chance to shop the rest of the collection."[129]

Despite all of this, I still followed Bernstein on social media, for the same reason I still read gossip magazines and click through *Daily Mail* photo albums when I should be doing more important things. She's entertaining as hell, the platonic

ideal of a millennial influencer, aspirational but still relatable, thin, well-dressed, and vaguely wealthy. She's the kind
of woman who sells *product* rather than clothes and wears a
singular pant, rather than a pair of them. She's an expert at
marketing without making it obvious, sprinkling her brand-
tagged "getting ready" outfit posts with outright ads designed
to look like getting-ready posts, sometimes with the word *#ad*
written in the same color as the post background, so that you
can only see it if you're really looking hard. To break up the
monotony, she also posts pictures of her dogs, including the
horny one, her mom's Westhampton beach house, and videos
of herself in designer workout gear dancing to knockoff versions of the Tracy Anderson cardio-workout routines made
famous by Gwyneth Paltrow, which have become ubiqui-
tous in the thin, well-dressed influencer community, due in
large part to how social media–friendly they are. (I imagine
even Elaine Benes would be able to stay on beat with these
jazzercise-style dances, and I'd be lying if I told you I didn't
routinely find laughter and joy in Bernstein's self-serious routines.)

In a sense, she's the version of me that I (and many other
millennial women) could be if I weren't too lazy to work out
regularly, if I had an unlimited clothing budget, fashion sense,
and a general lack of shame around dancing in public and referring to a plural item of clothing in the singular. Unlike my
own mismatched mélange of decor, everything in Bernstein's
home is perfect, au courant, and highly curated. Her couch
and rug, despite the presense of two different colored dogs,
are pure, unblemished white clouds floating above serene
wood tones. The truth is, I enjoy watching her curated life,
just like I enjoy watching the ladies of Bravo parade around
in their ridiculous designer outfits, and while I've never

purchased anything directly from her, I can't say with absolute honesty that I wouldn't one day in the future.

Quite simply, her reality does not look or function like my
own and it's fun to escape into when I'm bored on the subway.

In real life, of course, it is more likely that one of the brands
she works with would pay me not to tag them than it is that
I would get a sponsorship deal. But Bernstein makes it seem
like it could be possible. I was curious, so I looked it up, and
ten years and twelve thousand posts ago, Bernstein's Instagram
page was just like yours or mine. In fact, her very first upload, posted in 2010, was a generic, blurry, overprocessed picture of the chocolate birthday cake she had for her eighteenth
birthday, not unlike the one I posted for my twenty-seventh.

But Bernstein is Insta-famous (and I am not) because she
figured out over time how to post things that people want,
and by posting things people want, she's figured out how to
sell other things to them and that makes her valuable in an
increasingly online society. Of course, Bernstein occasionally admits to suffering from plebeian issues like depression
and anxiety, but she never posts a problem without a solution, such as Highline Wellness, a line of CBD-infused gum-
mies for which she serves as an advisor. (This also sometimes
puts her in rather interesting company—Highline Wellness,
for example, also counts among its endorsers an influencer
named Marisa Hochberg, a long-term spon-con relationship
that has apparently continued even after Hochberg was outed
as having squatted at a Montauk home during the COVID
outbreak, leaving behind an unpaid bill of more than $14,000
and an entire *New York Times* exposé into her alleged grift.[130])
But Bernstein has curated her life of any such ugliness—and
even curated her own body shape, if the watchdog accounts
@WePhotoshoppedWhat, @WePhotoshoppedWhat2, and

@WeOverWhat are correct—and served it to the public along with detailed information on how we can achieve it too.

But anyone can curate their lives to seem like something they're not, if they're determined enough (and skilled enough with a Facetune app), explains Dr. Roberto Cavazos, an economist at the University of Baltimore, who's published a number of studies on the influencer market. Ever the prototypical warm, rumpled professor, Cavazos met with me over coffees in a conference room on a rainy winter day in Baltimore to discuss what he refers to as the "influencer problem."

"Identity is just such a facile thing, but people think their identities are fixed. But some very successful people are able to craft an identity and realize that an identity is something very, very malleable, that it can be worked to an advantage," says Cavazos.

It's even easier to craft an identity—and sell products—when you have the assistance of agents, publicists, and managers. Add in a handful of experienced reality-TV producers and complete editorial control over your image, and you might ascend to a level like the Kardashians and Donald Trump, who have used their programming to successfully cement their carefully crafted identities as fact in popular culture.

Trump may not have been posting fashion Instagrams, but like the Kardashians, he studiously built his public profile until people reported his fictions as fact. When he wanted people to think he was dating models he'd never met before, he was said to have planted stories about himself by calling reporters under the name "John Barron," at least, until he transferred the name to his youngest son. Now it's part of the printed record that he stole Carla Bruni away from Mick Jagger with his supposed sexual prowess, despite the fact that Bruni and Trump have never been alone in a room together.

But it's really Mark Burnett we have to thank for molding a

bankrupt, corrupt real-estate developer into the platonic ideal of a successful businessman on *The Apprentice*, which reached twenty million households at its peak, just as we can thank Ryan Seacrest, the producer of *Keeping Up With the Kardashians*, for convincing tens of millions of Americans that we've been inside the Kardashian family's living room.

As it turns out, many of those exterior shots that open every episode of *Keeping Up With the Kardashians* are just random stand-in homes in which the family has never set foot. A long-running magazine column, "Keeping Up With the Kontinuity Errors," demonstrates how often the show reshoots and films out of order to craft their supposed reality. Even the most "explosive footage" the show has aired has been vetted and approved for broadcast by the family momager and executive producer, Kris Jenner. (The devil works hard, but Kris Jenner works harder, goes the aphorism.)

What really goes on with these people behind the scenes is, frankly, anyone's guess. In the run-up to the 2016 election, Burnett threatened his production company's employees with a $5 million penalty for releasing any unseen footage from *The Apprentice*, which the actor Tom Arnold assures me contains copious use of the n-word. Trump and Burnett both deny this.

And like any good influencer worth his salt (and unlike prior presidents, Trump's personal shakers always reportedly made several sizes larger than one provided to the guests at his table), Trump managed to use his show to market any number of products, including ties, wines, steaks, perfumes, and even a urine-test kit, which promised to diagnose vitamin deficiencies. And people bought them! Not because of the quality of his products or his discerning taste (he reportedly enjoys his steaks well-done, with ketchup), but simply because he was famous.

"Celebrities always have pitched products in some way. But

HYPE   157

normally, they were people that had become celebrities for
actually doing something, whether they were an athlete, or
movie star, or something like that," said Derrick Borte, the
creator of *The Joneses*. "But I think now, you've got people
that are celebrities just for being celebrities. Just for having or
creating a following from some combination of a reality-TV
show and a social media presence, they become a brand. And
I think that you have people that are captured by that, that
are mesmerized by that. And they think that, 'If I do what
they're doing or do what they're saying, I'm going to have this
life that they have, or I can come close to it in some way.'"

You don't have to be traditionally beautiful to make impressions and influence people, but it certainly doesn't hurt, says
Karyn Blanco, a thirty-eight-year-old Bronx native and self-
described Black butch lesbian. But her castmates on Netflix's
digital-reality show, *The Circle*, the filming of which was conducted in private and over social media with no face-to-face
interactions, knew her as twenty-seven-year-old Mercedeze,
who is "Fenty all the way down." Blanco, one of a number
of so-called "catfish" plants on the show, had used real photos belonging to her friend (and model) Chynna Cliette with
which to communicate with her fellow castmates. She credits
the feminine persona as helping her get along better with the
other girls on the show, as well as Chris, a gay castmate with
whom she felt a particular bond that she's not sure would have
developed had he seen her real face to start.

"We're all in separate rooms, and we can't speak to each
other directly. We never get to hear each other's voices, or see
each other's faces, other than what's projected on the screen.
It's kind of hard to be able to build a relationship with someone when you're limited on what you can, on how often you
can speak to them," Blanco said during a recent phone call.
"I feel it was liberating, because one, I was able to say and

move in a way that because of my dolled-up and pretty persona or character, I was able to glide through the game in a way where I was able to flirt with the guys, flirt with the girls, be friends with the guys, be friends with the girls, and not get picked up on. I feel as though, had I come in as myself, I would have been received, but I probably would have been a little bit less acceptable, simply because I would have been the only one there of a female gender but a masculine demeanor."

Blanco burst out laughing when I asked her if she thought there was any truth to the notion that influencing is similar to being a catfish, in the sense that they are presenting the most idealized version of themselves, but people receive it as their friends recommending products—or their friends modeling.

"That's one of the best explanations I've ever heard," she said. "It makes me laugh, because the way that you—I've never heard anyone explain it as well as you did. I'm sorry, I'm going to have to use that, so if you hear me say it again somewhere, I'm going to give you credit." (You heard it here first!)

But Blanco can see both sides of the issue quite clearly, because her catfishing on the show actually ended up turning her into an influencer. After the show's premiere, she suddenly found her face was being broadcast across Times Square, and her follower count started rising precipitously. Not long after came the brand inquiries.

"I posted a picture of me laying in my bed, like literally I was laying in bed. I had just washed my hair and taken a shower and I was just laying in bed," she said. "We actually ended up getting contacted by three companies that specialize in bed linens and houseware and home goods because of the reaction and the comments.

"Now it's like, no matter what we post, if it's ad or not,

people are automatically like, 'Oh, my god, I need that.' Or, 'Oh, my god, I want that,'" Blanco said.

Blanco's path to fame and influence was a funny one, given that she became a fan favorite on the show by coming clean about being fake, despite getting eliminated in the third round. That helped her become one of the few cast members to get blue-check verified once the show started to air, a designation that she said "catapulted everything for me as far as the representation, the brand contact, people wanting to work with me in the most sporadic ways."

But in the wake of the show, Blanco's newfound status as an influencer has completely changed the way she uses social media. She strategizes about what to post and when, something she says she had never thought about before. When she knows she has a brand post coming up, for example, she tries to pace out posts so it'll have the maximum impact for the advertisers. And she's far more conscious of what she posts from her so-called real life now.

"I make music in my real life. I'm used to having a fan base, but this show has catapulted me to a place where I would never have imagined in my wildest dreams. Now, when people are calling me an influencer, it's kind of like, an influencer of what? You have to be very careful on what you put out or what you post or it kind of makes you walk on eggshells," Blanco said. "Like, there are guidelines. You don't have the freedom to post how you want. You can't say certain things. You have to represent yourself a certain way in the industry. And it's kind of weird, because it's like, so I have to get all dolled-up and keep presenting myself as this fully polished person. When I really just want to lay on the sofa with my hair in a messy bun and some sweatpants."

Maybe that's why Blanco thinks apps like TikTok, which allows users to use technology to transform both their own images and other found material on the internet, is a more honest experience than Instagram, which revolves around the notion of stripped-bare authenticity, despite its inherently performative nature.

"On Instagram, you can only post a picture or a video. TikTok lets you emulate what someone else is doing side by side, unless you use voice-over, since you can be someone else. It literally allows you to be a whole 'nother person through other apps on the internet. It's one of the craziest things I've ever really experienced, but it's at a point now where this is what people want to see," Blanco said. "Everyone wants to be real—to an extent. No one wants to add up or own up to their own personal opinions, their own personal thoughts, beliefs, because of what the internet is portraying, for everyone to be on the same robot mentality kind of thing."

And even TikTok has its problems. In December 2019, a group of nineteen teens with millions of followers on the app founded the Hype House, a sort of *Real World* for content makers, set in a gated Los Angeles mansion with no parents allowed. Arguably the most famous of the Hype Housers was fifteen-year-old Charli D'Amelio, who gained close to thirty million followers with her Renegade dance, which, it turned out, had been lifted from Jalaiah Harmon, a Black fourteen-year-old aspiring choreographer. Harmon would not get credit for the dance until months later—the same month D'Amelio attended Milan Fashion Week as a guest of Prada. But it was a gold mine for the Hype Housers, who combined their star power on the app to gain millions more followers, a fawning *New York Times* profile, and a number of lucrative brand deals. D'Amelio, who has danced onstage at a Jonas Brothers concert and appeared on *The Tonight Show Starring Jimmy Fallon*, even filmed a 2020 Super Bowl commercial for Sabra—all based on her Renegade fame. (According to the *Times*, when

D'Amelio learned of the dance's true creator, she commented through a publicist, "I know it's so associated with me…but I'm so happy to give Jalaiah credit and I'd love to collaborate with her."[131])

Things fell apart quickly at the Hype House, however, and in March, just three months after putting her name on the lease, founding member Daisy Keech left the house in a fallout with her cofounders over copyright and merchandising issues that allegedly saw one Hype House member dismissing her as "an Instagram model with a shelf life." Keech, who filed a subsequent lawsuit against two of her former Hype House roommates, then opened her own house, called the Clubhouse, which was put under investigation in August after allegedly throwing wild parties during the Los Angeles pandemic shutdown.[132] (D'Amelio left the house before that happened, expressing her desire to film a reality show with her family.)

But whether it's through Instagram, TikTok, or whatever new app media influencers are using to communicate with the world at large, one thing is undeniable: the world is watching. And history suggests we've always been watching on some level.

Following, consuming, and internalizing the exploits of these people who are famous for no good reason is something we as humans have enjoyed as a valid form of entertainment long before Paris Hilton was even a star in the summer sky. Arguably, the prototype of the influencer exists as far back as the Holy Roman Empire, explains Cavazos.

"The earlier versions were sort of royals in rich countries, right? In the Habsburg Empire, you were a prince or princess, and what you would do was, you would go ahead and open restaurants and sponsor things, get involved in various enterprises, and lend your name to organizations," Cavazos said. "If you go way back to the Romans, they actually had an organization called United Artists, the gladiators and certain legionnaires and distinguished proconsuls would lend their name to the entertainments and get a cut. So this is an old thing. It's just an old thing but was enabled dramatically with technology."

Dramatic almost seems like an undersell. The social media platforms and advances in smartphone technology have spurred new levels of anxiety—and a willingness to be influenced previously unseen, even in the Habsburg Empire. Our phones are the first thing most of us touch in the morning, and the last things we look at before going to sleep at night. For many of us, it's our most intimate relationship.

And, for those of us without employees to hand us designer water and remind us to take a break, it's making us miserable. Even Bernstein admits she sometimes has to pause from social media—despite it making her millions of dollars—because of the negative emotions it stirs up inside of her.

"There's times where I go days without scrolling through my feed. Right? I'm still posting and I'm still doing what is technically my job. And I'll stop looking because you can look and you're exposed to so much then you always think the grass is greener and there's always something better. Someone looks better. The thing they're doing, or they're making more money or whatever it is," Bernstein told me. "And you're always comparing yourself to other people and it's super unhealthy. Even with other influencers, I can be like, 'Oh, shit, she got to go to that fashion show and I didn't.' Or 'Why is she working with that brand and I didn't?'"

Studies show that social-networking usage "is linked to increased social comparison and negative affective states such as envy and jealousy,"[133] and that these feelings are amplified when you're just passively scrolling. Social media is no longer something we can just opt in to—for most millennials who grew up with the internet, and certainly Gen Z, it's become a natural extension of our lives. And with the spread of COVID-19 and mandatory lockdowns across the planet, it's all but replaced IRL social interactions. We use it to seek out information, to form our identities—"often more favorably than off-line," notes Dr. Daria J. Kuss, a psychologist and program leader of the cyberpsychology department at Nottingham Trent University. And of course, we also use it for entertainment, hopping on in times of boredom or stress to experience fun and pleasure.

"Nowadays, social networking does not necessarily refer to what we do, but who we are and how we relate to one another," writes Kuss.[134] "There appears to be an inherent understanding or requirement in today's technology-loving culture that one needs to engage in online social networking in order not to miss out, to stay up to date, and to connect."

According to Kuss, it seems it's now possible to fulfill Maslow's entire hierarchy of needs—the theory of the five basic motivators of all human beings—all while sitting on the toilet.

Social networking provides "safety, association, estimation, and self-realization," by allowing users to customize their privacy, connect with like-minded individuals, and compare their performance online to others. "Finally, the need for self-realization, the highest attainable goal that only a small minority of individuals are able to achieve, can be reached by presenting oneself in a way one wants to present oneself," Kuss theorises, "and by supporting 'friends' on those social-networking sites who require help," she concludes.

The stress of social media performance can even affect those whose influence is supposedly divinely bestowed; the royals are the reason why the magazine *Tatler* exists at all, why

Kate Middleton's outfits sell out within hours of her public appearances, and why sites like Meghan's Mirror stay in business. Even the future Queen is not immune to the impetus to strive for maximum aspiration and attainability, as highlighted by the fashion expert Elizabeth Holmes (no relation to the Theranos founder) who analyzes the royal family's sartorial choices for her Instagram blog, *So Many Thoughts*. In one recent appearance, the former Ms. Middleton wore what I would define as a cute rust/salmon-colored suit. Holmes went a little further.

"Not just any suit, but a PINK TROUSER SUIT from Marks & Spencer," Holmes observed. "This suit is threading a needle like nothing else we've seen. It is (what I believe to be??) her first trouser suit, which is a style that is Serious with a capital S. But it's pink! And not just any pink, but a saturated yet soft hue, which is so approachable. And it's currently for sale for like $250 at Marks & Spencer, so for a royal it's supes accessible."

Holmes's description of a future royal consort's act of wearing relatively inexpensive pink pants in public as a radical act reminds me of a notion offered by Nick Viall, the forty-year-old apple of *The Bachelor* franchise's eye. I met the handsome, former dating-show star for lattes in Venice Beach. Viall is friendly, dry, and extremely self-aware, noting that the choices influencers make are often influenced by the public just as much as the public is influenced by them.

Viall was a breakout star on the reality series, appearing on two different seasons of *The Bachelorette* before nabbing his own starring turn as the titular *Bachelor*. The network then carried him from *The Bachelor* finale to the premiere of the ABC ratings monster *Dancing with the Stars*, where he ultimately placed sixth, ahead of stars like Nancy Kerrigan, Charo, and Mr. T.

Basically, Viall's American royalty. And thanks to his carefully edited star turn on *The Bachelor*, he's a Prince Charming in the eyes of the 7.4 million viewers who tuned in to watch him find love.[135] (Spoiler: he didn't.)

He's also one of a handful of *The Bachelor*–universe stars who've outlasted their appearances on the show in the popular consciousness. That staying power translated into more than a million Instagram followers, though he says that number tends to dip once you've been off-screen for a while. He laughs when he recalls how, in 2014, he gained fifty thousand followers just by appearing on TV for the first time.

"I thought that was an insane amount," Viall said.

But, "It gets old fast," Viall warned me. "What I mean by that is, you'll see it every season. Every season, the new fan favorites will get this overnight bump in following, and their engagement will be through the roof. Truly, everything they post is liked. And then, very quickly, once the show ends, that engagement is drastically, drastically reduced."

That drop, Viall recalled, "happens immediately, but it takes a good six months for it to kind of get to…" He stopped and made a flatlining motion with his hand.

"You look at other influencers, like YouTube stars. They build this loyal fan base, and this loyal fan base chose to follow them based off of this love that they felt for them. And then if you go on this TV show, it's a novelty. It's a curiosity. You don't even know this person," Viall said, suddenly sounding weary. "The novelty wears off. You're following him because you loved him on the show, but you don't really know about him. And then he starts posting things, and you're like, 'I'm not really enjoying it.'"

There's actually a technical term for that short-term enjoyment: *neophilia*. "It's the love of the new, right? So we like something that's new and it's exciting," Cavazos said.

By the time Viall formally stepped down as ABC's poster man for love in 2017 with a fiancée on his arm, he had amassed millions of followers on Instagram. And although the situation broke down almost immediately with his chosen fiancée, Vanessa Grimaldi, he held on to his followers—well, most of them, anyway.

"When my relationship ended, people were following for the relationship. And I was no longer in a relationship, so they unfollowed," Viall said.

He's spent the last few years figuring out how exactly to thread that needle and hold the attention of the ones who stayed, now that his brand isn't centered around performatively searching for and experiencing love on prime-time television. He tries to emulate other stars who have found ways to connect with their fans outside of their specific genres. "John Mayer's Instagram is awesome. He's like my muse," Viall said, referring to the esoteric musician's Instagram talk show, "Current Mood with John Mayer."

Viall is still trying to figure out exactly what his audience wants from him. "You get this following, and then you're kind of like, 'What do I do with this?' Because people are following you because of, really, just you," he said. "If you're lucky enough to come out of that experience in a relationship, then that's easy, because you're like, 'Oh, they're following you for your love story' or whatever. So you post a lot of pictures of your relationship. If you have a kid, the playbook is to post about your relationship and your kid."

By comparison, Carly Waddell, a onetime *Bachelor* contestant who married and has two kids with another contestant she met on an offshoot of the show called *Bachelor in Paradise*, has about the same number of followers as Viall, despite never starring in her own season. And JoJo Fletcher, one of the rare titular stars to actually marry her chosen fiancé, leads the pack with more than 2.2 million followers.

Viall shrugs and sips his coffee. "Ultimately, that's what *The Bachelor* fans tend to prefer."

But after spending four years searching for love on all the wrong soundstages, Viall decided to make that part of his life private (though it still occasionally erupts onto the pages of *People* magazine and *Us Weekly*) and has been working instead to craft his identity into something entertaining for the million-odd followers who have opted into updates on his life. Cavazos, the business professor who theorizes that we can craft our identities into whatever we want them to be, would be proud.

Because what Viall really means isn't, "What do I do with this?" it's "How do I make a business out of this?" If he hadn't become famous off *The Bachelor*, he says, he probably wouldn't have an Instagram account at all.

"And if I had one, it wouldn't be what it is. And I wouldn't ask my friends to stop and take a picture of me next to a nice sunset. And I wouldn't record myself painting. I just wouldn't. I wouldn't do it," Viall said. "For me, even though I try to show an authentic side of myself, it ultimately is a business. You know what I'm saying? I try to have fun with it. I try to be entertaining. And now that I have it, I try to do something with it, try to do positive things with it."

Viall says he still finds it "wild" that anyone would pay him to post a picture or video of himself, all based on a single app.

"And so I just look at it as, I just want to make sure that I'm forward-thinking," he said. "Instagram was down for a day, a couple weeks ago, and I had the thought of 'Well, what if this never comes back?'"

These days, Viall uses his page primarily to engage his large following, which skews around 90 percent female, with weekly live events that include shirtless, Bob Ross–style paint-ing sessions, and an interactive "Advice with Nick" series, which he finds rewarding because fans have stopped him on the street to thank him for his answers.

"Lots of times I'll not wear a shirt, and those get the most attention. I don't like leading with it, but I try to do it in a way that's kind of funny, where I'm obviously doing it be-cause I know it gets attention. It's silly. It's meant to be silly and funny. But it's honestly taken me kind of a while to fig-ure out what I want to do with it," he said.

When he's not maintaining his audience-slash-customer base and promoting an essential oils company he founded called Natural Habits, Viall still does work for other brands. He even appeared in an "Ice Cream for Adults" 2019 Super Bowl ad for the ice-cream company Halo Top, where he tells two young children that love just isn't worth it in the end. But he won't attach his name as a founder unless he's in control, after getting burned in a partnership with a company that he says turned out to be a pump-and-dump scheme.

"We had this idea, and basically my job was to promote it and their job was to source the product, or whatever. And I found out that they were waiting for me to create the de-mand before they did it. I wanted to create a quality business, quality products, and I quickly realized that they wanted to do a pump and dump. Create some demand, sell some crap, move on. I was like, 'No.' Ultimately, we just agreed to dis-agree," Viall said. "Ultimately, we just dissolved the business. My partners didn't live up to their side. Certainly not to that level, but these guys kind of had that same mentality of the guy in the Fyre Festival."

When it comes to advertising for Natural Habits, Viall says influencer marketing isn't worth the price of admission.

"I am fortunate enough to have my own platform, because I couldn't afford to pay the rates that some of my peers charge, or that I charge, quite frankly. Because I can't afford to not make money on a campaign. There has to be obvious ROI. I can't afford, necessarily at this point, for me, to pay for just awareness and goodwill. Which I think is of value in social media. Because you have to kind of keep hitting them with, reminding them of this DIFF Eyewear, or whatever," he said. "You hear it, now when you need sunglasses you think of DIFF. But that one push might only generate thirty sales, but if that cost you $6,000, you're not making $6,000 back."

According to Cavazos, influencer marketing is still lucrative for bigger brands with a marketing budget to burn because in general people follow brand accounts at a much lower rate than they do internet personalities and industry experts (who are potential influencers). And the influencer market is only growing, from an estimated $1.7 billion in 2016 to $4.6 billion in 2018.[136]

Still, advertising made-for-the-internet brands like DIFF Eyewear and FitTea, low-quality products whose value derives solely from the marketing dollars stacked behind them, can be so lucrative for reality-TV stars that they actually start to alter their behavior on-screen to be more attractive to advertisers. There's just so much competition for the agents and brands who work with reality stars that there's no room anymore for villains or unpopular contestants to snag deals— even for laxative tea.

"For all the people who watch the show and talk about 'the right reasons,' I think most people, before this social media explosion, went in for the experience. You really had no idea," Viall said. "And now there's definitely at least the illusion of a playbook. You go on the first show, you go to paradise. If you're on X number of weeks, you have a good chance of having this number of followers, and these are the opportunities.

"It's obvious. It's out there. You can see it. All you have to do is take a look to see who was on last season, how many followers they have, and the things they're doing. It's out there. If I were to go on now for the first time, I would probably look into what the experience means, and I would start doing a little bit of research and be like, 'Oh, I guess if I do this, I'll be able to do that. That's pretty cool.' It doesn't necessarily mean it's malicious, or calculated; it's just so clear that obviously it can change people's behavior," Viall said. "I don't think it makes people any more disingenuous, I think it just makes it more clear of what their options might be. Because I think five years ago, it was a lot of excitement, but a lot of unknown."

It's not so unknown anymore. According to one recent survey of 1,000 young children (aged six to seventeen) conducted by *The Sun*, three-quarters of Gen Z and millennials chose becoming a YouTuber as their planned career.[137] (Comparatively, only 6 percent expressed interest in becoming a lawyer, so at least there's something positive to take away from it.) Yes, the #spon life can be lucrative, but I think there's something more to it. When you're an influencer, personal and public successes are one and the same. Every like is a dollar, and every dollar is an ecstatic tithing.

It was perhaps the inevitable outcome of the same landscape and thought process that led to the explosion of the gig economy, the notion that people would eventually begin selling themselves as a brand. Cavazos likened the effect as "almost like a Willy Loman thing."

"I think they view themselves as the product," Cavazos said. "And so instead of saying, 'Oh, well look, I'm Roberto, I'm selling Toyotas,' instead they're saying, 'I'm selling me, I'm selling me, and my judgments, and then people will buy my judgment and buy this Toyota Camry or buy Dr. Bronner's baby soap.'"

Nowhere is that clearer than the British reality-dating series *Love Island*, where dozens of singles compete for the audience's favor—and a £50,000 prize. When the show started out, people submitted audition tapes. Last season, only six of the contestants actually submitted an audition tape. The other thirty were either recruited off Instagram—or pitched by their own agents.

The cash prize, it turns out, is the least valuable thing about being on the show, which airs nightly before an audience of about 2.6 million viewers in the highly lucrative sixteen-to-thirty-four age range.[138] Almost everything on the show is for sale, from the clothes the islanders wear to the blow–dryers they use on their hair to the personalized water bottles seen in the background of almost every shot. Even the suitcases they use to wheel out their sponsored clothes when they get kicked off the island are listed for purchase on the show's mobile app.

The payoff's even better for the contestants themselves. In a review of the 2018 cast, the *New Statesman* site found that only one competitor, Josh Mair, failed to get any brand deals at all, perhaps due in part to his "pitiful following" of only thirty thousand people.[139]

"Josh does not even seem to have a brand manager, making him the biggest loser from this year's *Love Island*," the outlet concluded.

On the other end of the spectrum was Eyal Booker, who had garnered more than 840,000 followers following his appearance on the show. (By press time, that number had dropped to 804,000, just as Viall predicted would happen once a reality star leaves the show that made them famous.)

"Eyal has done everything a *Love Island* contestant should: paid appearances, brand partnerships, and endless sponsored posts. What makes him the real winner, though, is that he's already landed himself a spot on another reality show, as one of the celebs in *Celebs Go Dating* 2018," the site reported. "Eyal is the only Love Islander that's guaranteed his way back on to reality television and it will inevitably catapult into more fame."

As of press time, Booker was also in a relationship with Delilah Belle, the eldest daughter of Lisa Rinna, one of the stars of *The Real Housewives of Beverly Hills*, where Delilah has made a number of appearances. (Her sister, Amelia Gray, was also recently linked to Kardashian baby daddy Scott Disick, and the reality show for which they're known also happened to be the launch pad for former Fyre Festival spokesperson Bella Hadid.) With 1.3 million followers of her own, Delilah Belle makes her living as a part-time model and full-time social media influencer. And, like Booker, almost all of her posts—even the ones that aren't specifically ads—contain detailed product information. Everything in their lives, at least the online versions, is for sale.

4

The Allegory of the Fave

With four months to go until the festival, the Fyre team had no infrastructure and no clue how to get it.

But they did have the best publicity, marketing, and social media teams that other people's money could buy, including the PR firm 42West, the digital agency VaynerMedia, and the social media gurus at Jerry Media.

The venerable 42West, which at the time repped stars like Rihanna and Charlize Theron, had started earning its monthly $20,000 retainer from Fyre in December 2016, according to internal documents, by seeding favorable coverage of the festival among 42West's more agreeable press contacts at outlets like *Vanity Fair, Billboard*, and *GQ France*. They also maintained relationships with a smaller subset of that group, a stable of writers who could—and, in fact, would—be relied on to counteract, post-publication, much of the negative coverage that might have otherwise warned off consumers.

The money paid off in dividends: "11 Things To Know About Fyre Festival, Because It's Unlike Any Music Event You've Attended Before," Bustle raved the day the Instagram campaign began. "Every Single Model is Promoting This Music Festival on Instagram," the *Observer* noted. A promotional photo from the campaign even graced Vogue.com, which declared that "Bella, Emily, and Elsa Have the Supermodel Antidote to Winter Blues."

42West, according to leaked emails, also spent a significant portion of time fielding overly detailed, often-irrelevant style notes that the festival's head of marketing Grant Margolin, then twenty-four, tended to send out at all hours of the day, including on Christmas.

But more importantly, they set a tone in media coverage that helped cover up the Fyre team's incompetence by pulling favors, offering freebies, and when all else failed, spinning the truth furiously on Fyre's behalf.

"To maximize press coverage in key media outlets, consider covering the expenses of select journalists/bloggers to attend the festival," the firm advised Fyre early on. "While many media are not allowed to accept free travel, there are a number of bloggers and freelancers who may be able to take advantage of this offer."

42West was right on the money. The mountains of effusive press that poured out of 42West's efforts to chronicle positive updates about the so-called exclusive festival would do wonders to boost its credibility, even as things were clearly crumbling. The Fyre team couldn't even afford to keep their website up.

"They didn't have any money. They kept paying the influencers and the models," former Fyre employee Nyla Coffie said. "After MATTE Projects made that video, they went down, they filmed one of the party weekends. 'Let's all have a great time, yada, yada, yada.' And Fyre never paid them. So the whole Fyre Festival website got yanked. And they had to create a whole new one within a day."

Outside of MATTE, which held the footage and maintained the site, the Jerry Media team stayed with Fyre the longest, in part because they knew the Fyre guys already and were willing to extend the benefit of the doubt despite repeated nonpayments on invoices. One reason, sources say, was Fyre's talent booker Samuel Krost had grown up with Jerry's founder Elliot Tebele.

Jerry Media had actually first gotten involved with Fyre months before, in August of 2016, when the Fyre Media team had been hired to put together a brand activation for Lincoln. As part of the project, Tebele offered to post a single promotional image on the FuckJerry account for $25,000—and offered up a few of his friends he thought might be open to the same deal, including Man Repeller founder Leandra Medine and Kardashian baby daddy Scott Disick, who, Tebele warned, might not be an ideal spokesperson but had a large following.

"Don't think he's is [sic] great person, however I know he's a sucker for a buck, has almost 20 million followers and his IG consists of that lavish lifestyle," Tebele advised in an email.

So, with the relationship established, and after a spirited round of negotiations punctuated by jokes about certain Jewish employees' membership in "the tribe," Jerry Media officially signed on as a partner in the festival in early December—for the low price of $35,000 a month.

Fyre then introduced their "key drivers for ticket sales": "Influencers, scarcity of tickets, treasures, talent, travel and friend groups."

"To leverage the impact of effective influencer marketing, we will direct a social media take-over with 400 selected influencers (models, artists, athletes, comedians). At the same time, we will send out a press release with the major points about the festival and curated press coverage of influencer involvement. This story will be crafted and sent out in collaboration with the PR agency. We will follow with a massive email blast through affiliate partners and promoters," the Jerry marketing plan read.

The four hundred influencers were instructed to post the orange tile with the caption *#fyrefestival* on Instagram, and to add the link to their bio. Using paid media, Fyre boosted the Instagram posts, and 42West simultaneously sent out press releases "including major points about the festival," and directing "curated coverage of influencer involvement (i.e. story about why 'Odell Beckham and your favorite athletes changed their IG image to an orange tile' on Bleacher Report)."

The next day, an email blast "from partners in Event, Ticketing, Fashion, Music, Travel & Lifestyle (see Excel sheet for full hitlist)" went out in exchange for free tickets or 10 percent of affiliated ticket sales. At the same time, the official Fyre account began giving out free tickets to followers who posted orange tiles in their own, non-influencer feeds.

To coordinate the paid ads, Fyre signed up for a $100,000 minimum spend with VaynerMedia.

But they still were woefully unprepared, even on the basics: the day before the launch, the Fyre site still wasn't up and running and the ticket-sales page gave users a 404.

To the Fyre guys, however, the Jerry team wasn't just a marketing firm. They were also influential players in the Instagram game, bundling ads for their millions of followers with other popular accounts for incredible sums. Around the time they signed with Fyre, Jerry was charging more than $100,000 for a single ad posted across their cohort of accounts and partners. For an additional $40,000 a month, they would also run the client's social channel, creating thirty pieces of content and growing its audience organically by "approximately 10-20k new followers per month." Part of that strategy, records show, required setting profiles as private to track incoming friend requests, a growth hack employed by a lot of large meme pages, which typically require you to request to follow them before you can see the funny image your friend direct messaged you on Instagram.

But beyond their algorithmic insights, the Jerry team knew how to get to and negotiate with the kinds of celebrities that might be willing to advertise an unknown music festival to their followers—for the right price, of course. But not all their ideas were genius. It was Jerry Media who also suggested the LinkedIn campaign, which involved paying influencers there to change their job titles to "I'm going to Fyre Festival," thereby flooding all their followers' inboxes with LinkedIn update spam.

Luckily, the team got more bang for their influencer buck than they had expected. Despite—or perhaps because of—the hefty on-boarding costs of the first wave of top models, the Fyre team didn't have much of a budget left over for the influencers lower on the totem pole. But those influencers seemed more than happy to get involved in exchange for free tickets to the festival.

In a series of emails, the Fyre team, in conjunction with 42West, decided to use the lack of information about the festival to their advantage, "creating intrigue," and "ending on a question: What were they doing there?"

And to answer that question, they decided to lie.

Faced with a launch date and nothing to launch, 42West proffered a two-prong plan: one soft press release, revolving around the presumed private-island location, and a second, hard launch later, which would reveal the acts they'd been able to book.

None of it made any sense. No one at 42West, for example, knew which pictures from the photoshoot were of the actual island, or which of the influencers were actually planning on going, but of course, none of it ended up mattering. Instead of the beach shots that Fyre had paid hundreds of thousands of dollars to produce, 42West decided to use the candid Instagram photos posted by the models instead, because, they determined, using "professional photos might have a clear marketing agenda."

And to distract from the fact that there were no musical acts in place for a music festival less than five months away, they pretended that the models—whose contracts stipulated nothing more than a Bahamian photoshoot and an Instagram post—were throwing the festival too.

"This weekend, beautiful mega talents including Alessandra Ambrosio, Bella Hadid, Hailey Baldwin, Emily Ratajkowski, Elsa Hosk, Paulina Vega, Lais Ribeiro, Rose Bertram, Gizele Oliveira and Hannah Ferguson flew down to Fyre Cay in the Bahamas where they gave the world a glimpse of the experience thrill seekers can expect at the first-ever Fyre Festival this spring 2017. During the 48-hour excursion, the 'Fyre squad' came together to dream up a one-of-a-kind festival experience. They worked to provide feedback on all of the activities that will be available to festival-goers this spring including seabobbing, yoga on the beach, water trampolines, snorkeling near a plane wreck off Norman's Cay and so much more!" the release crafted by 42West claimed.

"I think it's best if you follow those accounts and ensure everyone posts (they are but in the unlikely event there is a fluke want to be 100% truthful)," Margolin responded to an early draft touting all the influencer endorsements. But behind the scenes, Carola Jain—the wife of billionaire Bob Jain who first joined up with McFarland for Magnises—was privately urging the team to further blur the lines between fact and fiction.

"Grant, is there any way we can say they helped shape what's about to be unveiled for the festival? Did they provide any ideas or insights, could they be leveraged to really show they have an interest in the festival?" she asked Grant in an email. "Don't want to get sued by them, but you are closer with the crew and will know how much they want to be involved."

She ultimately found encouragement from 42West's Anna Miller, though Miller pushed back when Jain edited out of the press release an explicit reference to the models providing feedback for the festival.

"Carola—We've integrated your edits however do we want to remove the fact that they were providing feedback? I think that's key in order to help shift the messaging," she urged.

But 42West wasn't concerned about the press questioning their assertions. In fact, they seemed confident they'd be able to convince any suspicious journalists to update their coverage of the weekend with the new text.

"This is what we plan on sending out at 5pm ET. But we will approach the outlets that already ran and ask them to update their stories with the first paragraph," Miller advised.

The story ran that day in outlets including *Elle*, *Marie Claire*, and the *Daily Mail*.

But a follow-up plan to release the promo video exclusively with Refinery29 or Vogue.com turned out to be dead on arrival when the 42West team learned, too late, that the Fyre team had already dumped the video on the web, wasting their leverage.

The group also stumbled when it came to hashtags. Under the impression McFarland had purchased or at least put a down payment on a private island they planned on naming Fyre

Cay—something Margolin readily confirmed when asked—
42West started circulating *#FyreCay* on its content. At the
last minute, with no private island, or even any venue at all,
Fyre abruptly switched its messaging to *#FyreFestival*—and
completely neglected to warn the agencies.

Internal emails also show the team had the option of engaging FuckJerry to append *#ad* disclaimers on the models'
posts as required by the FTC—but definitively chose not to.

"FJ said nothing to worry about BUT can have IMG tell
everyone to #AD," Margolin wrote.

"No one is allowed to #ad that's lame as fuck," McFarland replied.

Margolin—desperate for cash—was offering potential sponsors access to individual influencers, who had zero clue that
their talents were being pimped out in festival deals.

In one sponsorship pitch, for example, Margolin promised an old friend—up-and-coming consultant and son of a
billionaire, James Sternlicht—that, "Due to our close relationship with these influencers, we have the ability to build
'advertorial coverage' in the deal—we will compensate the
influencers, negotiating directly with them (they are amena-
ble and excited for these opportunities)."

(To be fair, Margolin may have also had a personal stake
in bragging about his access. When his assistant, Cheyenne
Miller, emailed Sternlicht asking if he would be available for
a call the next day, records show, Margolin's heart sank. He
believed her email had been too casual to be sent on behalf
of an executive of his stature. "Especially given my past relationship with him (he was a bully at camp and made fun of
me—not the best way to start this—this is crushing me…..),"
he wrote.)

Otherwise, the launch went surprisingly well. Fyre's em-
issaries had no trouble finding influencers happy to post the

promo for free with nothing more than the promise of concert
tickets. At the time it certainly seemed impressive: in a typical
exchange, they'd offered models and influencers with more
than a million followers up to four VIP tickets, a package that
was to also include "private flights from Miami, villa accommodations, and food and drinks to the festival in exchange for
one Instagram post to your account." All for one little post!

But that ambiguity also served to cover up Fyre's ongoing
efforts to misrepresent the models' role in the festival. With
no confirmed acts or venue in place to advertise, all the team
had to show for their efforts was the series of paid celebrity
endorsements.

"After speaking with the team, we have too much riding
on this to abort our original plan," Margolin wrote in the
lead-up to the launch, which they'd decided to move forward
with despite not having any confirmed acts. "Let me know
when we can discuss—we need to push on the experience
and really really play to all of our advantages (i.e. the Angle
of all of these influencers posting orange around this common theme, i.e. the experience of Fyre Cay)."

But for the rest of December and into January, Fyre puz-
zled over how best to position the festival, all without taking
any real steps to book, build, or buy anything for it—outside
of an alcohol sponsorship through Randy Gerber, George
Clooney's business partner in the billion-dollar tequila company, Casamigos. Gerber also happened to sit on the board
of Tablelist, the company handling Fyre's ticketing, and he
and Margolin ended up together on a call.

"I kept deflecting numbers," Margolin reported back to
McFarland after. "He asked if that was for real, I assured him
that this was."

McFarland, in response, urged him to lie by telling Gerber the festival had "10,000 people per weekend. weekend 1 100% sold out, weekend 2 75% sold out."

When asked who in the fantasy pitch deck of influencers was actually coming to the festival, McFarland responded with confidence, "All in the deck are 100% coming. Call any of them." But when it came down to how much alcohol the festival needed, he demurred entirely. "Let's have them recommend. I don't know."

Still, the numbers appeared to appease Gerber, whose company provided the cases of tequila the Fyre team would ultimately use to placate angry guests demanding to see their tents.

Meanwhile, Margolin couldn't make up his mind what he wanted or who he wanted it from. In emails that stretched from Christmas Eve through the morning after Christmas, he demanded 42West help prep a release about Kendall Jenner's involvement, despite not having a deal with her in place. In fact, her contract wouldn't get locked in until later the next month, ultimately rendering the entire exercise useless.

Meanwhile, Jerry Media's contract didn't just require them to build out the company's social media assets—it also required that they earn out their retainer by "consulting on content strategy and follower growth for all key members of the Fyre Organization."

While not officially stipulated, those lucrative contracts also required them to endure Margolin's pedantic lectures, like when Jerry's former graphic designer Oren Aks accidentally posted an innocuous Boomerang of a New York City subway platform to Fyre's Instagram Stories instead of his own personal account and had to formally apologize, despite recognizing his own mistake and deleting it "within three minutes." And it required the Jerry team, along with 42West, to work around the clock through the Christmas holidays, with one email chain still active around midnight on Christmas Eve, all for a Jenner rollout that never actually ended up happening. An attorney on Fyre's legal team, also working on retainer, even submitted work product at 2:00 a.m. one morning, after Vayner's ad-buying team threatened to stop work if Fyre didn't immediately post a required set of terms and conditions on its website.

But between the efforts of Fyre, Jerry, 42West, and Vayner, the Instagram campaign was a runaway success, resulting in the reported sale of 95 percent of tickets overnight.

So it should come as no surprise that another scam arose out of the only successful beat the Fyre team hit. At least two individuals have stepped up to take credit for the Orange Tile campaign—even though neither of them actually deserves it, say sources with knowledge of the planning.

The first person to claim the idea was FuckJerry's former graphic designer, Aks, the man who, according to one blog headline, "Stopped the Internet with a Single Color."

"Though there's been plenty of finger-pointing in the aftermath of Fyre Festival, the guy behind the orange tiles… Oren Aks, has proudly raised his hand to take ownership of the campaign," the article notes.

Aks has been a bit more careful with his words, but he's taken the credit multiple times, claiming in one interview, "In the same meeting I came up with the infamous orange tile to complement the new design strategy. The color palettes of the time were highly influenced by all muted colors or with pops of neon. I decided that we needed to respond accordingly without feeding into temporary styles if we want to be the epicenter of all things pop culture and dominate the internet every time we push something out."

"My inspiration came from UPS trucks and how a UPS truck, brown, kind of stands out in a downtown setting because nothing around it is that solid of a color," he said in an-other.[140] "Because everything is life-colored on Instagram, a neon stood out. It was a combination of the two, and I think it worked out well."

Fast Company was even more explicit in crediting Aks for the influencer campaign, writing, "But Aks's crowning achievement wasn't the feed; it was the idea to pay dozens of influencers to post a solid orange square on Instagram at the same time as a way of announcing the festival."[141]

Aks also took credit for most of Fyre's imagery, even though a review of internal documents shows that MATTE, hired at least a month before Jerry Media, produced the logo, a pro-totype of the tile, and the first steps of the marketing plan used in the campaign. In fact, MATTE first proposed many of the festival's defining features, including the "Fyrestart-ers" influencer team.

Everyone I've spoken with, whether they worked for Jerry Media or Fyre, say Aks had almost nothing to do with the campaign. Even the most famous graphics, ostensibly under his purview, came from somewhere else, sources say.

"I think MATTE Projects was the one that actually de-signed it. I don't even think it was Oren, ironically. We did posters, the artist billing or whatever it's called. I'm pretty sure that was MATTE Projects," a Fyre source said. "It's not important to your story, but it wasn't even Oren, so I think it's funny."

At least, according to two sources with direct knowledge of the conversation, Ja Rule—who became the second man to claim sole credit for the orange-tile idea during an appear-ance at the 2019 Raleigh Internet Summit—was present for the moment of inspiration. Not that you'd know that from a recent speech, where the rapper formerly known as Jeffrey Atkins declared definitively that, "I was like, you know that's a dope thing. We should do, our color was orange, we should do orange blackout, or orange-out if you will, and get my celebrity friends to post at the same time, and they said, 'Yeah we should do that.'[142]

"And that was kind of the start of the marketing campaign." Atkins continued, "So I sat and started hitting my friends with lots and lots of followers, and it worked very well, because as people were scrolling up their timeline at this hour, they were seeing all of the coolest people posting this orange tile. That led people to say, 'I have to be a part of this,' not even knowing what it was."

Sources say that is indeed how the conversation went but dispute the notion that Atkins was the person who said it. He would also contradict himself later in that same speech, saying that it should be obvious he was innocent in the scam because "It wasn't even promoted to my people."

Either way, sources say the orange-tile plan actually came from Margolin, who came up with the idea aboard a Bahamas-bound jet.

According to my sources, Margolin, McFarland, Atkins, and Ian Browne, Fyre's talent officer, had been spitballing ideas when someone brought up Jay-Z's recent ad campaign for Tidal, a minimalist rollout that focused on the brand's distinctive turquoise color.

Fyre, Margolin suggested, should copy the idea and blanket Instagram with its signature orange. The agencies, including Aks's employer, Jerry Media, were later informed of the plan in early December, according to internal emails.

"We were sitting on a plane, and Billy said to all the models who were in the back, Billy was trying to impress everybody, so he called all the guys. This was probably early in October, and he goes, 'What are we going to do?' He goes, 'You know what I remember growing up, there was something called, the shot heard around the world. It was around the Revolutionary War.' So I said, 'Why don't we get, just like that, why don't we get hundreds of people to post at the same time?'" said a former Fyre employee who would speak only on the condition of anonymity. "Right when I said that, Grant was like, 'Oh, my god, that's such a great idea. And then we could do an orange tile.'

"I came up with everyone posting at the same time and then Grant piggybacked off that and came up with the orange-tile idea," the employee said.

"Perfect. We'll do the orange tile at the same time, and as you're scrolling through," Margolin said, "all you'll see is everyone's posting the same time. Everybody follows one of these people, and all you'll see is an all-orange screen as you scroll."

The real marketing happened after the festival imploded, sources say, when Aks and FuckJerry used the notoriety of the festival to position themselves as the brains behind the plan.

"I have nothing bad to say about Oren, but I think it is funny, where people on the outside… He tried to take advantage with that, with his new marketing company. But the orange tile was us, and FuckJerry was supposed to do the graphic works for stuff. They had very little to do with anything which is a good thing and bad thing," the Fyre employee said. "Grant was the orchestrator of everything. FuckJerry were the executors of certain things, but there was no visionary or creative aspect."

However you cut it, the orange campaign was an undisputed success, drawing tens of millions of eyes to the brand. But it was also a smoke screen. They were selling something that didn't exist.

All along, the team had been struggling to book artists, and the ones who did show interest were demanding outra-

geous fees to take a chance on a first-time festival. Krost recalled paying around $500,000 for Blink 182's commitment.
Records show they also paid $800,000 for a Disclosure com-
mitment and $350,000 for the G.O.O.D. Music endorsement.
The German DJ Tensnake got an additional $25,000. In all,
bankruptcy attorneys for Fyre Media estimate the company
paid out about $14.4 million to secure talent that never per-
formed, including $300,000 to Ratajkowski, and an as-yet-
unaccounted-for $350,000 payment to...someone.

"It would be very easy to spend many millions on that talent. I know that they had to start paying 100 percent in advance. Usually it goes from 50 percent up front, usually, with
reputable shows and venues," said a publicist with knowledge
of the deal who was not authorized to speak on the record. As
an unknown entity, however, "They had to lay out all that
money in advance or else people would start feeling that it
wasn't going to happen."

The deals were good, but McFarland kept running out of
cash to close them. His team would secure contracts and then
find themselves unable to pay. Internal records show McFarland would routinely swear to various concerned employees
that he'd wired payment to a vendor—even emailing over
purported copies of the wire receipts—only for the money
to fail to appear. This happened over and over, and not just
for outside payments. Even his own employees were often reduced to begging over email for wire transfers to reimburse
their office expenses.

Around that time, Fyre's CRO Jason Ve started privately
pushing Margolin to "plant a seed" for him with McFarland,
part of what the money manager described as an underground
effort to get his hands on then-top-secret documents, like
"the festival budget."

"Now that we sign the contracts directly, lots of risk. We

can't miss payments. 90 days til festival. No time," he warned in one email.

"Will relay ASAP," Margolin replied, although there's no indication he did.

"I know the artists thing was 100 percent true, that they hadn't paid them until late, and they broke up the payment into two. Because I had access to their bank accounts, and it was often zero," Coffie said.

It was only thanks to a last-minute investing round led by McFarland months later that the artists were even paid on their contracts—and only then after a *Wall Street Journal* article threatened to derail the whole thing.[143] Then, with less than a month to go, Fyre suddenly switched to a cashless, RFID system that would require that concertgoers prepay to load their wristbands with funds in order to pay for things like food and water—despite the lack of Wi-Fi at the site.

"The numbers they were attaching to this were the kind of numbers that make it exclusive, but in reality the reason they were doing that was because they ran out of cash. By the end they were inventing, like, 'a trip to the moon with Elon Musk' $800,000 package," Wells said.

But they had little choice—McFarland had secured a last-minute loan secured on receivables, a lien on their presumed sales, but one that would enable the festival to open as planned. Without the wristband money, he would have been shut down well before the first plane ever took off.

"You're moving into a criminal element when you're factoring receivables and lying about your receivables," Wells said. "Stuff like that. That's bad hombre–type stuff."

It was a disappointing, ignominious end to months of rumors that the Kardashian-Jenner-West family were on the verge of signing on as partners. After much back-and-forth, Fyre had successfully arranged for Kendall Jenner to post in January about the festival, with a caption hinting that her brother-in-law, Kanye West, might be involved via his G.O.O.D. Music label—in exchange for a cool quarter of a million dollars.

"She got $250,000 and she's involved with G.O.O.D. Music, so they booked her brand. And they [the Fyre team] perpetrated this rumor that Kanye was gonna be there. It's really weird," Wells said. "Kanye costs more. I think he would do it for $3.5 million. That's probably what it would have cost to have him for two weekends," said Wells.

According to a November sample budget circulated to potential investors, McFarland actually expected to pay Kanye $2 million, with another $2 million allocated toward marketing. The brief hiring of Nate Brown, a former creative director for Kanye West, increased their optimism about getting the deal done.

"Kanye and Bieber," McFarland assured one customer who emailed to inquire about a $50,000 yacht charter predicated on the festival's lineup. (According to the SEC, McFarland also told prospective investors that Drake had been confirmed to perform—another lie.)

On December 23, Margolin even emailed the 42West team to confirm the news that both West and Jenner were on board. The only catch was, they couldn't tell anyone.

"As everyone knows, the entire GOOD Music Family (including Kanye West) will headline both weekends of the Fyre Festival (Friday show date). As everyone knows, the legal discussions between Kanye West and Live Nation are quite intense. Thus, we cannot use Kanye West's name in connection with the festival. We cannot confirm his performance," Margolin cautioned. "While we can debate the merits of announcing without the use of Kanye's name, but as Kanye will be there, and as he will design assets, we are in agreement this is a good move."

Still, at least one outlet—Condé Nast *Traveller*—ended up running a print story listing the location as "Fyre Cay" and citing West as a headliner. It wasn't an accident; in February, 42West knew they had sent out the wrong information but declined to do anything about it since they had already "passed the deadline to make any changes."

But in the lead-up to the big Jenner post, the Fyre team couldn't agree on what they wanted her to say, in part because they needed the copy to look like more than just a paid advertisement. One unpublished press release, prepared by 42West the morning after Christmas, shows how much more involved they believed she and her family had become.

"THE ENTIRE G.O.O.D. MUSIC FAMILY ANNOUNCED AS HEADLINER FOR FYRE FESTIVAL. Kendall Jenner Posts the News on Instagram and gives First Clue in $1 Million Treasure Hunt that Will Take Place During Fyre Festival," read the unreleased headline.

"Kendall Jenner took to social media today, to officially announce that the entire G.O.O.D. Music family will headline Fyre Festival—the brand new festival coming to the historic private island of Fyre Cay, in the Bahamas. The G.O.O.D. Music family is the first to be announced as part of what will be a stellar lineup for the first ever Fyre Festival on April 28–30, 2017 & May 5–7, 2017. In addition, Kendall Jenner posted a custom orange tile that is the first clue to the more than $1 million of real treasures and jewels hidden on the island that will create a once in lifetime experience for ticket holders."

But when it came time to post, there was no deal. It wasn't until weeks later, in mid-January, that the team settled on the bizarre compromise of having Jenner's post look both spammy as hell and make absolutely no sense at all.

"So hyped to announce my G.O.O.D. Music Family as the first headliners for @fyrefestival. Get tix now at fyrefestival.com. VIP access for my followers… use my promo code KJONFYRE for the next 24 hours to get on the list for the artists and talent afterparty on Fyre Cay. #FyreFestival," is what Jenner finally ended up posting. For this, she pocketed $275,000.[144]

And it was one of the last fees the Fyre team paid up front and in full, in part because one of Jenner's reps had shown up at the office demanding the money.

"I don't know who it was I was talking to, but I remember Kris was complaining they didn't get the money yet. She was standing next to me, waiting for me to process it. Would not leave until Kris got her money," Coffie recalled.

Jenner's caption might not have been the most legible phrase, especially given that it had been written for her by a group of self-proclaimed "marketing geniuses," but at least it included a link to the festival. McFarland and Margolin were so pleased with the result, it appears they almost paid her more. In the wake of her post, they engaged 42West to prepare a release announcing Jenner as the festival's emcee, host, and face of a private after-party on the "Fyre yacht"— only to quietly cancel the agency's work on it just a few days after they proposed it.

McFarland had already spent millions of dollars on influencers before the Jenner deal. He'd spent hundreds of thousands more on private-jet rides his employees thought he'd been paying for out of his own pocket. Had he saved some of that money, he might have been able to throw a successful festival. But the festival wasn't the goal for him, it was the means to another end.

While McFarland was trying to convince more people to buy tickets, the people who already had were desperate for answers. They didn't know when they were flying, or how, in part because Fyre wouldn't book the planes until the month of the festival. But they didn't know that. They didn't know anything, and the response online had gotten so overwhelming and negative by February 12 that at least three people were required to actively manage the Fyre Facebook page: FuckJerry's Mick Purzycki and Oren Aks, as well as Margolin's assistant, Deanna Smith, who, records show, had been tasked with checking the page hourly for any negative comments the FuckJerry team had missed in its sweeps. Margolin, who had never had an assistant before, outsourced much of his work to Smith and seemed to take a distinct pleasure in having a job that came with office support. When he traveled, for example, he'd have Smith prepare travel itineraries and send them to his parents, along with hour-to-hour updates about his flight status.

So in February, with less than two months to go until D-Day, the team—fully aware how behind and unprepared they were to execute the festival—prepared a series of make-up dates: November 3 to 5 and 10 to 12. In collaboration, 42West prepared a press release and general game plan.

"We recommend grouping the announcement of the last headliner along with the location change. While we don't anticipate this change will garner much negative press, especially since you are offering guests an upgraded experience, we feel announcing a big headliner will help to shift focus and eliminate any risk," 42West's Erika Tuzkov advised.

The proposed press release read, "After listening to feedback from our fans, Fyre is excited to announce that the sold out, two weekend festival will now be taking place on Grand Exuma in the Bahamas. Here guests will have the option of staying at the luxurious Grand Isle Resort and Spa, private condominiums or villas with the festival taking place nearby on the stunning, seven-mile Coco Plum Beach. Located just a quick 15-minutes from the airport, guests will now get to spend more time living it up Fyre style and less time traveling."

It might have saved Fyre from itself. But records show Margolin had started researching reputation-management firms the same day, and the proposal went ignored.

As the bills mounted, the agencies started to worry, and rightly so. By the time the festival collapsed, McFarland would owe 42West, Jerry Media, VaynerMedia, and MATTE Projects, among other agencies, hundreds of thousands of dollars—monies they've never fully recouped.

"Billy seemed to get a lot of family friends to be investors in his companies. They were probably investing anywhere between $50,000 and $150,000 with him in either of his companies. There were some cases where Magnises investors wouldn't invest in Fyre and vice versa, but I think he basically shared the same pool of investors," said a former Magnises employee, who asked to remain anonymous because he signed a contract containing a nondisparagement clause.

And despite their subsequent denials, records show the Jerry team was well aware of the growing issues—even sending out a memo outlining how the festival could spin a postponement in the press.

In the email dated February 20, 2017—under the subject line "PR Spin"—Mick Purzycki outlined what had become clear to everyone: the festival simply could not go on as planned. The email was sent to Margolin, Tebele, and Aks and recommended rescuing Fyre by recruiting a celebrity with a good reputation to become the new face of the operation.

"Grant, please see our suggested plan of action below," Purzycki wrote. "Situation: Fyre is postponing the festival to November. Objective: To avoid brand degradation and legitimize reason for postponing. Strategy: Fyre Festival is acquired (in name only) by another established and recognizable entity (i.e. Jay-Z, Kanye West, Kendall Jenner, etc.). The involvement of such a massive partner warrants significant changes to the style, lineup, vision, and most importantly, LAUNCH DATE of the Fyre Festival."

To distract from the festival's shortcomings, Purzycki proposed a series of high-profile announcements, including a press release about the established celebrity's acquisition, video of the established celebrity getting involved in the planning, a notable change to the festival's branding that would reflect the established celebrity's involvement, and, finally, a direct outreach to ticket holders explaining that the festival was being delayed in order to incorporate the established celebrity's "exciting" new ideas. To really hammer home the point, he proposed, all the announcements would be targeted at the feeds of the Fyre ticket holders.

"We believe the involvement of this partner will give way to a new narrative about the festival that will minimize degradation of the Fyre brand. Considering only GOOD VENTURES get acquired, the acquisition itself will serve as testimony to the legitimacy of Fyre Festival," Purzycki concluded. "If executed correctly, this strategy could strengthen the overall perception of Fyre's brand, and could even generate additional excitement and suspense, despite the postponement."

"Thanks Mick. This is a very infesting [sic] take which I will run by team," Margolin responded.

It was as good a plan as any, but once again, McFarland ignored it. For one thing, after asking apropos of nothing whether festival insurance would cover the event not happening for reasons other than force majeure, he'd never bothered to purchase it. (According to the SEC he did, however, lie to prospective investors by claiming he had, which ended up being "material to the decision of at least one investor to invest in Fyre Festival.")[145]

But despite it all, Jerry Media continued to work.

"It was just an absolute nightmare. But the thing that pisses me off is that they never owned it. It was never like, 'Hey, you know what? Fuck, we messed this up. Guys, give us a year.' Or like, 'Hold your applause and hold the tickets. Give us a year. Our bad.' Instead they've been perpetrating the stuff. Now it's turned into true fraud," Wells said.

So by February, when it was clear that McFarland wasn't going to be able to place a music festival on a deserted private island, he decided that an undeveloped gravel pit next door to a Sandals resort, overlooking forty-foot-high cliffs was as good a place as any.

VaynerMedia quit in March too, a vacuum that was quickly filled by FuckJerry, which took over media buying on March 10. MATTE Projects, which had ceased work pending payment, also started to come back on board, partnering with FuckJerry to design a plane wrap.

And 42West, working until the last minute, planted a positive *Vanity Fair* piece that, while a total puff piece, did note one major risk associated with Fyre: concerns that all the publicity might "compromise the islands' exclusivity."[146]

In retrospect, social media users and the influencers who star on these platforms couldn't have been more primed to get snookered en masse by something like the Fyre Festival. The only surprise is that it took so long to happen.

For one thing, we're hopelessly addicted to social media. What started out as a way for Mark Zuckerberg to rate attractive Harvard students quickly turned into a way for all of us to judge—and be judged. It was so fun and exciting, consuming this constantly updated feed of all the things our friends, family, and the celebrities we identify with were consuming that we didn't even mind as we became the product and our feeds turned into lifestyle catalogs.

"In today's age, we're the commodity and we're kind of being sold over and over again on social media. There are all these ideological and moral inconsistencies in how we behave on social media, and how our tech giants behave. And there's a lot of room for concern and it can be very scary. You can get scammed and you can be lied to and you can be catfished," explained Natalia Antonova, a security expert and former Bellingcat editor. "I think we could all learn from this story and maybe encourage our tech giants to tell people, 'Hey you have to mark this as an ad,' if it is in fact an ad. But you know, our tech giants don't always have our best interest at heart do they? So that's kind of the other elephant in the room here, right? Instagram makes so much money, they even revamped their entire platform just to appeal more to shopping."

"I think it's just an evolution of what we've had for a long time already, but I think that the peer-to-peer interaction that happens with social media makes it obviously much more direct. You don't have multiple layers of approvals, and people making decisions and policing these things," Borte, the writer and director of *The Joneses*, said. "You have people say, 'I'll pay you to do this.' And you have a direct connection to those followers at that point, without really any guidelines."

The average social media user might be the customer for influencers, but at some point down the line, we also consented to selling our own data for the privilege. In exchange for some social interaction and a big hit of affirmation, these apps get to track us across the internet—and off it—and sell the information to advertisers and shadowy data brokers who compile profiles of us and then sell them to other advertisers until every ad we see has been carefully targeted just for us.

But worse than that, the platforms are constantly learning how to keep us locked into their sites for as long as possible, which means algorithmically learning how to arouse our emotions in a manner not unlike a slot machine until we're drunk, spinning around on our digital swivel seats, pulling the refresh screen like a lever hoping that maybe this time we'll hit.

"We have become more isolated, we're lonelier, our emotions are therefore more easily manipulated, and this is why we fall for scams," said Antonova. "When you see how lonely we really are on a regular basis, I think that's one of the big factors as to why, even though we have the tools at our disposal, a part of us just wants to be fooled just so we can feel less alone. And I'm very sympathetic to that."

And it's not just the algorithms doing it to us—many of the people we follow are also trying to arouse our emotions to sell us things. In a sense, we're all trying to sell something, whether it's accompanied by a swipe-up link or not. Every post we make is essentially just an advertisement of our personalities that we're hoping someone might deem worthy of an investment of a like or comment.

"Something I've been very interested in lately is this phenomenon of this aspirational culture, where everyone I see feels like they're just one Instagram post away from fame and fortune. I think people see that as a path to success in some way now. And I think that it's interesting, because on one hand, you're finding people that are becoming content creators in some way, with the technology that they have," Borte said. "But if used incorrectly, I think it can lead to some pretty vacuous character and behavior, and I think that some of that is probably relevant to your Fyre Festival stuff. I think seeing some kind of lifestyle that you feel like you should be part of, it's… I don't know. It puts everything at your fingertips, and in a way that… I'm not sure where it's going, but I think that it sort of ties in with these prosperity preachers, that are out there that are talking about essentially you deserve whatever it is that you want. And there's never any sort of consciousness of any sort of price to pay. It's just about short-term gratification in some way."

I think he hits on an interesting point. Social media has become so hopelessly commodified that, even as a consumer, we're also the marketer. It's just that most of us are not profiting from it, monetarily or spiritually. But we also can't stop using it.

According to Nir Eyal, a former Stanford professor and author of *Hooked: How to Build Habit-Forming Products*, 79 percent of smartphone users check their device within fifteen minutes of waking up every morning,[147] a stat that, frankly, seems low to me. My phone often tends to be the last thing I touch before I sleep and the first thing I touch when I wake up, often before leaving bed.

Part of it is seeing what the people I know have been up to in the hours I've been offline. But a larger part of it is seeing what's been happening in the world outside of my own—and for me, that includes the news, the jokes, and, of course, the Kardashians.

In fact, in a February 2019 experiment in weaning himself off his cell phone, the *New York Times* tech columnist Kevin Roose cited "maintaining ambient Kardashian awareness" as one reason to continue using social media apps like Twitter and Facebook.[148] But he had found that using social media so frequently had made him "angry and anxious," so he attempted to unhook his brain from it by quitting the apps for thirty days. To aid his efforts, he wrapped a rubber band around his phone and changed the lock screen to ask three questions: *What for? Why now? What else?*

Escalating things further, he locked his phone inside a safe at night and took up pottery to distract his empty hands. For an incredible forty-eight hours, he even left his phone at home and traveled to an Airbnb in the country, using only paper maps and directions from strangers. Horrifying, I know. And yet he persisted.

"For the rest of the week, I became acutely aware of the bizarre phone habits I'd developed. I noticed that I reach for my phone every time I brush my teeth or step outside the front door of my apartment building, and that, for some pathological reason, I always check my email during the three-second window between when I insert my credit card into a chip reader at a store and when the card is accepted," Roose noted. "Mostly, I became aware of how profoundly uncomfortable I am with stillness. For years, I've used my phone every time I've had a spare moment in an elevator or a boring meeting. I listen to podcasts and write emails on the subway. I watch YouTube videos while folding laundry. I even use an app to pretend to meditate."

By the end of the experiment, Roose had diminished his average daily screen time from five hours to one and gone from picking up his phone one hundred times a day to twenty. His resolve lasted for about a year—and then COVID-19 hit.

"I am trying to claw it back!" he told me recently when I checked in to see how the experiment had held up.

It reminds me of what I found to be the most shocking moment in the recent Netflix docudrama *The Social Dilemma*, which gathered together a group of former Google, Instagram, Twitter, and Pinterest employees to reflect on the impact of social media: most of them ended up addicted to the products they had helped build. One former ad exec resorted to bargaining with himself—promising himself that he would leave his phone in the car, or swearing that he wouldn't use it in the bedroom—only to realize he was missing out on his family life because, despite his plans to quit, his phone had never actually left his hand. Another coder had to write a program to stop himself from using Twitter. (The damning allegations in the docudrama even prompted Facebook to issue a rare four-page statement with subheadings like "Facebook builds its products to create value, not to be addictive" and "You are not the product."[149])

At least the warning message in the Netflix documentary could be viewed without logging on to a social media platform. In a recent video called "Stop Being Your Phone's Slave,"[150] the actor-cum-activist Russell Brand tackled the issue, though he may have perhaps defeated the purpose by disseminating it across his verified Facebook, Instagram, YouTube, and Twitter accounts.

"Unless I deliberately decide not to check my phone in the morning, I will check my phone in the morning," Brand mused, a tiny avatar in the YouTube app on my iPhone. "And so begins a descent into caring too much about what other people think, placing my well-being into the hands of others."

He continued, "The rush through the phone is necessarily man-made. A reappropriation of an ancient kind of reward system. Like, 'Oh, look, so and so liked me, I feel temporarily validated!'"

A two-minute clip of Brand's rant has been viewed six million times on Twitter and one hundred thousand times on YouTube, where the full six-minute video is led into by an ad. Thanks in part to the deeply ingrained, habit-forming sites like Instagram and Twitter, I've noticed the same Pavlovian response to boredom and quiet moments that resulted in me watching Brand's videos. I even recently deleted the Instagram app from my phone, only to find myself opening— literally dozens of times a day—the app that slid over to take its place. I'd absentmindedly be holding my phone in my hand only to sort of come to and find myself staring at the screen in confusion, wondering why I'd just opened the Podcasts app again. Roose suggested treating it like I'd been reaching for a bag of cocaine.

"With some hindsight, I think the key is replacing things with other things," Roose said, noting that it's an insight he derived from the addiction-recovery world. "So instead of checking Twitter, I trained myself to pick up a book or a magazine. Instead of checking Instagram, I'd play with my dog."

And because Roose is far smarter than I, he said when he was writing his book he'd lock his phone in a box and tell his partner not to let him open it until he'd written a thousand words. Meanwhile, I spent the majority of my quarantine panic-scrolling through Twitter, sometimes opening the app just to realize I'd closed it not two seconds before.

According to Eyal, we activate these "automatic behaviors triggered by situational cues," a clinical way of describing a habit, many hundreds of times a day.[151] Sometimes we're consciously prompted by external triggers, like alerts or red notifications indicating something new has occurred, but we're also motivated by internal triggers, like the banality of waiting in line at the supermarket or even stopping at a red light. Internal triggers also tend to be negative, which is something we'll get back to in a bit.

"Instead of relying on expensive marketing, habit-forming companies link their services to the users' daily routines and emotions," Eyal says.[152] "A habit is at work when users feel a tad bored and instantly open Twitter. They feel a pang of loneliness and before rational thought occurs, they are scrolling through their Facebook feeds. A question comes to mind, and before searching their brains, they query Google."

It doesn't take long for these apps to become shortcuts in our brains, hence the theory of Google brain, which holds that we've started remembering less now that we know the information is being stored handily in our pockets. And once we're inside the apps, we're rewarded by a constant stream of new content, tailored to our tastes. Like a slot machine of status updates, vacation photos, and sponsored content, social media sites prime us to expect rewards by constantly providing us with variability. This reward expectation triggers dopamine neurotransmitters in our brain, "creating a focused state, which suppresses the areas of the brain associated with judgment and reason while activating the parts associated with wanting and desire."[153]

That element of never knowing what'll come up next is the most exciting part of the addiction.

According to Eyal, "More recent experiments reveal that variability increases activity in the nucleus accumbens and spikes levels of the neurotransmitter dopamine, driving our hungry search for rewards. Researchers observed increased dopamine levels in the nucleus accumbens in experiments involving monetary rewards as well as in a study of heterosexual men viewing images of attractive women's faces."

So we're hopelessly locked into social media, which builds our investment in their platforms in escalating steps from even before we've signed up for them, and we tell ourselves stories in order to go live: for example, we're not bragging about our own exploits, we're keeping connected with our friends and family. Similarly, the Fyre ticket buyers didn't just anticipate having a good time—they anticipated being as popular as the influencers they were following.

As humans, we're always searching for ways to feel part of a "tribe," online and off, and apps like Facebook, Twitter, Pinterest, Instagram and TikTok provide that buzz that we might otherwise find IRL. "With every post, tweet, or pin, users anticipate social validation," Eyal notes. "Rewards of the tribe keep users coming back, wanting more."[154]

It's a little bit like that old "No soap radio" joke, where a group collectively agrees to laugh at a nonsensical punch-line just to see if the odd man out pretends to get it. Plus, the platforms know that once they've handed over their personal information, built up a following, and followed accounts representing their own interests, users are extremely unlikely to squander all the time, effort, and social capital they've built up.

But we're not just passive users. The more we observe people being rewarded for particular behaviors, the more likely we are to emulate them, a tendency first observed by the Canadian–American psychologist Albert Bandura. In a series of experiments that formed his core social-learning theory, Bandura found that "most human behavior is learned observationally through modeling: from observing others one forms an idea of how new behaviors are performed, and on later occasions this coded information serves as a guide for action."[155]

That's never been truer than on social media. Take Thomas Gültzow, a PhD candidate at the Care and Public Health Research Institute in the Netherlands, who applied this notion to photographs of male bodies on Instagram and found that the bodies represented on the app were overwhelmingly lean, muscled, and white.[156]

"Based on Albert Bandura's social cognitive theory, body image pictures on Instagram may, through positive modeling, help to counteract the obesity epidemic, with the portrayals leading men to lead more healthy lifestyles. On the negative side, the skewed images may lead to male body dissatisfaction, depression, and eating disorders. We can use this knowledge to educate our patients about the false sense of reality often portrayed on social media," said Brenda K. Wiederhold, the editor-in-chief of the *CyberPsychology, Behavior, and Social Networking* journal, where Gültzow's study was published.[157]

Which is to say, when we see influencers rack up thousands of likes and comments, we're likely to follow suit, whether that's by emulating them in real life or Photoshopping our digital images to look like theirs. But when we don't receive that same adulation ourselves, we tend to feel worse.

Is it any surprise, then, that the most popular people on social media are also the ones who keep other people on social media? Whether your reaction to them is positive or negative, you're there, reacting, and the mysterious algorithm rewards them.

The problem is, social media isn't easing the emotions that trigger their use—it's exacerbating them.

In a 2011 study of college undergraduates, researchers "identified several features of internet usage that correlated with depression… For example, participants with depressive symptoms tended to engage in very high email usage… Other characteristic features of depressive internet behavior included increased amounts of video watching, gaming, and chatting."[158]

Unfortunately not using social media can also make people feel worse, at least in the short-term. "A habit is when not doing an action causes a bit of pain," Eyal says, though what he really means is more of an "itch, a feeling that manifests within the mind and causes discomfort until it is satisfied."

"The habit-forming products we use are simply there to provide some sort of relief. Using a technology or product to scratch the itch provides faster satisfaction than ignoring it," he said. The only problem is, "Once we come to depend on a tool, nothing else will do."[159]

He compares the transformation of our relationship with digital products over time to using painkillers. At the outset, they're nice to have, but over time we become hopelessly addicted.

Eyal points to Instagram in particular as an example of how our psychological impulses have been weaponized against us—and subsequently normalized into part of our daily routines. We all want to seek pleasure and avoid pain, and these apps have synthesized those urges into a never-ending process.

"Emotions, particularly negative ones, are powerful internal triggers and greatly influence our daily routines," Eyal writes. "Feelings of boredom, loneliness, frustration, confusion, and indecisiveness often instigate a slight pain or irritation and prompt an almost instantaneous and often mindless action to quell the negative sensation."

Plus, "seeking pleasure and avoiding pain are two key motivators in all species."

According to Dr. BJ Fogg, the founder and director of the Behavior Design Lab at Stanford, three "Core Motivators" drive most of our actions: seeking pleasure and avoiding pain, seeking hope and avoiding fear, and seeking social acceptance and avoiding rejection.[160] The Fyre Festival, with its fantasy world targeted toward the average losers, hit all three square on the head.

"When bored, many people seek excitement and turn to dramatic news headlines. When we feel overly stressed, we seek serenity, perhaps finding relief in sites like Pinterest. When we feel lonely, destinations like Facebook and Twitter provide instant social connections," Eyal says.

Once we find a scratch for the itch, we tend to become addicted quickly. In a 1950s experiment that reminds me of my own Instagram-app experiment—where I deleted the app and found myself constantly opening its replacement, anyway— James Olds and Peter Milner, a psychologist and neuroscientist respectively, placed rats in a box and provided a lever that would stimulate their brains' pleasure centers. What they found was astounding.[161] The rats would forgo food, water, family, sleep, and sex to press the lever—as many as seven thousand times an hour. They had to be manually unhooked to keep them from starving to death.

The response in humans was even more extreme. In one particularly egregious 1970s experiment on homosexuality, a subject attached to the electrode "stimulated himself to a point that, both behaviorally and introspectively, he was experiencing an almost overwhelming euphoria and elation and had to be disconnected despite his vigorous protests." In another experiment, a female subject developed "a chronic ulceration" on the finger she used to adjust the amplitude.[162]

Once the subjects had been given a way to experience pleasure from a button, researchers quickly found that nothing else would do. Not only did the subjects continue pushing the button even when it had been turned off—some of them had to have the buttons forcibly removed from their hands.

I think Olds and Milner would be horrified to find we've been carrying around their levers in our pockets, keeping at our fingertips that unhealthy yet pleasurable "escape from life's more mundane moments."[163]

"Many years later, experiments in both humans and critters have revealed that most experiences in our lives that we find transcendent—whether illicit vices or socially sanctioned ritual and social practices as diverse as exercise, meditative prayer, or even charitable giving—activate this pleasure circuit in the brain," writes David J. Linden, a professor of neuroscience at the Johns Hopkins University School of Medicine.[164]

Which helps to explain in part why, when hundreds of attractive and wealthy models and influencers began posting about the Fyre Festival—the pleasure experience to end all experiences—people began buying tickets without giving it a second thought. It's painful thinking about how much fun people are having without you, and here was both a trigger and a solution in one. Could you think of a better platform to sell access on than the place where people who are feeling bored and insecure go to see how the other half is living? Now they were being told that the lives they followed day in and day out could be theirs.

Part of the Fyre response can be explained by a series of experiments, conducted by the Stanford psychology professor Brian Knutson, who hooked up his subjects to an MRI machine and found a clear link between emotional stimuli and financial risk-taking. In one experiment, he showed a group of heterosexual males photographs of beautiful women and then asked them to gamble either a dollar or a dime.[165]

"What we saw is that when they viewed the erotic pictures, the activation in their nucleus accumbens increased compared to the other stimuli, and also that they had increased activation in that region before choosing the high-risk gamble," Knutson said. "After people had seen those erotic pictures, they tended to pick the high-risk gamble more often, especially if they had been picking the low-risk gamble before."

What's more, Knutson found in a subsequent experiment that the nucleus accumbens wasn't activating when the reward was received—it was activating in anticipation of it.

"The study revealed that what draws us to act is not the sensation we receive from the reward itself, but the need to alleviate the craving for that reward," Eyal concludes.[166]

Which helps explain why the onslaught of Fyre marketing didn't just entice buyers with its images of beautiful models in bikinis and pristine sand beaches—it also triggered an equal and opposite powerful emotion: fear and, in particular, the fear of missing out.

"Everyone likes experiences, and I think if you think that

cool people are going, like all those social media influencers, everyone's obsessed with being famous," Billy's high-school classmate told me. "Everyone's just obsessed with having followers or having likes. By doing things like Fyre Festival, they thought they could get that maybe, or get close to people that have that."

The most-cited definition of FOMO comes from a 2013 study, which cites the feeling as "a pervasive apprehension that others might be having rewarding experiences from which one is absent."[167] Researchers also found high levels of FOMO to be associated with "lower general mood, lower well-being, and lower life satisfaction, mixed feelings when using social media, as well as inappropriate and dangerous use (i.e., in university lectures or whilst driving)."

Studies have also shown direct links between the use of social media sites like Instagram and Facebook and "increased social comparisons and negative affective states such as envy and jealousy."[168] These feelings then spur us to use social media even more to alleviate the negative emotions, resulting in a feedback loop most of us aren't even aware we're in. As many as three-quarters of internet users back in 2011 reported experiencing unease when they felt they were missing out on what their peers were doing. Instagram, which confirms for you that's true, has only made things worse.[169]

And it appears to be a universal experience, judging by overseas studies done on *kiasu*,[170] a word that originates from the Chinese Hokkien dialect to describe a cultural behavior so competitive it encompasses not just the fear of missing out, but the fear of losing out to others, and the Hong Kong phenomenon of *par chup sue*, which translated literally means, *scared to lose*.

"I think FOMO is human behavior. I think every youthful person, or young-at-heart person knows what FOMO means," said Lois Sakany, the editor of *Snobette*. "Who doesn't feel bad when they go on their Instagram Live and, say, see friends hanging out without you?"

And lonely people are more likely to use social media, which makes you feel even lonelier, which increases feelings of FOMO—and has a direct correlation against maximization, the act of looking for the best options. And as a result of this FOMO loop, we're more likely to buy into something blindly.

Even the celebrities who help inspire FOMO are not immune.

Speaking by phone, Sakany, who has been covering streetwear trends for almost twenty years, pointed me to a social media pile-on involving Maisie Williams, the young *Game of Thrones* actress, who was photographed in 2016 wearing what certainly appeared to me to be a Supreme box logo T-shirt.

"But the kids who really followed Supreme immediately picked up on the fact that it was fake, that she had bought it… I don't know, like a knockoff copy from wherever she bought it. And she was ripped to shreds for that," Sakany said. "So in that case you could see where, she just thought she was buying something cool, she didn't know all the rules about Supreme, maybe she didn't even know what Supreme was, you know?"

The teenage actress's supposed gaffe made headlines, from *Esquire* to *Teen Vogue*. "Few things are as nauseating as celebs wearing niche brands that they otherwise would have never heard of had their stylist not picked it out for them," a writer for Highsnobiety opined. "It feels so completely fake, something that's poetically illustrated by the sight of a Supreme tee that looks like it was bought from a Chinese eBay seller."[171]

But people forget that Supreme itself was created off the backs of pre–social media influencers—the cool skaters, DJs, and club kids in New York City. The brand launched to much fanfare after it supplied the wardrobes (and the extras) for the Larry Clark film *Kids*, but the designs didn't come from the young creatives who ultimately caught the nation's eye. They came from James Jebbia, a British businessman who had moved to New York as a teen in the early eighties and saw dollar signs in the then-underground downtown scene. After working behind the counter at a store called Parachute, he opened up his own shop, Union, where, according to lore, he noticed Shawn Stüssy's designs were selling the best and partnered up with the legendary skateboarder and surfer to open a New York Stüssy flagship. But when Stüssy, then the father of streetwear, decided to retire, Jebbia launched Supreme to fill the hole he was leaving behind.

"I know James started Supreme when I was leaving, so maybe just for that fact—that that was the impetus of him starting," Stüssy told *Acclaim* magazine.[172] "Because he was worried like, 'Wow, I'm a shopkeeper and if Shawn leaves and Stüssy dries up, what am I going to do?'"

Supreme launched in 1994, and Jebbia suddenly stepped into Stüssy's shoes—without ever skateboarding in them himself.

I asked Sakany, point-blank, what is it that's so special about Supreme, which mostly seems like a T-shirt store with long lines and rude security guards.

"It was always meant to be street-inspired items that people in the hood wore, and that could be a hoodie, a T-shirt, a crewneck shirt. And it's really more about creating this insider boys' club appeal through collaborations, through subtle silhouettes," Sakany said. "From the outside, it looks like T-shirts and hoodies. But if you're in the club, you understand the language, the storytelling, the game-changing moments."

Leah McSweeney, the creator of the clothing line Married

to the Mob and one of the newest cast members of Bravo's *The Real Housewives of New York City*, has another theory.

"I haven't been in the Supreme store in so long, but part of the appeal is that when you would walk into Supreme, the people that worked there would treat you like shit. And people love that. It's like some masochistic weird thing," McSweeney told me. "You would see in message boards and old articles, people would talk about that. You go in the store, no one wants to help you, don't touch anything, they're looking at you like you're a total fucking loser. And people loved it."

But it was Jebbia's clever use of influencers to gain street cred that enabled Supreme to become such a big brand, she explained.

"The guys that worked at Supreme, when it first opened, for so long, they are really what made Supreme so cool, because people were interested in these skaters that were in the movie *Kids*, that were native New Yorkers, that dressed the way they did. And they were young," said McSweeney.

They were, in a sense, an early prototype of influencers, only their cachet was genuine and measured in sales orders as opposed to follows and likes.

"The thing is before social media, the people who were part of the Supreme crew, those were guys from the city that people from all different countries were looking at and they were obsessed with. It was really about those guys," she added. "I'm telling you, a lot of it has to do with that beginning foundation and people looking at the Supreme, loving it had to do with the guys that worked at the store."

It's something Jebbia himself admitted in a rare interview with GQ.[173]

"I really liked what was coming out of skate culture at the time. So I just thought, 'Okay, let's do a skate shop,'" Jebbia said. "We opened the store and it was very bare-bones. The guys I hired were very key. Everybody who worked in the store was a skateboarder."

McSweeney started her label a few years after Supreme launched, giving her a unique perspective of the largely male downtown skater scene.

Jebbia wasn't really a part of it, she recalled, but he saw how monetizable the scene could be—and capitalized heavily on its underground stars.

It's not unlike the Fyre marketers laundering their message through the feeds of America's most beloved supermodels, which Sakany agreed with when I asked her.

"I like the word *launder*. I think that's exactly what they do. I think, again, humans are social animals. It's painful for us to be apart from each other. As a rule, we like to follow a leader, you know? And I think a lot of these brands, they tap into that, and they understand that if you invest money in collaborating with the right people or brand...everything they do is meant to send a message that, 'We're so cool, we're so clever, we get people to collaborate with us that won't collaborate with anybody else,'" Sakany said.

In 2004, McSweeney thought it would be a funny commentary to co-opt the Supreme logo for her first collection under her female-focused brand, Married to the Mob, with a graphic that read "Supreme Bitch." After all, Supreme had co-opted its logo, color, and font from the anticapitalist artist Barbara Kruger. And they had very conspicuously declined to design for or include women in their vision (outside of outright objectification), which is part of what inspired McSweeney to start her label in the first place.

For almost a decade, Jebbia was cool with McSweeney's appropriation, even granting his permission for her sales and offering the design for sale at his store, Union. Superstars like Rihanna and Cara Delevingne were pictured wearing it. Everything was copacetic, at least until the brand took off and she tried to trademark the Supreme Bitch logo in anticipation of a large order with Urban Outfitters.

That's when Jebbia filed a $10 million lawsuit against her.[174] Suddenly both designers found themselves playing a corporate game over their anti-corporate message.

The action prompted the then-sixty-eight-year-old Kruger to make her first and only public comment on the brand, which she provided to former Complex editor Foster Kamer in a Word document named "fools.doc," which she attached to a blank email.[175] "What a ridiculous clusterfuck of totally uncool jokers. I make my work about this kind of sadly foolish farce. I'm waiting for all of them to sue me for copyright infringement," Kruger had written in the file.

It also marked the turn of a new era that would see Supreme, revered for its independence, begin to sell out, first slowly with a private-equity minority investment, and then all at once with a $500 million deal with the Carlyle Group,[176] a shadowy investment cabal with ties to absolute icons ranging from the bin Laden family to the Bushes.

"Jebbia's a corporate dude, 100 percent. And I think people saw that once he sued me, to be honest. It changed everything," McSweeney said. "His personality, his interests, his background is not indicative of what Supreme is. That's not why people are buying Supreme. It's the people he was using to have represent it, and the guys that worked at the store, that I feel like he took advantage of."

Before the internet, "only the streetwear illuminati, downtown skate rats, and well-informed creatives were blessed with the knowledge of just what lay behind that enigmatic red emblem," noted Highsnobiety.[177] But with the rise of social media, "People across the globe [were] drawn to its hysteria-inducing collaborations, esoteric subcultural influences and blink-and-you'll-miss-it product drops." David Shapiro, the author of *Supremacist*, a book about the company, even acknowledged as such in his intro, dedicating it "to those who posted, and to those who moderated, as I lurked."[178]

It was early collaborations with more underground artists like Rammellzee, Dondi White, and Kenneth Cappello that helped position Supreme as more art than apparel, but it's the image of Kate Moss smoking in a box logo shirt and leopard-print coat and Dipset posing in matching Ts that sold the brand to the masses. The appeal of the brand is less the brand itself than the vast array of cultural tastemakers who have agreed to collaborate over the years: Damien Hirst, Roy Lichtenstein, Jeff Koons, Larry Clark, Sade, Gucci Mane... and Oreo.

On the other hand, in 2016, they sold an actual brick for $30. It almost immediately resold on eBay for a cool $1,000.[179] And despite creating a brand that is premised, according to Shapiro, as a "long-term conceptual art project about consumerism and theft...and corporate ownership,"[180] the reality is Supreme is corporate as hell and has been since the get-go.

Because what's kept the brand popular all these years isn't its design instincts (though Sakany tells me they made the anorak fashionable) or its artistic independence or even the quality of its products—it's the social currency that wearing their logo seems to bring to its consumers. Part of the draw comes from how hard it is to get your hands on it; you either have to snap their wares up on sight or pay an obscene markup with resellers, whose industry is thriving thanks to these restrictive "drops," just like concert scalpers clean up outside Madison Square Garden, thanks to Ticketmaster's obscene restrictions.

That's one of the most astounding aspects of this so-called hypebeast culture: these kids aren't just spending money on clothes—they're giving up their time just to have the opportunity to part with their cash. These brands could easily print enough T-shirts to clothe every fan on the internet, but they deliberately limit their offerings to goose demand. And goose it they do: the thirst for these marked-up goods is so great that a secondary market for "sneakerbots" run by AI is now thriving as more and more consumers invest in technology to enable them to buy expensive, supposedly collectible sneakers. This is despite the fact that Beanie Babies are currently offering better returns on investment.

On a cold night in late February, I was walking my dog down Mott Street when I saw a young man fumble a stack of red boxes propped up in one hand as he opened the door to the vestibule of a walk-up building with the other.

A young-looking group was also walking by, and I heard one of them say to the others, "Yo, that's Supreme." The young man in the vestibule looked up and said just one word: "Reseller." The group stopped to check out his wares, and as I continued on with my dog, I could hear them begin to hash out a deal for what appeared to be a pair of sneakers. SoHo, once a red light district, is now a red box logo.

"On the perimeters of any subculture, you have your inner, core group, who are like the creators, and, for lack of a better word, the influencers. And then you ripple out a little bit, and then along the perimeter you do have that impact where there's people who don't quite get it, or who don't deeply care, but they want to fit in," Sakany said. "The whole concept of influencers is definitely that you have this core group of people who are viewed as cool, and they're often creatives themselves, and they tend to amass a following. And then if you go further out, you're going to have people who have no clue about any of the sort of intricacies of that subculture, but it looks cool to them."

These days, it's a delicate dance between the $185 billion streetwear industry[181] and the dedicated millennial and Gen Z consumers who reliably line up by the hundreds in sunshine, freezing cold, and rain alike, just to have the chance to spend hundreds of dollars on a T-shirt that cost the designer $10 to make. Their marketing departments may talk of quality, but in the end, it largely comes down to who's photographed wearing it. Is it any wonder that after his involvement in the Fyre Festival, the talent booker Samuel Krost—himself a former Onia intern—created a sweatshirt company with a line called Support Your Friends, which he got his own childhood buddy Gigi Hadid to promote by wearing it out during Fashion Week? Just like the Fyre Festival tickets sold out by offering its customers entreé, however temporary, into a supermodel's world, so too does purchasing the clothes they're wearing.

"Like many religious and nationalist illusions, consumer freedom fulfills a narcissistic function, offering us opportunities to enhance our self-image and raise us above those around us," writes the Greek-British sociologist, Dr. Yiannis Gabriel.[182] "If the therapeutic function of freedom is attained by exercising it, its narcissistic function is attained by exercising it in a discriminating manner. It is not surprising that the psychoanalytic concept of narcissism has proven so valuable in discussions of contemporary consumption. Consumerist ideologies appeal to people's narcissistic desires, offering to enhance their image and attractiveness through a wide range of beautifying accoutrements."

Or as Shapiro put it in *Supremacist*, "I think you have a Freudian collector thing going on with Supreme… Freud said that people collect things as a way of channeling their surplus libidos into objects of desire."

But it's not just niche brands like Supreme and Krost's

Friends-focused label that market their low-cost gear by marking up the price as the cost of membership in an exclusive
club by appealing to our basest instincts. It's all the big athletic
companies, like Nike, Adidas, Puma, and Vans, who promote
their products through celebrities people look up to. It's Beyoncé rolling out her Ivy Park line with gifts, sorted by size
for each level of celebrity, spread over her friends' and family's Instagram accounts.

The Ivy Park PR missives, coincidentally wrapped in Fyre
orange, were sent out to a select and diverse group of celebrities like Reese Witherspoon, Cardi B, Kelly Rowland, Megan
Thee Stallion, Yara Shahidi, Zendaya, and Ellen DeGeneres.
The celebrity-caliber made the Adidas x IVY PARK the
drop of the year.

"I think, again, it goes back to being part of this club,
where you understand what's cool, you buy it, you wear it,
people recognize it, and if you're a top-top-dog, the brand actually gives it to you. Even better if they give it to you before
the launch," Sakany said. "That's sort of the order of things.
You'll have this sort of flex order where you have an A-list
influencer who will splash the sneakers on his Instagram Stories, or his Instagram feed before even official images, but
then shortly after, official images will come out. Little by little they drip out stuff, and it's done in a very orderly manner,
you know? And again, they use a language, and they use a set
of characters that everybody understands."

Thanks to Beyoncé's A-list fame and the sheer number of
celebrities who heeded her call to organically promote the
line, the media response to the Ivy Park launch quickly turned
away from the clothes themselves and into an adjudication on
clout. BuzzFeed, among other publications, tallied up "All
The Celebrities Who Were Lucky Enough To Get An Ivy
Park x Adidas Box From Beyoncé,"[183] and publications and

fans alike began questioning why Kim Kardashian, the queen of social media promotions, hadn't posted about her box.

Almost two weeks after the product launch sold out, Kardashian finally posted an unboxing video of her own, writing "Sorry I'm sooo late!" That too made headlines. "Kim Kardashian Swears She Didn't Mail Herself a Giant Orange Ivy Park Gift Box," Jezebel reported.[184] And, "For everyone keeping score," Revelist noted, "Kim Kardashian got an orange Ivy Park box."[185]

"It feels like a club," Sakany said. "Like this small club of people who understand the language and recognize it. It's a way of sort of identifying the person."

"All of these things are done in an extremely limited sort of way," she continued. "They're affordable, nothing's crazy priced, and people want those shoes, and they want to be able to go out and flex with that pair of shoes on."

By using celebrities to launder the brand's promotion, the companies create a frenzy that is stoked by the fact that they keep the product stock low to signal exclusivity. The frenzy for social media clout has grown so loud that in November 2020 Kim Kardashian took the final step and began selling a limited-edition version of the KKW makeup PR box, which all her famous friends got for free, for $295. The "crystalized box" which is wrapped in a nineteen-photograph collage of her face, contains $190 worth of makeup and an apparent $105 worth of celebrity street cred.

It's a symbiotic relationship between the brands and the influencers they rely on to build out the hype for their products, Sakany said, pointing to a recent collaboration between Nike and Scottie Beam, the model and cohost of *Black Girl Podcast*, who also runs an Instagram page with over 160,000 devoted followers.

"She posted a pair of the Stüssy Nike sneakers. And in the

caption, all she put was 'Love these.' Right? And a bunch of people are going to be like, 'Oh, my god, I'm trying to get those.' And then a whole bunch of other people will be like, 'Oh, those are cute,' but they don't have any idea what they are, or what they mean. Probably she was given a pair. Nike probably gave her a pair because she's got a big following, and she's an influencer. Beyoncé sent her an Adidas package. So that's another flex for her too, where she can be like, 'I got these, Nike gave these to me,' because Nike is known for being very stingy with product seeding," Sakany said.

Put simply, Nike is now aspirational. Where once they sold sneakers, now they sell a lifestyle.

"Nike isn't a running shoe company,"[186] writer Naomi Klein wrote in the tenth-anniversary edition of *No Logo*. "It is about *the idea of transcendence through sports.*"[187]

But if a shoe drops and nobody's promoted it on social media, can you really call it cool? It's exactly what the Fyre Festival capitalized on, using four hundred famous so-called Fyrestarters to whip up excitement about something that never existed. And it's the same anxiety the influencers who weren't included in the marketing felt when they started posting the orange tiles unbidden on their own feeds so that people wouldn't think they were out of the loop.

It was, in fact, specifically the kinds of kids who line up to buy Supreme that the festival was targeting with their marketing, at least according to them.

"I'm twenty-eight, and I lived in Manhattan in Chinatown on Canal Street. I do my $7-coffee bullshit, eat avocado toast, I have a design job—that's a bull's-eye millennial," said Oren Aks, the former FuckJerry designer who tried to take credit for the orange-tile idea, in an interview with *AIGA Eye on Design*.[188] "I had to cater to a different generation of rich— not just the type of people who show up in a limousine and smoke cigars on the beach. It's the people who want to fly in from Manhattan and wear their Supreme fannypack."

It was the idea that buying the tickets would make them part of the club they'd spent so much time and energy following online.

"I feel like hype is created because people are really trained, or it has something to do with people not thinking for themselves," said McSweeney.

"It's like people not being happy with their own lives and having to cling on to something else, whether it's a T-shirt or a fucking music festival," she said. "It's just a fucking Instagram opportunity. Back in the nineties, it's not like you could go on Twitter, you had to go out to see what people were wearing, you had to go out to see who was deejaying, you had to go out to see if the club was good. You couldn't look on Twitter or Instagram or anything. And also, you were in the moment. Social media has taken so much away from us."

Pair that with rampant consumerism framed as individuality, and you have a recipe for disaster.

"It's what happens when the mind internalizes a lifetime of brand conditioning and marketers achieve their ultimate end goal. In the modern consumer model, our purchases are framed as expressions of our personality and identity," notes the fashion editor Alec Leach.[189] "And when you define your identity by the brands you purchase and the products that you consume, you become locked into an endless cycle of purchase and consumption in order to justify to yourself that identity."

Our commodified world means tons of tiny in-groups that people want to be a part of, brands launder their marketing through trusted insiders, and then people identify with those brands to show their allegiances.

In 1997, the writer Tom Peters defined personal branding in a piece called "The Brand Called You"[190] for *Fast Company*.

"That cross-trainer you're wearing—one look at the distinctive swoosh on the side tells everyone who's got you branded. That coffee travel mug you're carrying—ah, you're a Starbucks woman! Your T-shirt with the distinctive Champion 'C' on the sleeve, the blue jeans with the prominent Levi's rivets, the watch with the hey-this-certifies-I-made-it icon on the face, your fountain pen with the maker's symbol crafted into the end..." Peters wrote. "You're branded, branded, branded, branded."

Peters's article made me think of a recent meme that saw social media users eagerly dividing their lives to fit certain parameters: there's the "Facebook You," the "Instagram You," the "LinkedIn You," and the "Tinder You." And somewhere, outside of those defined boxes, lives the "real you." But who exactly is that?

Thanks to technology ranging from deep fakes to the photo-editing software conveniently contained within the apps we're using to post photos—to say nothing of the myriad Facetune-style apps we can use to doctor our image on our own time—it's now possible (and a somewhat accepted practice) to lie about where we are, who we're with, and who we are—and show evidence to support our claims.

This collective agreement to accept our virtual lives as accurate depictions of who we are is a funny bug of the post-truth era.

That's something Marc Weinstein, the investor and producer who tried to help salvage the wreckage of the Fyre Festival, found most disturbing about looking back on his Instagram feed from his time in the Bahamas. He might have been inside his own personal hell, barreling toward oblivion, but to his followers, he was having the time of his life. The historical record did not match the reality.

"Instagram started off as this showboating platform, and I

think it still is to a large degree, but it also has become something different as the platform's evolved. And so for me, no matter what I post on Instagram, even today, I've been struggling. I don't enjoy posting on Instagram, because no matter what I post, whenever I see it on the other side, it always feels too promotional to me," Weinstein said during a phone call mid-pandemic. "If it's real, I might ask, 'Why am I sharing all of this with a bunch of people that I've never met in my life? What is the intention behind the use of that platform? Is it for attention? Do I think that I'm having an impact on people's lives by posting this?' You can't really separate those two sides of yourself. The attention-seeker and the do-gooder are merged into one body, one mind, and one spirit. And so, I don't know, it's just challenging."

Even when we try to buck the trends and just be ourselves, there's still a performative element, points out Weinstein, who launched a podcast called *Look Up!* after the Fyre debacle to highlight the collective problematic relationship between our mental health and social media use.

"We're all creating these little digital avatars of ourselves on a day-to-day basis, and those avatars are often informed by the platform itself. So, whatever you put on Instagram is going to come out the other side through an Instagram lens, just because of the rules of that game that you're playing on Instagram," Weinstein said. "You try to be different. You say, 'Oh, I'm going to be vulnerable today on my Instagram Story. I'm going to share with you something hard that happened to me.' And if that starts to pick up steam, then before you know it, you'll have an Instagram feed full of people that are sharing their most vulnerable moments with their communities, and then you get this performative vulnerability, which is well intentioned, but also just another attention-seeking habit that we all are susceptible to."

What's worse is that it's incredibly difficult for us to admit we're even doing it in the first place. We've become primed to make decisions based on what feels right, rather than the objective facts of a given situation.

"The real problem here, I claim, is not merely the content of any particular (outrageous) belief, but the overarching idea that—depending on what one wants to be true—some facts matter more than others," writes Lee McIntyre, a research fellow at the Center for Philosophy and History of Science at Boston University, and the author of *Post-Truth*.[191] "The main criterion is what favors their preexisting beliefs. This is not the abandonment of facts, but the corruption of the process by which facts are credibly gathered and reliably used to shape one's beliefs about reality.

"When a person's beliefs are threatened by an 'inconvenient fact,' sometimes it is preferable to challenge the fact. This can happen at either a conscious or unconscious level (since sometimes the person we are seeking to convince is ourself), but the point is that this sort of post-truth relationship to facts occurs only when we are seeking to assert something that is more important to us than the truth itself," McIntyre says.

These practitioners of post-truth, according to McIntyre, are "trying to compel someone to believe in something whether there is good evidence for it or not."

It's a perfect distillation of the Fyre Festival. McFarland had obvious financial reasons for perpetuating the lie that Fyre ticket holders would be touching down for a weekend of extreme luxury in the Bahamas. But why, given all the available evidence to the contrary, did the ticket holders take that chance?

That's something Wells, the investor who tried to sound the alarm about the festival, is still grappling with.

"Truth cannot disturb the cacophony of paid advertisements," Wells said, looking back. "I felt like one of those people that knew Madoff was cheating. Like Markopolos, what was that guy's name, Markopolos? Jumping up and down at the SEC for five years."

But—to quote Harry Markopolos's own book title—no one would listen.[192]

"The cacophony of sound, using the influencers and their social media strategy, was so overwhelming, that not only did various smart financial guys give them money, but, like, facts were just totally ignored, based off of the strength of the social media strategy," Wells said.

It wasn't just the unsuspecting public. "I had friends who were like, 'We should buy tickets to this!'" Wells said. Some of them were stranded on the island when everything finally fell apart.

Wells says his alarms were drowned out by the lure of the influencers and the pay-for-play press pliantly directed by 42West that crowed about the exclusive, sold-out festival. Wells couldn't believe what he was seeing.

"Anyone who did any type of work at all would, for one, recognize the festival is not sold out because there are tickets for sale on the website. And then two, obviously it's not the hottest festival because people can't even fucking get there," he said. "Any research, any cursory information or research, would reveal these horror stories that people are talking about, that I knew were gonna come."

Even the notion that Kendall Jenner would be there, hanging out on the beach with festivalgoers was ludicrous to him.

"If you think you're going to be hanging out with Kendall Jenner…if you think she's going to be hanging out at the Sandals Resort? You're out of your mind," Wells said. "She may stop by and post to Instagram because it's contractually obligated, but she's not hanging out there. That's insane."

The saddest part, to Wells, is that one critical post from one of the influencers could have stopped the whole thing in its tracks.

"Just owning up to it like, 'Hey, guys, it turns out everything I was showing for isn't legit.' Just one of their posts that goes to three million followers would have solved this shit," Wells said.

But the influencers had good reason for not marking things as ads or stopping the festival in its tracks: their brands depend on authenticity. That's what makes them so attractive to advertisers. It's a sort of laundering operation that preys on the general public in a number of insidious ways.

Part of it is plain human psychology. What exactly are we experiencing when we look at a Kendall Jenner post inviting us to fly private to the Bahamas with her? It all comes down to the science of anticipation—what happens to us when we anticipate a pleasurable event, the role dopamine plays in how we respond when we're emotionally connected, and how our brain chemistry can be easily manipulated.

The dark side of that, outlined by C. T. Bauer College of Business professor Vanessa Patrick, is that too much hype can be detrimental due to the concept of "affective misforecasting," a term she and her co-researchers created to describe the gap between the anticipated experience and the actual experience.

But it's also a reflection of the scarcity principle, wherein we place more value on things we perceive as harder to get. Both the Fyre Festival and the streetwear industry derived great value from this phenomenon, and there's a wealth of examples and experts to interview to create a wry portrait of this principle at work, including Dr. Robert Cialdini, the author of *Influence: The Psychology of Persuasion*, and Barbara Kahn, a marketing professor at the University of Pennsylvania, who has studied how social media can amplify its effect. (Sample quote: "It's not about the product per se, it's really about the hype being magnified by social media.")

Meanwhile, tens of millions of fake accounts are proliferating online, just waiting to interact with us. One 2017 study[193] found that on Twitter, "our estimates suggest that between 9 percent and 15 percent of active Twitter accounts are bots," which means close to fifty million users on the platform are actually fake. Twitter puts a nice spin on it, explaining that "many bot accounts are extremely beneficial, like those that automatically alert people of natural disasters...or from customer service points of view,"[194] but that doesn't tell the whole story. That's because bots are good business, even as companies like Social Blade try to discern which users are real and fake to give advertisers a clearer picture of what kinds of audiences they're working with.

Because influencers aren't just buying fake followers to charge advertisers more—they also want their followers to think more positively of them.

"In her experimental research, Utz (2010) empirically demonstrated that social-networking site users with many friends are judged to be more popular and socially attractive than those with fewer friends. Similarly, Tong and colleagues (2008) found a significant relationship between the number of friends one has on Facebook and their perceived social attractiveness," a 2014 study conducted by Seung-A Annie Jin of Emerson College and Joe Phua of the University of Georgia found.[195] "As such, the number of Twitter followers a celebrity has can be seen as a type of cue used by consumers to gauge the celebrity's trustworthiness and credibility.

"When a celebrity has a larger number of followers... consumers who view this information may see the celebrity as being more attractive, trustworthy, and competent," the study concluded.

It feels sometimes like an arms race to sentience, because in our modern society, followers are currency, whether you're advertising for money or not. Some actors and models report a minimum following required for an audition; according to one gossip site, Kim Kardashian buys followers not to raise her own prices but in order not to fall behind her younger sister Kylie, who can expect to earn upward of $1 million for a post to her 202 million, and growing, followers.[196]

And as the tools to detect bots grow stronger, the bot companies are responding in kind. These armies of bots are controlled by companies like Devumi, which the *New York Times* recently discovered had served around "200,000 customers, including reality television stars, professional athletes, comedians, TED speakers, pastors and models" in their quest to look more popular online.[197]

Before the company shut down and settled with the FTC for $2.5 million its customer base reportedly included social-media users as varied as John Leguizamo, Michael Dell, Ray Lewis, Kathy Ireland, Akbar Gbajabiamila, Louise Linton, and even Martha Lane Fox—a Twitter board member.

Meanwhile, the analytics site SparkToro ran a 2018 analysis of Donald Trump's following and found a whopping 61 percent (more than thirty-three million accounts) following him are fake. And they're not even particularly good fakes either.[198] According to SparkToro's analysis, 35 percent of his following are quantified as "low-quality," as "accounts that trigger 10+ different spam/fake follower signals." And that's up from the 50 percent *Newsweek* found in 2017,[199] and even more surprising following Twitter's supposed 2018 purge of fake accounts from the site that saw Katy Perry lose close to three million followers.[200]

But these influencers are learning that you can't rely on the placebo effect to move product. Just ask Ariana Renee, an Instagram influencer with more than two million followers who wasn't able to sell the minimum thirty-six T-shirts required for her company to launch.

"It breaks my heart to have to write this post. I've poured my heart into this drop," she wrote in a now-deleted post. "Unfortunately the company that I'm working with goes based on your first drop sales. In order for them to order & make my products (even to keep working with them) I have to sell at least 36 pieces…but I was getting such good feedback that people loved it & were gonna buy it. No one has kept their word so now the company won't be able to send out the orders to people who actually bought shit & it breaks my heart (don't worry you'll get a refund)."

And one successful sale isn't necessarily predictive of the next, especially when the brand is inseparable from the influencer's reputation. The fashion influencer Arielle Charnas, who posts under the handle SomethingNavy, set a record with her 2017 clothing line launch with Nordstrom, selling a reported $1 million of merch in twenty-four hours.[201] Her second collection, launched in 2018, apparently crashed the site. But by 2020, the partnership had dissolved for unannounced reasons that seem likely linked to the drubbing she received online after it was revealed she had traveled from New York City to the Hamptons after contracting coronavirus.

The problem for advertisers, when they're not worrying about tracking quarantine violations, becomes how to track whether influencers are being honest about their metrics. According to Unilever's former CMO Keith Weed, at least 40 percent of influencers have bought fake followers,[202] which frankly seems like a lowball figure. But it's created a booming industry around fake accounts—there are companies that create them, companies that sell them, and companies that find them.

Even when the followers are real, you can't necessarily trust it. As an experiment, I recently paid a company called Jumper Media $500 to make my incredibly cute and well behaved French Bulldog Colette (you can follow her at @good_dog_colette) into a bona fide Instagram micro influencer. And they did...for a few days, anyway.

Almost overnight, Colette's account had jumped to more than 3,000 followers, which is about double the number of followers on my own verified Instagram account, where you can always follow me if you want at @gbluestone. And it felt like all of her new followers were suddenly enthusiastically commenting on her delightful doggy photos. Even though I knew I had paid for it, it was still exciting to log on to the account and see the notifications steadily growing. But then, just like that, it all stopped. By the next morning, she lost 1,500 followers—almost half of what she had gained the day before. We were back to obscurity before Petco even had time to take notice of us.

It was the obvious outcome, but the warm glow of going viral still felt so promising. The thousands of new followers had come to her page under the impression that a YouTuber named Zane was raffling off a prize for his 3.5 million followers. To be in the running, all Zane's followers had to do was follow the people he was following—a list that had been leased to Jumper Media that included my four-year-old French Bulldog and dozens of other nobodies who were willing to pay for the experience of being popular. For two days, I watched as Jumper ran the promotion, rotating people on and off the list as they hit their promised follower accounts. To game the companies trying to spot bots and promotions like the one I'd paid to participate in, Jumper had also been encouraging new followers to comment on each account's newest posts, hence the "cute doggies" and red heart emojis that piled up under her photos. ("How much?!" asked one new follower, as if she were a swipe-up link.)

For a brief moment, it had felt like my content was actually engaging and connecting with people. Sadly, no one has commented on my perfect dog since.

5

Fyre in the Hole

About a month before the disaster unfolded, McFarland and Margolin had a very real logistical problem. The festival didn't exist. Millions of dollars raised and spent, and months gone by, and all they had to show for it was a beautiful video produced by a company whose bill they never fully paid. Though the SEC would later estimate McFarland had fraudulently induced over one hundred investors to invest more than $27.4 million with him, by March 2017 the company was almost dead broke.[203]

Forget the outrageous amenities like villas with private pools. They had no tents. They had no toilets or showers. They had no electricity or basic emergency medical services. They didn't even have ice for the drinks. And the ports were closed two weeks before the festival, because it had been scheduled for the same weekend as the Exuma Regatta, the island's biggest annual event. All the hotel rooms on the island were booked too.

"I warned Grant from the years of experience me and my team have, I was like, 'Look, this is false advertisement that you guys are putting out. If you can't deliver on these drawings and the failed paragraph you guys are touting here, you're gonna be in trouble when that comes through,'" said MDavid Low, the product designer who worked on the Fyre Media app out of the company's Portland office. "And they continued to push forward with it regardless."[204]

To make matters worse, Fyre's leaders had intentionally given themselves less than two months to plan the whole thing. They'd conceived of the festival in November, which only gave them five months in the first place—an insane proposition for an event in a major metropolitan city, much less a remote island. And then, instead of pouring themselves into the planning, McFarland and his team spent most weekends chartering private jets to Norman's Cay at their $50,000-a-week party house, all paid for with company money.

"They absolutely hoped to sell as many tickets as they can and then just kind of figure it out," Low said.

As bad as things looked on the outside, things were ten million times worse on the inside at Fyre. They'd promised the headliners multiples of their regular fees but had no way of paying them.

At that point, the company was so broke, it couldn't even afford decor. According to internal emails, Fyre had hired an interior design firm called Workframe to kit out the offices, but when the lookbook came back, the company couldn't afford to buy any of the furniture listed inside. Ultimately, the only furniture in the office could be inventoried as follows: an assortment of rented office desks, one conference table, a handful of leftover vanity desks from the previous tenant, and a single IKEA dining room table.

Most employees were not given work computers and had to use their own personal computers. McFarland and Margolin were two of the only people in the office with desktops. Still, despite the lack of cash or experience on the marketing side, Margolin's position only grew at Fyre. In spite of—or perhaps because of—his singular year of marketing experience, Margolin was permitted to hire two different assistants to help him oversee the festival—despite never having attended one before.

(Weinstein also points out that this wasn't an obvious red flag to anyone because start-ups are expected to have to bootstrap. "A lot of people think that founders should be hungry and scrappy, and that necessity breeds genius. So, something like not having furniture was maybe a sign that they were scrappy, and therefore someone that would be a good steward of capital because we're not spending on wasteful things," Weinstein said, pointing to the founders of Airbnb, who raised $30,000 selling Obama-themed cereal and lived off soup for years before the company took off.)

But that wasn't even close to what was actually happening at Fyre: sources say the festival idea had developed largely because McFarland needed a business reason to justify what had by then amounted to months of alcohol-fueled team trips aboard private jets en route to private-island parties in the Exumas, trips on which they were sometimes accompanied by models, athletes, and potential investors.

"He loved the Bahamas and the Exumas more than anybody," said a former Fyre employee. "He started going down there with investors, models. That's sort of the trick. Once they all came down, they had the best time. That was part of his reasoning. He called it the three-day rule."

After attending at least one of those trips as a guest, Stadiumred's Ryan Giunta signed on as a festival manager in the fall of 2016, according to an early Fyre investor pitch deck. But unlike the rest of the team, Giunta had real experience with large-scale events. As a first order of business, he prepared for his new coworkers a $34,500 feasibility study, billed separately from Stadiumred's $10,000 monthly retainer.

His conclusions, diagrammed and explained in granular detail, were immediately concerning. With an outrageous amount of money up front, he concluded, the team might be able to throw a giant party on a private island. But certainly not the one they were planning.

"Upon considering all the above, and the quickly approaching launch date of May 2017 for the Fyre Festival, it is Empire's best recommendation that Stadiumred consider scaling down year 1 to a 1–2 day soft–launch concert/festival event for 2017 with a small audience size (i.e. 2,000–5,000), with the sights on 2018 for a full-scale festival, when on–island infrastructure, facilities, and capabilities are improved and further developed," read one portion of the fifty-four-page report emailed internally.

And if there was any chance of pulling it off, Giunta said, the Fyre team would have to stage it on Norman's Cay, the larger of the two islands Fyre had been considering.

Unbeknownst to Giunta and most of the Fyre team, however, McFarland had recently been served with a cease and desist on their lavish promo video by the owners of Norman's, whose one rule was that the company not promote that it had once been linked to an attorney for Pablo Escobar. After the video not only referenced Escobar but claimed that he himself had actually owned it, Saddleback Cay was the only option left.

Unfortunately, the feasibility report concluded, "Upon

scouting Saddleback Cay, we do not foresee a plausible solution to this island hosting FYRE Festival 2017, and recommend a date target of 2018 and beyond for Saddleback as the potential festival grounds."

A few days later, Giunta resigned, citing nonpayment and a lack of cooperation from the Fyre team.

"The funds for Empire, Robbie, and the expense advance still have yet to be received despite being told on numerous occasions that the wires had been executed," he wrote in his January resignation email. "At this stage, I do not feel we have the ability to proceed as a production partner or leading brand-partnerships given the now-unrealistic timeline the group is faced with, the decision to promote and sell tickets to a festival that we have not yet determined to be feasible given the change in proposed venues, and most importantly the lack of follow-through across the board."

One reason the wires hadn't been executed, CRO Jason Ve confirmed later that month in an email, was because there was no money left in Fyre's accounts. (They were, however, able to scrounge together enough to make a $10,000 payment to Status Labs for "reputation management." The payment was supposed to make a negative article about the festival on a fashion blog disappear from Google; unfortunately, it had already reappeared on the first page of Google results before the month was over.)

But McFarland, who was renowned for his ability to seemingly pull money out of thin air, pushed on. (According to the SEC, McFarland was able to fraudulently induce at least $27.4 million out of more than a hundred people who invested in one or both of his companies, Fyre and Magnises, by doctoring "private placement memoranda, PowerPoint updates to existing investors, income statements, and emails, all of which materially exaggerated the number of talent bookings made via fyreapp.com, the revenue and income derived from these bookings, and the Fyre companies' assets." In one example, McFarland took a legitimate report prepared by Fyre's chief revenue officer and, according to the SEC, "tripled the stated goal for completed bookings—from $50 million to $150 million—and increased the number of 'talent represented' from 200 to 1,200." In another example, McFarland instructed a contractor to "make sure 35% [of the locations are] international cities;... sprinkle in a couple of higher offer amounts;...and show $30.1 mm total bookings in January with strong repeat buyer percentages." It was all a lie, the SEC charged, concluding that Fyre had really made just $57,443 in bookings that year—barely enough to cover a single round-trip private-jet flight to the Bahamas.)

Meanwhile, McFarland's employees had all somehow arrived at the mistaken impression that he had been paying for the private jets and party weekends out of his own pocket.

"Everybody was like, 'How is Billy paying for these flights?' Everyone said, 'Oh, Billy made a lot of money in Magnises.' Everybody said it was Billy's money. You see what I'm saying?" one former Fyre employee told me, looking back almost three years after the festival. "There was a Chinese wall. Nobody knew anything, and so because of that, you can keep on going. Yeah, looking back on that, how douchey do I feel going on those jets now?"

But McFarland was successfully raising money selling other people the same thing he was searching for: the opportunity for an average loser to live like a celebrity. And for a time, he was living that way. He just needed other people's money to do it. Like a hedge funder who dealt solely in social media clout, McFarland had, over the years, rigged together a fund that he could use to invest in celebrity access. Instead of paying himself management fees, he was expensing his entire life. And he arranged it so that he could do the fun parts—let's call it due diligence—and then offer a watered-down version back to his investors, like little Instagram-friendly dividends.

Things were dire. McFarland needed to sell something—and fast—or it was all going to come crashing down. Magnises had all but fallen apart, and, according to the SEC, McFarland had taken to pretending that he had found a third-party buyer willing to purchase it for $40 million.

"As part of this scheme, McFarland concocted an ever-changing cast of purported Magnises buyers. First, the purported buyers were an unnamed consortium of five companies (including Magnises and Fyre). Next, the purported buyers were a group led by a well-known fashion mogul. Then, the purported buyer was a Connecticut-based broker-dealer," the SEC charged. "Indeed, as recently as April 2017, McFarland appeared to still be changing the identity of the buyers, with McFarland proposing in an email to a colleague that the buyers could be a mixed group of celebrities (such as Jay-Z and Sean 'P. Diddy' Combs) and Fyre Media investors."

When that scheme failed to take off, the SEC found, McFarland invented a consortium of buyers, which he named Saddleback Media, with Magnises's New York City address.

"In other words, McFarland falsely claimed that Magnises's purported independent buyer was headquartered at the *same* location as Magnises," the charging document alleges. "To imbue this scheme with a gloss of legitimacy, McFarland engaged two large and reputable law firms to prepare transactional documents to unwittingly 'paper' the fictitious deal. McFarland also created a fake employment retainer agreement between himself and Saddleback Media. This agreement bears the electronic signature of Saddleback's purported President, a certain 'G. Smythe,' an individual who—on information and belief—does not exist."

Despite the impressive financial records McFarland had

been handing out to potential investors, Fyre Media hadn't been making much money either. They were occasionally able to book Ja Rule out, in one notable case delivering a three-song Hamptons performance to the infamous publicist Lizzie Grubman, but they had claimed to be making millions of dollars a month. The true amount, authorities say, was somewhere closer to $60,000—*in its entire lifetime.*[205]

When McFarland was running really low on cash, meanwhile, his desperation would manifest in absurd add-on offers, like a $100-per-year service that he claimed would allow any cardholder to book a room at the Dream Hotel in Midtown, as long as it was after midnight, for $99.

That same month, records show, he began circulating a new pitch deck to investors, asking for $5 million investments that would help cover the festival's initial capital requirement before the ticket sales began. In exchange, he promised investors would see a 150 percent return by the end of the year. And in the event something catastrophic happened, their investment, he promised, would be "secured" by Fyre's revenue, which he estimated between $20 and $40 million.

But here on Earth, the ticket sales were more like $1.5 million, according to an accounting done by the trustee currently overseeing the Fyre bankruptcy case. Though the team calculated it internally as closer to $3.5 million, that may be because they didn't have the technology to separate comped tickets from paid ones.

But the facts were clear. Tickets did not sell out in the first week. In fact, by February, they were still at less than 50 percent, and McFarland had to reduce the size of the festival from 10,000 to 2,500 attendees.

Whatever money there was, McFarland spent it almost as fast as it came in, chartering dozens of private jets back and forth from the Bahamas and shelling out tens of thousands of dollars to Margolin's then-girlfriend, the interior designer Amanda Stoopler, for decorating McFarland's $25,000-a-month Chelsea penthouse.[206] And those were just his personal expenses, even if they were paid out by company money.

"It was just the rich boys' playground, and they never got serious," then-Fyre employee Nyla Coffie said. "They would pay for people to go out to lavish dinners, like, friends of friends, on the company dollar."

Even at home in the city, a single night out at 1 Oak with the boys and their potential clients could top more than $10,000 in bottle-service charges on the company card, records show.

According to expense reports, McFarland spent outrageous sums leading up to the festival that far exceeded the income he was making at the time. For example, prosecutors say, McFarland spent $215,090.59 on interior design and furniture between January 1, 2017, and April 25, 2017.

Records show that even while he was bouncing checks to suppliers, producers, and staffers working on the festival, he was spending hundreds of thousands of dollars on personal expenses, including $41,359.41 on clothing at Barneys over a four-month period in 2016. He also dropped more than $100,000 on dining, entertainment, and hotels between May 2016 and April 2017, when the Fyre Festival took place, according to court documents.

In all, prosecutors say, he spent at least $631,925.58 of other people's money on himself in the year leading up to the Fyre Festival, including more than $30,000 on hotel rooms in the Hamptons during the summer of 2016. During that time period, Fyre Media made only $57,443, and McFarland was drawing a salary of $100,000 per year, according to court documents.

"Throughout the period of his fraud, McFarland received

money, benefits, and perks, which enabled him to live an extravagant lifestyle, including maintaining a Manhattan residence, employing a private driver of a luxury vehicle, taking frequent trips by private plane, and making seemingly magnanimous donations to charitable interests and friends. These activities were funded, in substantial part, with investor money," the sentencing document reads.[207]

According to emails, following the departure of Stadiumred, a new production company called DPS entered the arena to the tune of $850,000. After accompanying them to the Bahamas to check out a potential site—an undeveloped gravel lot next to a Sandals resort on Great Exuma, a commercial island—Margolin prepared a memo for McFarland laying things out quite plainly.

There was a lot they could do to stage the festival, but one thing was clear, he wrote: "It is not the idyllic beachside location we've marketed." And it was going to cost them at least $16 million to pull off even a bare-bones version of what they had promised ticket holders.

He attached a budget: "DPS says they can do this in May. I would take this with a grain of salt. To do this in May, we would in essence, be putting a gun to our head, lose leverage and not have any ability to negotiate," Margolin wrote in a section analyzing whether to change the festival dates. "Coupling this with Regatta, it is not the wise decision to keep the dates as-is. We may be able to leap-frog; however, we would need 3.5MM++ in less than one week."

But McFarland didn't have $16 million. He didn't even have $3.5 million. He didn't even have enough to pay the $307,000 he still owed MATTE Projects or the $100,000 he now owed to VaynerMedia.

So McFarland reached into his bag of tricks for one of his famous short-term cash grabs. The same week DPS made its visit and the invoices came due, McFarland announced a new idea for the Fyre team. In addition to planning the festival, he ordered, they would also be responsible for launching an international tour of pop-up parties that would cross the US and even stop in Tokyo. He reasoned the project would help the company raise a quick $4 million by "selling 500 tickets per city (expecting 20% don't attend after buying) for $100/ticket," partnering with high-end hotels for free event space, hiring artists on the cheap—oh, and selling bar and table service for at least $100,000 a night.

"Plus brand sponsors," he added.

"Ja [Rule], as you say every performance, 'one thing is for sure, and two things are for mother fucking certain' everyone in the world wants to go [sic] this festival no matter how rich, poor, cool, or non-cool they are," McFarland promised. "We've proven, by way of instagram posts in exchange for a couple of tickets, that we have tens, if not hundreds, of millions of dollars of free influencer marketing at our disposal. It's time to leverage these influencers' desires to attend by having them market other Fyre initiatives in addition to the festival."

The entire Fyre team loved the idea. Only Julian Jung, an investor in Magnises and the CEO of the ticketing company Tablelist, responded with alarm.

"Do you think this will end up distracting from the Fyre Festival and cannibalize sales?" he wrote in an email questioning McFarland's conclusions. "When we have a crazy night IE Dan Bilzerian and only have that as a single event, we only do $100K. So having all events cross markets at 100K each is a tough projected number. Maybe we do a smaller number of cities?"

In the end there wouldn't even be one city. After cutting the international tour down to five US city dates, they raised less than $35,000 in ticket sales after paying more than $15,000 to advertise it. The failure was certainly in part because Mc-Farland refused to divulge any details about the events beyond that they would take place at a "secret location to be revealed soon." (There were, of course, no details to divulge.)

"We are launching it today with artist, location and date TBD, and…prices subject to change," Tablelist's Jung replied. "That might look weird in the event description when we put it up."

"We are going live with sales for cities ASAP per Billy," Margolin replied. "We create a sense of urgency through limited inventory and a coordinated launch plan."

But the other problem was that they were pushing it out to the customers on their email list—as in, a list of already existing, angry Fyre ticket holders still waiting for concrete information about the festival. That, more than anything, seemed to finally push Jung over the edge.

"Who is getting this? And when are you guys sending this email? Do you have another list you are going to hit? To existing Fyre purchasers? I thought the point was to drive more business to the festival? You want existing festival purchasers to buy?" he wrote with concern.

McFarland later sent out an email to the team with no text, just the subject line, "pros/cons of emailing the people who've bought ignite the fyre?"

On this, even Margolin had to admit things weren't great. "We haven't sent out any material information, and every email has been transactional." On the plus side, he noted, "We capture more revenue from our guests."

At McFarland's direction, the Fyre team had also dropped thousands of dollars on Fyre-branded passport covers and hats to hand out to guests at stops along the tour.

But no one was interested.

"We cancelled the Miami, SF, Boston, Las Vegas, Chicago

and DC dates due to low ticket sales—we do not want to communicate this, but wanted to advise you on this to create messaging around—please let us know your thoughts," Margolin wrote Fyre's reps at 42West. "We postponed, the NYC and LA dates to create a better experience for attendees (we were developing a partnership with 1 Oak for their 10 year anniversary, but the branding opportunity didn't make sense, so moving dates will allow us to really, really create a dedicated and amazing experience for all)."

"We would like to call each person and advise them that the show has been canceled for those respective cities and invite them to the LA or NY shows. We feel via phone is better than putting anything in writing," 42West advised. "Also, a thought: if there is further pushback on the NY-specific event as to why, you can use the storm as a reason to postpone. It won't work for all cities, but at least NY."

The whole thing was abruptly canceled, first in every city but New York and LA, and then there too, all using the same convoluted language the team would later use to cancel the Fyre Festival.

"Due to circumstances beyond our control, we have to postpone the event to a date in the very near future. Your ticket will most certainly be honored for the new date, or alternatively, we can refund you for the ticket purchased."

That same day he pitched the ill-fated Fyre Tour, McFarland also ordered the Fyre team to drop the prices of the yacht packages they were selling online. A week before the festival, realizing they couldn't fulfill any yacht orders, the team decided to ax them and refund people. McFarland, who had been ignoring the thread, suddenly emailed back in a panic asking why.

Coffie says that was the same story behind the extravagant villas McFarland had advertised on the Fyre Festival website.

"They were literally just rendering someone's mind. The whole thing. Like the villa, the big, big villa, apparently they did it as a joke to see if people would pay for it," she said. "Never existed. And then people did pay for it, so they kept it. And they laughed about it."

Instead, records show, McFarland spent around $42,000 at IKEA a week before the festival, which accounted for most of the furniture and mattresses, much of it still in boxes, that festivalgoers encountered in the Bahamas.

The truth was McFarland and the Fyre team weren't interested in creating experiences. They just wanted to see what they could get people to pay for. The people buying tickets didn't care about the musical acts—the fact that there were none was testament alone. Their ticket holders cared about the photos and how their vacation was going to look to other people following them online. And Fyre was ready to cash in on that.

"Our 'value add' is priceless, ie getting access to a party at a private house with all the celebs ppl go crazy for," Carola Jain noted in late January. "Have to look at what motivates buyers of these luxury experiences, don't think its [sic] privacy, its [sic] probably more wanting to be in the mix as a big shot so access to very exclusive experiences is key (and hard to quantify)."

At the office, the expenses were mounting exponentially. In addition to all the monthly agency fees, artist payments, and production invoices Fyre was now paying out, Fyre Media's team in New York had moved from a WeWork to a flashy $30,000-per-month, three-story office space on Lispenard Street in Tribeca.

"They had an office in Tribeca that they paid a ton of money for. They didn't care enough to put furniture in the office. So people are working on borrowed furniture, looking like they are squatting. They paid a company to source the furniture. They did all the work, and then they didn't buy any furniture. They didn't have the money," Coffie said. "They gave it all to Kendall Jenner, I'm sure."

"No furniture or anything, but like three stories of prime Tribeca. I'd go there and meet with Ja and all his entourage, and there's like ten people there, but nobody's working in the whole place," said the former publicist. "This place was literally a big mezzanine, overlooking the main floor and another floor below and boardrooms and marble bathrooms everywhere. I mean, really just blinged out, with no furniture and no people working, except in the boardroom. And they said, 'Yeah, we're going to put on this festival.' It was really kind of the blind leading the blind."

If there was ever a time they could have and should have turned back, it was in early February, when almost every outside contractor—and in particular, the beleaguered Tablelist staff bearing the brunt of the public dissatisfaction—was starting to freak out.

"I mean, I kept urging them. I work on big projects. I never worked on a project that big, but just like a small project, that's how much work it takes, you know? I wanted to introduce them to the people who put on Art Basel. They're right in Miami, and they could have actually implemented the infrastructure for this," the publicist said. "But they were just, like, oblivious and traveling back and forth to the island. It was just crazy."

"Ja Rule," Cal Wells said, "who's not known for his financial acumen and a failed tech entrepreneur, can't throw a music festival together in nine months if it was on dry land in the middle of Ohio, much less the logistical nightmare of flying in aircraft, dealing with foreign governments, passports, permitting, insurance. All of this stuff just isn't done, right?"

Internally, Fyre employees were worried too. Emails had been pouring in to Tablelist, the company McFarland had contracted to handle their ticket sales, in a deal he'd strong-armed to his advantage. Now if the festival failed, Tablelist would be on the hook for those ticket refunds. And they were running out of excuses for the angry Fyre ticket holders.

"We're so sorry for the extreme delay. Due to technical issues, we were not receiving emails to the concierge@fyrefestival.com email and had redirected everything," Tablelist responded to one angry email. "The flight profile will be sent out in the next couple of days (if not tomorrow), and more information will follow."

After hearing about what had been happening, Jain urged the team not to respond.

"I think we should stall them for now and go silent for a few days and not ask people to provide more information, as I think it will reflect negatively on the brand if we 'string them along,'" she wrote in a February 4, 2017, email. "Thinking Madoff, etc. The pretending everything is normal strategy makes people really question the honesty of the individuals behind it so the more we ask people to fill out questionnaires and tell us when they want to fly to the island, etc., the more ppl are going to 'time track' and say they were misled. Just my POV. Don't think we can go from 'send us your preferred time of travel by jet' to 'we can't make it happen within 24 hours.' I think a bit of dark time in between is better—i.e. stay tuned and we are going to provide more info."

Though Jain would later file her own lawsuit against Fyre[208] amid a storm of bad press, internal emails and employee interviews show she had been involved on a granular level.

Coffie says that however much Jain did know, she was still bombarded with false status reports from the Fyre team. "Like, 'Everything's going good.' I remember seeing plans of infrastructure they were building. There's clearly no infrastructure! It never happened," Coffie said. "They were like, 'Yeah, they're breaking ground today.' No ground was broken."

On February 4, however, Jain knew enough to email McFarland advising he call the whole thing off or at least move it to Miami.

"Dear Fyrestarters," Jain drafted. "Unforeseeable circumstances are preventing us from creating the experience that we have envisioned for everyone. We strive to exceed your expectations and had to take the hard decision to postpone the Fyre Cay venue. We don't want to let down our community of Fyrestarters that has formed over the past months and are moving the party to Miami. We have confirmed an amazing lineup (see below) and are taking over xx space and bringing the island mojo to Miami. Everyone who has purchased a ticket will receive a complimentary VIP upgrade with full access to food, vip [sic] lounge areas etc…"

Jain's email also included detailed financial notes for McFarland.

Later that week, McFarland missed a payroll altogether.

At the same time, multiple employees recall, McFarland's parents were more clued in than the average entrepreneur's. Though it's never been reported before, sources say his mother and father were on the island the night everything imploded, enjoying a preshow investor dinner before things fell apart. And that wasn't even their first sign that things were going very badly at their son's company.

"They were there [in March] and they were like, riding around, and his mom and dad and his uncle, and like they acted like we were like peasants," producer Tiffani Harris recalls of her month on the island. "Everyone did. They just acted like…they wouldn't really talk to us. I introduced myself because they were with us all the time, like on site visits and stuff. His parents knew, yeah. It was very strange."

On February 21, Tablelist—which would ultimately get left on the hook for $3.5 million, forcing layoffs of about 40 percent of its staff—asked in a roundabout way if McFarland was running a scam.

The Tablelist team had reached "a point where we are unable to successfully do our job until we have more information to provide to guests. 'Apologies for the delay,' 'thanks for your patience,' and 'you will have info soon' is no longer an acceptable response," founder and CEO Julian Jung wrote. "We have to fend off angry guests all day, through the different channels we are managing until we have more details for them. People are threatening legal action, calling this a scam/fraud, asking for refunds, and we have no justified response to this."

Attached to the email, Jung provided examples of the kinds of messages he'd been fielding approximately "50-100" of per day.

The last one came from a friend of Jung's.

"It's getting to the point where I am risking my own credibility as well as Tablelist's," Jung concluded. "I know my team is really reaching their breaking point and we are doing our best to keep people at bay. I'll look to hear from you later today or tomorrow. Let me know if there is anything else that I can do to help. I am confident you'll make this happen as originally planned."

McFarland replied blithely, "We are going to hell and back to make this the best experience ever. I got you. This is going to be put us [sic] on the next level. We will have hard details asap. In the meantime, for people unhappy, let's refund anyone who wants. Let me know if we need funds for them.

We will come out with a bang with more detailed info asap. Back to you by tomorrow am."

But he never got back to Jung. And internally, McFarland kept pushing for more attendees to come, not fewer, even as it became clear there would not be any place to house them.

"A month in advance you know that you're going to have mattresses lying on the sand. That's not like a day-of thing. You knew you didn't have those tents. Well, actually, they did know they didn't have those tents. Because I know they were rendered, and I said to them, 'Those don't exist,'" Coffie said. "I actually found a vendor in Vegas who could create them, and they said, 'Too expensive.' Same thing happened with the caterer. They got the quote, said too expensive; wouldn't pay for it."

"We should say that all accommodations are tents btw. kenneth pointed that out to me," Jain finally realized at the end of January.

"I feel unbelievably uncomfortable about this, my reputation is seriously on the line here—and I feel like we are being quite dishonest in our marketing of the festival," Brown, the former Kanye West creative director, wrote in a February 3 email. "Especially if we are having conversations about throwing blow up mattresses on the floor."

Things were in a dire place, and with two months to go and still nowhere to throw a festival, the Fyre organizers turned at last to the Bahamian government for help and set their sights on the Roker Point Estates, the gravel pit located next to a Sandals resort.

"Billy said that they had met the governor of the island, and he needed…like his term was ending. And he wanted to give everybody in his family a job. And that's kind of who hooked this whole thing up," said the publicist.

Not that the Fyre team was honest with those officials either. In a pitch deck presented to government officials and Bahamian landowners, Fyre responded, with a slideshow, to the age-old question that nobody asked: "What if together, we introduce thousands of high–net worth millennials to the Exuma Islands?"

"Billy is not very smart," explained Harris. "When he talks, he doesn't ever say anything."

When Fyre contractors tried to bring him back down to Earth, "It was one of those like, 'You guys should smile more and have better attitudes about everything.' And everyone was like, 'We have great attitudes, we're just letting you know the reality of this that it's not going to happen,'" said another female producer who was also hired in the same wave as Tiffani Harris.

Going with the gravel pit meant the festival would be less likely to anger the wealthy neighbors, who were paying close attention at that point. One of them, a Floridian contractor who owns land in the Exumas, had been following their attempted land buy with a sharp eye. He found out in February the deal had fallen through amid a pile of broken promises from the Fyre team.

"You have to understand the Exumas are… They call them the family islands. The Exumas, these islands, the chain of 365, except for Great Exuma, aren't set up for a festival. They were promoting ten thousand people, they were promoting luxury tents and houses. When I looked at the renderings and I saw what they were trying to do, knowing the festival was five months away at that point, I felt it was a scam," the Bahamian landowner said. "There was just no way, there's no power on that island, there's no water, there's a small airport that you can get a private jet on next to it, but the fact that they had sold it based on renderings for that particular island, it was false. It wasn't going to happen."

Plus, no one in the area wanted "five, ten thousands kids coming in, doing ecstasy, and trashing the Exumas. It's a national park."

"The people in the Exumas, where they wanted to host this, they don't want people there. I mean, Johnny Depp's our neighbor, okay?" he said. "There's a reason, forgive my French, but there's a reason he calls his island Fuck You Island."

But the problem would eventually solve itself. Out of time and money, McFarland had abandoned the island idea—conveniently neglecting to inform anyone outside the core team—and set about getting a venue for free by convincing the owners of the Roker Point Estates that Fyre's audience "comprised... global professionals between the ages of 25 and 45, with an average annual income in excess of 200,000 USD.

"In addition," he added, "we have confirmed the presence of UHNW [ultrahigh net worth] individuals of great interest to Roker Point Estates."

In exchange for the free land rental, McFarland promised to "furnish thousands of guests for both weekends of the festival, creating a unique opportunity for Roker Point Estates to capture a relevant demographic who might be interested in purchasing land on Great Exuma or directly know qualified purchasers" and to "make commercially reasonable efforts to introduce the Roker Point Estates to Snapchat who will be running a global story during the festival. If Roker Point Estates chooses to buy media on Snapchat, they may expect millions of impressions." McFarland did, at least, deliver on that last promise.

Still, somehow, McFarland had a deal. Around the same time, Brown resigned abruptly from the festival, sending along with his termination an invoice for $68,106 for services rendered by his company, Institute.

By March 14, when newly hired talent producer Chloe Gordon visited the site for the first time, there was still nothing to show. "This was not a model-filled private cay that was owned by Pablo Escobar. This was a development lot covered in gravel with a few tractors scattered around. There was not enough space to build all the tents and green rooms they would need. There was not a long, beautiful beach populated by swimming pigs. There were, however, a lot of sand flies that left me looking like I had smallpox," she observed in *New York* magazine's The Cut a few weeks later. She had been hired to join an eleven-person production team and assumed there would be something to show with only six weeks to go.

"Nothing had been done. Festival vendors weren't in place, no stage had been rented, transportation had not been arranged. Frankly, we were standing on an empty gravel pit, and no one had any idea how we were going to build a festival village from scratch."

About the only thing they did have, Gordon observed, was an alcohol sponsor. And even that had been fraudulently obtained, if their internal recaps of the Casamigos deal were any indication.

About two weeks before the festival and right before the shipping ports closed for the rest of the month, they got a few shipping containers filled with Amazon Prime boxes full of sheets, sleeping bags, and extra tents onto the site. As it turned out, the tents they set up trapped so much heat that they were essentially uninhabitable during the day—not that there was anywhere else to take shelter from the beating sun.

On Thursday, April 27—the day before the festival was officially supposed to kick off—McFarland started quietly warning people not to come to the island. First he delayed, telling one well-known agent that things on the island "weren't quite ready," and offering to pay his airline change fees if he'd switch his flight to the following weekend. The Fyre team eighty-sixed another reporter outright, telling her that her ticket to the island had been canceled because the site wasn't ready and they didn't feel comfortable with her seeing it. Most of the VIPs, like Bella Hadid and IMG model Shanina Shaik (who had posted a now-deleted video of herself and several other models with McFarland pouring Champagne aboard a private jet), stayed in Miami instead. Other influencers who were flown to the festival for free in exchange for social media promotions were housed on a cruise ship offshore, away from all the chaos.

"They called all the A-list names and the modeling agencies and told them not to come," Page Six reported. "They were just like, 'Oh, come next weekend when all the kinks have been worked out.' This was before the chaos even started."[209]

On Thursday night, as hundreds of people who had arrived at the site as planned were trying to find shelter from hordes of sand fleas and looters rummaging through unsecured tents, Shaik told someone at Miami's Ora Nightclub how "relieved" she felt to be in the club's VIP section instead.

McFarland and his team weren't as concerned about the people who actually bought tickets or the vendors who are still waiting on payment for their services. The models would be among the only people who got paid in full for their work on the project—as clear an example of McFarland's priorities as the fact that he spent the final hours of Thursday night partying on a yacht and filing last-minute cease-and-desist letters to people sounding the alarm while festivalgoers were chained inside an airport overnight without access to food or water. (The next morning, revelers on his yacht were told to be quiet inside the main cabin because he was rehearsing his statement, which he would repeat almost verbatim to both myself and a *Rolling Stone* reporter.)

The date had finally arrived and nothing had been done. They didn't even have the flights in place to get all the ticket holders to the island, where there weren't enough tents waiting even for the people who did arrive. And yet, they started flying people over, hoping maybe they'd get away with it, somehow.

That's when the rain started to pour down, destroying what precious little they had managed to set up.

Weinstein remembers thinking that at least the flights would be delayed thanks to the rain.

The first plane landed half an hour early.

By the next morning, the Fyre Festival would be a national punch line. But that Thursday evening, it was still an unfolding disaster. Thousands of ticket holders were loaded on school buses and shuttled to a nearby beach hut. A young blonde woman in a tiny bathing suit DJed on the porch, and Fyre staffers kept the party going all day, pouring bottles of rosé and Casamigos tequila directly into people's mouths. Later that night, one of the bottle girls would end up curled up in a fetal position, sobbing, in the front seat of a car, but at that early point the free alcohol was still soothing the sting of a few troubling details—the fact that no one could access their luggage, for one thing, or the complete lack of food beyond cocktail garnishes.

But despite the glaring inconsistencies between what Fyre had promised and what it ended up delivering, it ultimately wouldn't have mattered much if anyone had caught wind in advance and demanded for a refund. The organizers were only reachable by email, and they had stopped responding months before, outsourcing the job to Tablelist, whose employees were just as in the dark as the ticket holders. The festival's official Instagram page was kept current, but the FuckJerry team manning it refused to respond to concerned commenters and instead spent their time deleting the most critical public comments.

"Can someone confirm the status of the festival? Supposed to be flying out in the morning but photos and updates from people there now say it is unsafe and not at all what was advertised. How can we guarantee the status and guarantee refunds?" one woman asked by direct message on Instagram the day everything imploded. She noticed the message was quickly marked as Read, meaning a real live person had viewed the message. But no response followed.

"YOUR READ RECEIPTS ARE ON," she messaged back. Whoever was reading her texts sent a heart emoji in return but declined to respond again.

One reason why no one was responding was because most of the company's employees were on the island in crisis mode, desperately trying to direct Bahamian employees in an effort to cobble together enough beds for the hundreds of ticket holders who had managed to make it to the island. Those unfortunate travelers would be the only ones to make it: after dozens of canceled flights, the government finally shut the whole thing down late Thursday night, disallowing any more planes to land and later padlocking the site shut, citing customs fraud. The 130-odd Bahamian employees who had assembled the bare-bones site over the span of about two weeks never got paid. One carpenter's electricity and water would later be turned off when the festival stiffed him.

But no one on the ground knew that yet.

They were, however, starting to figure out the beach party was just a distraction. As the ticket holders spent the day drinking copiously on empty stomachs, the sparse festival staff was at the gravel pit, frantically assembling IKEA furniture and lobbing wet mattresses into the tents, which were infested with bugs and too hot to stay in when the sun was out. With no secure areas, they had thrown all the designer suitcases collected from the airport into a large shipping container attached to a truck cab.

Now, thousands of drunk, sunburned twenty-somethings wanted their belongings and a place to lie down. They had paid thousands of dollars for this. With no clue what was going on, the attendees congregated around McFarland, who was standing on a table holding a conch shell. People gathered around him described the scene as ripped from the pages of *Lord of the Flies* or *The Hunger Games* but with better luggage. Eventually McFarland gave up trying to assign lodging—he asked one woman, sarcastically, "Okay, who's the next person to ask me the same question for the hundredth time?" and eventually told people to go take what they could grab, before he melted away into the night. As the situation escalated and reporters started calling, he joined his friends on a nearby yacht where they could party in peace. Meanwhile, ticket holders were left to rummage for their belongings in haphazard piles of suitcases, which had been dumped in the dirt, using their cell-phone flashlights because there was no other light.

The ticket holders weren't the only ones starting to freak out. Investors had poured millions of dollars into the project. Employees at both of McFarland's companies, who had been getting paid in wire transfers and cash since payroll abruptly stopped in October, had spent months working on the project. They had warned McFarland and Margolin that it wasn't possible to provide what they were advertising. The vendors had warned McFarland and his team too. So had all three production teams who had worked on the event before they were fired or quit. So did the guy who they'd contacted to provide showers.

Just about everyone involved had warned them.

They just didn't care.

"Let's just do it and be legends, man," Margolin had said when a member of the production team urged him to postpone a year.

He had predicted the outcome—just not in the way he'd hoped.

A number of people I spoke to at both Fyre and Magnises saw the writing on the wall. But McFarland had pulled money out of nowhere before to save the day, so they believed him when he told his teams that Comcast had invested millions of dollars. As a result, many of them kept working for the company, even after the festival had failed, because they believed there was money to cover their paychecks. (As we know now, there wasn't, and not only did McFarland decline to pay them, he also refused to fire anyone, which would have enabled them to apply for unemployment benefits. This too was intentional, because he had also declined to pay unemployment insurance. Several employees also complained they had no pay stubs to prove they had ever worked for the company.)

It wasn't just Tablelist and McFarland's own team that got screwed in the fallout. A group of National Event Services (NES) medics who had been hired to work the event almost walked off the job when they saw the bug-infested, bloodstained mattresses they were expected to sleep on. They ultimately stuck around anyway "in response to obvious safety and health concerns for the people trapped on the island, which left NES exposed to serving distressed patrons for an unprepared festival site," but filed a lawsuit for damages just a week later.[210]

The writing was on the wall, and as everything fell apart, on April 25, Jain floated hiring Richard Rubenstein's crisis-management firm.

"Hey, guys, we are getting a massive number of refund

requests and potential charge-backs. Can we please initiate a wire first thing in the am so that we can refund these people? We are going to go through our reserves in a day," Julian from Tablelist begged in an email.

On April 27, Jain started offering options in the company to anyone who could help them redeem the mess.

And at 2:00 a.m. on April 28, McFarland had one of the whistleblowers served with a cease and desist. Then he started planning how he was going to spin things, eventually settling on offering his victims free tickets to the next year's Fyre Festival if they'd agree to wait on a refund.

Not a single musical act or influencer ever set foot on the island. And despite McFarland's confident claims that planning was already underway for the 2018 festival, none of them ever would.

6

On the Internet No One Knows You're a Fraud

By a funny twist of fate, the "influencer" Caroline Calloway went viral for her "scam" creativity workshops right around the same time that I was at the influencer Danielle Bernstein's house talking about the festival on her now-deleted podcast. I had never heard of her before, but once the headlines referring to Calloway as a one-woman Fyre Festival began landing in my Google alerts on a weekly basis, it became impossible to ignore.

From what I could tell, though, it wasn't really Calloway who went viral, but rather a Twitter thread about her that had been compiled by a journalist named Kayleigh Donaldson.

"That Instagram influencer I occasionally check in on because she's The Worst is now charging $165 for a 4 hour 'seminar' on how to be yourself," Donaldson wrote in the first tweet of what would become a month-long thread.[211]

It documented Calloway's Fyre Festival–esque plans to conduct seminars across the United States and Europe at which she promised she would cook for her guests and honor them with elaborate gift bags. Perhaps most whimsically, she also promised to give up her secret to creating the perfect flower crown.

Calloway's path to internet fame and infamy was an interesting one, in that it seemed wholly of her time. She was, at the time, a twenty-something social media influencer who had gained a large audience on Instagram by documenting her life as an American in Cambridge, a narrative culled from YA stories like *Harry Potter* and *The Princess Diaries* that read as equally fictional. Still, her sizable social media following landed her, in quick succession, international media coverage, a celebrity lit agent, and a reported $500,000 book deal about her charmed life abroad.

Suddenly, online at least, she was a literary star. But in reality, she was just playing one on TV. Calloway was someone who was clearly determined to become famous, but her goals didn't appear to extend all that far beyond her follower count. After all that buildup, after all those *Daily Mail* headlines, Calloway never actually wrote the book, although she did manage to spend all the advance money.

So by the time her creativity workshops rolled around a year after the deal had collapsed, it seemed clear that the real point of the tour was to sell her 800,000-odd followers the chance to meet her in real life and take a photo that might suggest, if posted to Instagram, some sort of friendship. At that point, Calloway had never held a real job or even published a real piece of writing. Who could blame her for trying to cash in on her fame? But such an outright cash grab would be "off-brand" for a woman who built a fan base writing from the perspective of a wealthy insider in a rarefied world. And, anyway, her previous efforts to sell $2,500 sponsored Instagram posts[212] and $10,000 appearances hadn't gained any apparent traction with advertisers.[213] So she dressed the meet-and-greets up as traveling writing workshops, and sprinkled them with extras like Billy McFarland in an MFA program, offering her followers additional perks like personalized journals with handwritten notes inside, a "home-cooked salad," and a "portable DIY wildflower garden to take home" (influencer-speak for a bouquet of flowers in a mason jar) in exchange for the $165 tickets.

Just as McFarland had poured all his time into marketing, leaving him no time to actually plan and execute a large-scale event, Calloway had left herself very little time to plan her global tour and appeared to be relying on ticket sales to provide enough capital for her to pay for the next stop. So she started subtracting perks. The goody bags were the first to go—there just wasn't enough time, for example, for her to read through the goals she had asked every ticket holder to email to her, much less for her to write the personal notes she'd promised back inside the commemorative journals.

Worse, Donaldson soon realized, despite selling her followers tickets, Calloway hadn't even bothered to secure the venues necessary to host them. She had reached the gravel construction pit phase of the Fyre Festival of self-improvement seminars. "Important update: Said 'influencer' just put down a deposit on a venue for her 'seminar' and is conveniently upping the number of available spots for attendees. Methinks she just realized how pricey her scam was going to be and is now trying to widen those profit margins," Donaldson continued on Twitter, estimating that Calloway had netted a gross profit of at least $15,000 with her ticket sales—a nice chunk of change, but nowhere near enough to stage the elaborate event she'd conjured up in her Instagram Stories.[214] She had even been asking her followers if they would consider bringing their own food in exchange for her agreeing to spend an extra thirty minutes with them.[215]

It was an amusing saga to be sure, but Donaldson's thread didn't go mega-viral until mid-January, when she documented Calloway's reaction to the delivery of a pallet of twelve hundred mason jars. The crates completely filled the influencer's cramped studio apartment and appeared to imbue her with a burst of capitalistic fervor.

"I AM GOING TO REARRANGE SOME FURNITURE AND LIVE IN ~THIS HALF~ OF MY APARTMENT BECAUSE IT TURNS OUT EVERYTHING COSTS MONEY AND EVEN THOUGH THE TOUR TICKETS ARE $165 EACH THEY HONESTLY SHOULD HAVE BEEN MORE EXPENSIVE BECAUSE THE STUFF I GOT YOU IS REALLY NICE AND I'M WORKING EVERY HOUR OF THE DAY ~PLUSSSS I THINK THE THINGS I HAVE TO TEACH ARE REALLY VALUABLE~ SO YEAH. I REALLY UNDERSOLD MY TIME. NEVER AGAIN!!!! NEXT TOUR, TICKET PRICES ARE GOING UP. WAY UP. I WILL LEAVE TICKET PRICES AS THEY ARE ~~FOR THIS TOUR~~, BUT IF YOU WANT TO COME TO THIS TOUR... COME. I AM NEVER DOING AN EVENT FOR THIS CHEAP AGAIN," Calloway wrote.[216]

As it turned out, ticket prices were the least of her problems. As Donaldson noted, the first out-of-town event was only a week away, and Calloway still hadn't booked a venue for it.

That same week, citing an *overwhelming demand* from her out-of-state fans to force them to travel to her by holding all the events in New York City, Calloway blamed her "staff" for the decision to cancel and refund the Philadelphia, Boston, Portland, and Denver events, explaining she would lose money if she continued. But she assured her followers in DC,

LA, San Fran, Atlanta, Chicago, Dallas, Austin, Charlotte, London, and the greater European area, however, that the tour was still on, despite the already-obvious issues.

I'll cut to the chase. After all that hype, Calloway ultimately held just two workshops on that tour: the one in the New York loft, and one in DC.

It was a funny, if lopsided, comparison between Calloway's aborted tour and the Fyre Festival. Despite Calloway's large following, she hadn't sold all that many tickets in the grand scheme of things, perhaps because, as an audit conducted at the time showed, her followers were at least 43 percent bots. But in what would later become a clear pattern, Calloway had charged her social media fans for an event on which she had overpromised and underdelivered.

"I went to her workshop and was HIGHLY disappointed. No notes, no flower crowns, only about 1.5 hours (max) of actual 'teaching,' if you can even call it that," one attendee told Donaldson.[217]

Calloway, for her part, blamed Donaldson's thread for her poor showing. At one point, she actually admitted, "I was overconfident in believing that I had something to offer people that was worth $165 dollars, and this experience has been incredibly humbling." But then the next day, she blocked Donaldson on social media and "un-canceled the tour."

Though Calloway had refunded her ticket holders, per the terms of Eventbrite's service, she may still yet have made a profit. In a final email, she sent out a PayPal link requesting ticket holders "put your hand on your heart and decide what the experience I created and the time we spent together was worth to you. Maybe your full ticket price; maybe less; maybe nothing at all." And that secret to flower crowns she promised? She finally revealed it on her Instagram, free of charge: "There is no secret."

It wasn't the first time Calloway had leveraged her social media presence into payments for services she had no reasonable expectation of performing, as her book deal clearly demonstrated. Calloway herself has admitted she scammed her way into the book deal the old-fashioned way: by creating a fake online person. To do that, she hired a college friend named Natalie Beach to ghostwrite her whimsical Instagram captions and subsequent book proposal. And to get it sold to a publisher, she lied her way into the office of the literary agent and head of publishing at UTA, Byrd Leavell, and convinced him to sign her based on her fake following, according to Leavell.

(In a phone interview in early 2020, Leavell told me, "I never would have worked with her for a minute if I knew she had bought followers.")

"I think Caroline is a victim of growing up steeped in that culture of it's more important what you appear to be than what you actually are. Who you are is one thing, but who you are on Instagram is how most people are going to know you," explained Natalia Antonova, an internet security expert and former Bellingcat editor, who's well-versed in the infamous personas who rise up to the level of what's pejoratively referred to as Twitter's main character of the day. "I think it's a convergence of all of those things. For the same reason that Billy McFarland threw the Fyre Festival and the same reason that people bought the tickets to it. It's two sides of the same coin."

But the funny thing about Calloway is that unlike McFarland, she's never really faced a reckoning for any of it. She often reminds people that although her name is associated with Fyre Festival and Delvey, the Soho grifter, she's never actually been arrested for anything. Nor is it clear that Calloway has committed any prosecutable criminal offense.

"I think that we have to differentiate between grifter and scammer," Antonova said. "As long as they introduce enough vagueness into their statements they can also get away with it on a legal basis."

It reminds me a bit of a tweet that's been going around since 2016:

"Well, I'd like to see ol Donny Trump wriggle his way out of THIS jam!

★Trump wriggles his way out of the jam easily.

Ah! Well. Nevertheless."

Donaldson seems inclined to agree. "The tricky thing with writing about Calloway has always been that it's nigh on impossible to create a comprehensive account of a serial liar whose main mode of communication is Instagram Stories," Donaldson told me.

I had reached out to her for guidance after feeling a bit dizzy trying to navigate Calloway's curated online legend. She responded almost immediately, though not in the way I'd hoped. That being said, I understood where she was coming from.

"I must admit that I am hesitant to wade back into the murky waters of all things Caroline Calloway. Aside from the immense mental and emotional distress the entire workshop thread led to alongside being targeted directly by Calloway, I've been trying to ensure that my career isn't wholly defined by this one incident," Donaldson replied. "It's also tricky territory because Calloway herself is a master manipulator who seems to be enjoying a new wave of pseudoironic 'scammer queen' celebration by people who call her ineptitude and active targeting of women 'performance art.'"

Calloway's preternatural ability to cull the "fame" from infamy is basically her entire source of income: in the months leading up to this book, I watched her announce at least five times that she was planning to discontinue a series of Matisse knockoffs she had been selling over Instagram, only to watch her launch sale after sale post-retirement. She's since sold a second book, which she also hasn't finished, and then spent the last year writing Instagram captions explaining why it's still not done.

Her mode of communication and penchant for blocking critics—I myself have never directly communicated with Calloway but am blocked on every platform nonetheless—may make her hard to track, but people are still trying. There exists, on the message boards of Reddit and in small clusters across the United States, a loosely aligned group, composed primarily of women, whose mission is to expose Calloway, no matter how small the transgression.

"I really think the reason that she has so many people following along is because of the lack of repercussions. I think that there are so many people that want to believe that if you act in the way that she acts, you are going to have consequences," explained one woman, who is well-known in the "snark" community for her parody posts under the handle tcurb. tcurb, who is twenty-six and works in the health and wellness industry, agreed to speak by phone but requested anonymity because, "I'm just a normal person."

"She calls her Instagram captions her art, which is objectively just dumb when you think about the amount of people writing Instagram. Like, am I a writer? I have an Instagram and I write captions. Does that make me a writer? Absolutely not," tcurb said. "So it's like, she sees the world through her lens, and I think a lot of people just buy into that, but she absolutely hasn't written anything. This is her second chance to prove everybody wrong and write a book and where is it? You know? It doesn't exist, and I would be surprised if it ever exists."

To bolster the point, tcurb pointed to Calloway's Patreon account, a revenue stream she had set up in August 2019, promising exclusive access to her "close friends" content on Instagram, a setting that allows users to post to a specific group of people.

"For $2 a month, I'll add you to my Close Friends list on ig and I'll create exclusive content for you everyday [sic]," Calloway wrote.[218]

But the content never came. According to watchdog accounts on Instagram, she rarely posted, even though she collected money each month for it, a situation that happens to be something Patreon expressly provides for. According to the site, "We understand that some months you get busy and might not be able to make a post. Or maybe you're taking a well-deserved vacation and don't want to charge your patrons while you're away. When this happens, you can choose to pause your creator page for one month."

But Calloway opted not to pause the charges to her followers accounts for some reason, though tcurb says she can guess why.

"I think that the best example of that is her Patreon because you can really see how little intention or follow-through she has on her Close Friends account. If it was really just unintentional, then she could absolutely be like, 'Hey, I'm not posting this month. Everybody gets refunded.' But she doesn't do that," tcurb said. "As far as I know, I don't think she has ever, out of her own way, like gone and refunded people for a month where she's missed content, and there's been more months where she hasn't been seen with her Close Friends than she has. At this point, I think she's making over a thousand dollars a month on it, and she's not refunding people... At this point, there's absolutely no excuse for not knowing about herself that she shouldn't sell something before it's even made."

tcurb says that Calloway sometimes seems to have so many scams running concurrently that it can be hard for even her most dedicated detractors to keep up. "I also do think that she has so much content and so much of it is nonsense that it probably would be really hard to do a deep dive on her because I think she intentionally just keeps churning crap out, and it's hard to find those things," tcurb said. "But they are there, and I just think people hadn't really taken the time to dig those up, but all of it is literally available on her Instagram, and if you go back and look at it chronologically, you're like, 'Oh, my god, what is happening?'"

She's not wrong—every time I've reached out to Calloway's reps for clarification, they inevitably issue me a generic directive to "look at her Instagram page," even though they know I've been specifically blocked from viewing it.

"You go to her Instagram page and you're like, 'What is reality? What is the real world?' And then you go on Reddit, you're like, 'Okay, I'm not crazy. She's crazy. Other people see this too,' because she's created such an echo chamber with deleting comments and blocking people," tcurb told me.

tcurb is referring to the thousands of followers who trade sanity checks and compare intel on Calloway on a subreddit called SmolBeanSnark, an eight-thousand-odd-strong group with any number of additional lurkers, where updates on Calloway's activities have garnered tens of thousands of comments. The threads had originally started on another sub called BlogSnark, but grew so popular the group spun off onto its own page. (At the height of Calloway's fame, in the wake of a viral *New York* magazine exposé about her ghostwritten captions, the discussion even expanded into two dueling subreddits and an invite-only Discord thread. Things have since quieted down to the current iteration found today.)

The Reddit threads are, in a sense, the natural progression

of decades of internet celebrity discussion boards and Gawker comment threads that you can find with minimal searching around almost any person famous for being famous. (A number of people in the SmolBeanSnark sub told me they stumbled upon the threads after googling her name incredulously.) The Calloway page is, in form and function, almost indistinguishable from those that discuss Bravo's *Real Housewives*, which makes sense, since, to her fans on Reddit, Calloway is essentially the star of a reality show airing live on her Instagram Stories. (Not for nothing, Calloway's manager, Adam Krasner, also manages Bravo's Summer House reality star Hannah Berner.)

But it also seems to me that this kind of reflection on the lives of reality stars and influencers is also sort of human nature, and not something that's necessarily divided between the star and her audience. Bravo's *Real Housewives* subreddit boasts more than 110,000 members who convene each day to recap new content, including *Summer House*. But Berner, it turns out, is also getting paid to do the same thing, as one of the hosts of Bravo's *Chat Room*, a weekly thirty minute panel show that dissects the slate of reality-TV franchises currently airing on Bravo. If something airs and isn't recapped and then discussed below the recap in the comments, did it ever even happen?

I popped into the forum one day to try and understand the appeal. Why follow her exploits so closely? Was it entertainment, justice, or something else entirely.

I heard from people who said they had known her from college and were amused by how much her captions differed from their own experiences, people who said they knew "trust fund wannabes" just like Calloway, and people who had never met anyone like her at all, and found her whole schtick fascinating. Some had been following her for years, well before the book deal, while others had learned of her only a few months before in the wake of the viral *New York* magazine exposé. "I'm here for the drama," was one phrase that came up over and over, as were comparisons to reality television. Most people also clarified that they viewed the Reddit thread as entertainment.

All of the respondents seemed to agree, however, that the real value of the thread was far more personal: the reassurance that there were other people out there having the same reactions they were. One respondent, searching for an outlet for her negative reactions to Calloway's stories, said she found the thread after googling "Caroline Calloway Reddit" in frustration, while another poster jumped into the comments to share their old thesis paper on Goffman's theory on performance of self. At least two people clarified that they were less interested in Calloway's behavior than other people's reactions to it, and most of the respondents took it even further, citing their interest in ongoing discussions about privilege, white feminism, narcissistic behavior, influencer culture, and other societal ills.

A number of people also noted that observing Calloway's mistakes made them more determined to work harder in their own lives, a notion I can't deny occasionally crossed my mind whenever I panicked about my own ability to finish this book.

"It's interesting that scammers, the way they operate online is that their whole agenda is to push our buttons, to manipulate us a certain way, whether it's to give them money, or to enter a relationship with them or something else," explained Antonova. "I find that if you're suspicious about somebody, you have to kind of figure out which ones of my buttons are being pushed right now and with what intent? When people tell us what we want to hear we are excited and happy. And we don't want to shatter the illusion."

In Russia right now, for example, Antonova said, there's a big trend of scams related to animal shelters.

"Because who doesn't want to save a cute puppy or a cute kitten? So people create these fake animal shelters, sites, and profiles. There was a case on a Facebook profile for an animal shelter that basically didn't exist, and the person just used some stolen pictures of animals, but had managed to rake in quite a bit of money in donations, saying 'Come save these little Pomeranians.' Or, 'Come save this German Shepherd, he's going to be put to sleep,'" she said.

Antonova says she's also seen a recent proliferation of military scams that she believes are particularly potent to older, lonely people feeling isolated by the pandemic.

"Technology is a wonderful tool, but technology can also blunt our instincts and it can create these situations where we're not able to process information correctly. There's a mirage, and we fall for the mirage because we want to feel better. You have these vultures who prey on people's sympathies and prey on people's desires. And again, these people have a profile and a demographic that they appeal to," she continued. "In the case of the Fyre Festival, for example, you're preying on people's desire for fun. You're preying on people's love of influencers and glamor and they want to be part of that excitement. They want to be part of that world. And so you create this fantasy that caters to that, basically."

Which makes sense. Like McFarland, Calloway is skilled at spinning a fantasy. And it did seem to me that a lot of people in the Reddit sub were just looking for a friend to elbow about a niche celebrity to say, "Hey, you seeing this shit?" In fact, a few of them have even started doing so in real life.

Rowan Castelhano was certainly feeling that way when she started the "No Close Friends" Instagram account, designed to track how often Calloway was actually providing her monthly content. "Every time recently she's done something, people are like, 'Oh, she's just so naive,'" Castelhano told me. "Well, no. If you look there's clearly a pattern."

Castelhano, who left home at sixteen and has supported herself ever since, says she started following Calloway after the Donaldson thread and initially thought she was just clueless and funny. "But once I started learning more about her, I was like, 'Oh, she's just not a good person.' And I think that it's important to, I wouldn't say hold people accountable necessarily, but just be like, 'Hey, this information deserves to be out there,'" Castelhano said.

What Castelhano didn't anticipate was finding a community in Washington, DC, of other young women from the Calloway Reddit thread. One of the main rules of the sub bans having direct contact with Calloway, but she and her fellow snarkers have found creative ways to get the full experience anyway. At one meetup, Castelhano said, they had dinner at a Chinese restaurant Calloway had posted about eating at following her dad's funeral.

"We have a WhatsApp group with ten or eleven people. We meet up, we had brunch a couple of times. We've had *Bachelorette* viewing parties. It's pretty awesome," Castelhano said. "I mean, that's people that I keep in contact with basically every day at this point."

Castelhano said the entertainment they derive from following Calloway comes from the gaps between her public and private personas. But she says she would draw the line at actually meeting Calloway.

"I think that it's hard for me to see in the media, the people that are critical of her written off as trolls or weird stock of people. Because I personally have never interacted with her. I wouldn't. I am actually very against breaking the fourth wall, so to speak, because I honestly don't think it's going to do any good," she said. "And generally it just makes you look like an asshole.

"I just want to see less white mediocrity being rewarded," she added.

That's how a twenty-two-year-old woman, who is also named Caroline, felt when her original artwork from Calloway—a Matisse knockoff—finally arrived, months late and in terrible condition. It changed her relationship with the influencer, and not in a positive way.

"Whatever I got is not what I was expecting. It's literally a piece of Michael's paper with the tag still on it," she said. "I kind of had sympathy for her, she seems kind of relatable, she has mental health problems. So, for a while I felt like I could kind of forgive her stuff. But then when I actually put my money into it and that was the result of what I got, I was like, I can't support this anymore because I know there's other people like me who just aren't watching ironically and aren't spending their money because they are fine getting a shit product."

Ironic or not, however, she is still watching Calloway's content.

"I mean, there's nothing else for me to do except watch Instagram, and even in my real life, I work at Starbucks, I'm 22. So, I go out with my friends and stuff, but we're all consuming Instagram all the time," she said. "And it was fascinating for me for a little while to watch these influencers. And then I guess it flipped on its head and it was fascinating for me to see all these people feel the complete opposite way."

Leavell said that's what happens when you're more concerned with who people think you are rather than who you actually are.

"Caroline manufactured an illusion of herself as an author,"

Leavell said. "And it became more important to keep the illusion up than actually being an author."

She's certainly gone out of her way to keep the illusion up. She claimed for years that the Flatiron Books deal was still on, even though the editor who commissioned the book had long since left the company, before posting a topless photograph of herself December 2020 announcing that she'd bought back the rights and was no longer under contract. For the last year, she's also been running a presale on her personal website for a book called *Scammer*, though whether or not that actually exists is similarly unclear.

Calloway first began selling preorders for *Scammer* in January 2020 with a promised publication date of either February or "Spring 2020." Despite her literally naming the book *Scammer*, the announcement got positive coverage at outlets like Buzzfeed, the Guardian, and Nylon. It sure felt like history repeating itself. So I reached out to Krasner, her manager, to ask, "Given Caroline's checkered history, how can purchasers of the preorder be sure the book *Scammer* will be completed and shipped as promised?" and, "Is there a hard publication date for *Scammer*? If so, what is it? If not, how will buyers know whether the book is coming or not?" In his response, Krasner declined to provide an unambiguous shipping date, but I noticed the copy on her website was almost immediately updated to express that the presale would close at the end of February and that the novel would be sent out for printing on April 1.

The entire time, she continued to solicit orders, and, as time went on, offered her followers enticements reminiscent of her failed tour, including personalized love notes, exclusive art prints, and branded baseball caps. During one week in February, she even claimed that presales would soon close forever. But the link remained active, even though the book seemed no closer to completion. On March 19, she claimed that the book had been completed, copy edited and sent to an independent printing press that had subsequently been shut down by the pandemic. (The press, run by Krasner's father, later confirmed in an email that, "The design of the cover (image and type) was created and production was stopped. The severity of the pandemic in NY, cuts in amount of work load, production work and work force hindered thus limited ability for 6 months. No production has been finalized since the manuscript was 'increasing' and I am waiting for final files for creating 'spine width' with direct correlation to page count." Krasner affirmed separately that Calloway had provided the press with a completed manuscript.)

Still, nothing seemed to make any sense. On March 31, I reached out again, noting that Calloway was still accepting presale orders with a ship date of April 1—despite Calloway repeatedly noting on social media that the book would not be shipping anytime soon. Her team responded that "the ship date was always tentative" and updated her website to reflect that after my inquiry.

The only things that seemed clear were that I would not be reading *Scammer* anytime soon, nor would I be able to get a satisfying reason why. Despite claiming separately in March, June, July, and August that the book was finished and set to ship by the end of the month, Calloway had also acknowledged in June that she would be taking a break from writing it to observe the Black Lives Matter movement and later, in August, announced she planned on completely rewriting it to better reflect the events of 2020.

Meanwhile, Calloway had confusingly begun selling access to what she promised would be a three-part essay called "I Am Caroline Calloway." Although no one asked, she promised that each part would be comprised of fifteen thousand words, using some text from the *Scammer* book she still hadn't written. And she said she would post each section on Tuesday at 8:00 a.m. for the next three weeks in a row.

It reminded me a bit of McFarland's desperate bid to launch a nationwide Fyre party tour to raise money for the slumping festival. Calloway's execution was also similar.

Despite the clear parameters she had set for herself, the first installment dropped hours late and contained only six thousand words. When I asked her reps what had happened, her attorney Anita Sharma told me that "Originally she thought it may be about a 15k word piece, but during the creative process and upon receiving feedback on her drafts from trusted advisers, she realized that she was able to edit her original piece down and convey what she wanted to in about 6k words."

It was a confounding response, but one I was willing to accept until I saw Calloway had posted a nude photograph on Twitter along with a caption reading, "I fucked up. I said Part One would be 15,000 words, but it's actually 6,000. I wrote it in a Word doc with a bunch of other notes and I must not have selected the text properly when I checked the word count. My bad! Please accept this uncensored nude along with my humble apology," she wrote.[219]

I asked Sharma in an email if she could explain the discrepancy. "There were a number of factors involved with the decreased word count. I would also point out that Caroline's Twitter account is a parody account which allows her some artistic license," she replied.

I was, to be completely honest, starting to feel as if I had absolutely no sense of reality.

Because we're so primed to look at influencers as someone we're friends with, it turns out their betrayals can cut a bit deeper than a celebrity we only get to see in character.

They can also create insecurities that might not have otherwise been there.

"I think, with these people who are very good at appearing that they are very successful and happy, and Photoshopped into beautiful, perfectly done hair and makeup and clothes, we automatically feel like that there's that pressure that we want to have the same type of happiness," said Lisa Moskovitz, a registered dietician and CEO of the New York Nutrition Group. "And we feel like the only way to do that is to either eat the way that they're eating, or wear the clothes that they're wearing, or join these organizations that they're a part of. It's like, we feel like that's our way of feeling like we belong to something."

I'm guessing that's also where the rise of Snapchat dysmorphia, or Instagram Face, depending, I guess on your generation, is thought to originate. While part of it is also undoubtedly tied to the ubiquity of pocket cameras and their ever-increasing pixels, whatever the cause, the outcome is clear. More and more young people are seeking out cosmetic surgery to look more like they do in edited photographs.

"A lot of people really, it affects them. They really just internalize that and start to feel so much, so much less than because they don't look this way and don't have this life that the influencers make seem so attainable," Moskovitz said.

The surge in technology has undoubtedly affected the plastic surgery industry, said Dr. Garth Fisher, a Beverly Hills plastic surgeon who is also known for his work on *Extreme Makeover.*

"Back in the day, you looked at TV, movie stars, maybe magazines, and that was the access that people had to what was cosmetically desirable or aesthetically appropriate," Dr. Fisher told me.[220] "Now with Instagram and social media, it's become so just in your face. Everybody's a movie star, everybody is looking at themselves to do selfies, videos, posting on a page all their photography or photo shoots."

Fisher says the most popular procedures these days are: "Injectables. Tissue injectables, facial injectables, they're the most popular procedure. I just hate it, the overblown lip and face. I just think it's the worst thing ever." Breast implants, liposuction, and buttocks enhancements round out the list.

Fisher suspects the plumped-up beauty trend has been driven largely by algorithms attuned to a Kardashian standard of beauty.

"Aesthetically, what is pleasing or what's appropriate is driven so much by personalities, whether it's movie stars or who's hot," Fisher said. "When you look at different features, I think people before were looking at models, actresses. Now they're just looking at Instagram. Who's got the most followers? Who's the prettiest? Why are they being followed so much? Why are they pretty? They're trying to emulate that."

Never mind that the Kardashians edit all their selfies—occasionally beyond recognition—and even reportedly pay a paparazzi outfit to take flattering, staged photos of them. Never mind that we've all seen what their original faces looked like. "You're not ugly," the meme goes. "Just poor."

That's part of what led Dana Omari, a registered dietician with a masters in biochemistry, to start the @IGFamousBodies page on Instagram while working through her conflicting feelings about her patients at a Texas medspa.

"It wasn't just that they didn't know anything about cosmetic procedures. They also would bring in insane pictures, like Photoshopped, crazy pictures of celebrities who would say something like, 'Oh, I use this cream from my friend's line and all of my wrinkles are suddenly gone.' And it's definitely a super airbrushed picture and they don't look anything like that in real life," Omari said.[221] "And they're like, 'Do you have a cream that could do this to my face?' Like, yeah, it's called Photoshop. I can do it to all your pictures right now."

Instead, she started posting before and after photographs of celebrities who had had obvious work done. Even then, she says, people weren't convinced.

"I always have people in the comments that swear it's puberty or something. It'll be a model who's 23 years old and her face has dramatically changed in the last few years and they'll say, 'It's aging and weight loss and she's lost four pounds,'" she said.

"Celebrities like influencers and Kylie Jenner, they are the commodity. And so I think it's unethical for them to say, 'Oh, if you want a body like me, you should just get fit here, buy my workout program,' or whatever it is, when that's not what they're doing," Omari said. "So please don't sell me your skincare routine when what you've actually been doing is a bunch of laser treatments.

"It's okay if you get stuff done, it's okay if you don't get stuff done. The only thing that's not okay is lying to people about it. And especially if you're profiting off of it, which is these influencers that get their lips done and then say that it's just their lip liner and you need to buy their lip liner now, or whatever it is. Whatever they're selling," she concluded.

The older women who come into her medspa are more concerned with the work being subtle, tasteful, and personally tailored. Millennials and Gen Z, however, "are like, 'Make my lips as big as possible.' Bring in pictures of whoever. 'I want this done.'

"People will come in with a picture of themselves with a Snapchat filter or an Instagram filter. And a lot of those things are actually not possible to do with procedures. I mean there's no way that we can just make your face into a heart shape if it's not," she said. "But they would come in and say, 'I want to look like this.'"

It's not just the patients feeling the pressure. The celebrities and doctors are also under stress. "It's just gotten so easy and so competitive both for the doctor and patients, that a lot of them are turning now to, 'Hey, I've got to look better. I've got to do better. I've got to do Photoshop. I've got to put on filters,'" Fisher said. "Even doctors are, I think, Photoshopping their results."

Fisher said a doctor caught doing something like that could have their board certification revoked or get kicked out of the society, but he's not as confident as to its efficacy in practice.

"Regulation…it's hard to regulate. How do you know? You find somebody, you say, 'I think that's Photoshopped.' You do some maneuver to find some way to access the records. There's a lot of steps that you'd have to take to call them out, to have something done about it. But, it does happen," he said.

That's not the only fraud in the business, Fisher said. There's a real problem with snake oil treatments getting dragged into the feeds of regular people, thanks to all the social media algorithms vying for our attention.

"I'm constantly asked by TV shows, by magazines, by reporters, 'What is the newest thing? What is the newest thing? What's the newest thing?'" Fisher said. "That has driven this market into a cesspool of different technologies that really don't represent an improvement in technology. It's just a different marketing angle. There's so much just marketed, just marketed and marketed as brand new that doesn't work."

Fisher declined to name any specific procedures, citing a disinclination for being sued, but did let on that he had a laser treatment in mind.

"Back in the past, what happened was the companies would come to the doctors and say, 'What do you think of this?'

They'd spend a million dollars building a machine or whatever they have to do. You tell them, 'That looks terrible. It's terrible. It didn't work,'" Fisher said. "Nowadays, they say, 'Well, heck with you.' They just go straight to the media. They say, 'We've got ABC laser. Look at this before and after picture.'

"Then you're the doctor sitting in your office and after they spent $1 million advertising it, you got 100 people calling you saying they want the ABC laser. You say, 'I don't even know what this is. I better get it.' Then you get it," he continued. "Who knows if the patients are happy or not because you don't even know what it is. You're kind of forced to do it because the competition's buying these lasers or whatever the technology is."

"Then the doctor's stuck with a machine that may not work and it's going to ruin his credibility. The patient's not going to get a great result. But guess what? That technology company is going to just make something else and advertise that," he concluded. "Here we go. The wave just keeps going and going."

It hit me much later that he could have just as easily been describing the Calloway brand. Months later, her website's still open for preorders with the August 31 ship date, her inactive Patreon is still live with more than 300 paying customers, she found a new Matisse painting (*Goldfish*) to copy and sell to her followers, and she even recently launched a YouTube channel. So far, she's posted only two videos: "The Tumor in My Mom's Asshole," and "Reading Mean Comments About the Tumor in My Mom's Asshole."

7

The Fyre Next Time

Six months after the Fyre Festival crashed and burned, Mc-
Farland was out on bail and purportedly building his defense
from his parents' basement. Or at least that's what the US Attorney's office thought.

The truth was McFarland never really left the city.

After he was released on a $300,000 bond, he went home.
But he was soon back. For a few months, he bounced around
hotels and at one point, according to the FBI, stayed rent-free
at a friend's $31 million town house. (According to his presen-
tence investigation report, "[t]he seven-floor, four-bedroom,
seven-bathroom luxurious town house features, among other
things, a Zen garden, four kitchens, elevator access, a wine
room, a media center, a home spa and fitness center, a billiard
room, and a rooftop for entertaining."[222]) There were sight-
ings of him at strip clubs and nightclubs. One night not long
after his release, he was photographed partying at a Lower
East Side nightclub with an NFL player.

In a letter to Judge Naomi Buchwald, McFarland later reflected on this period, writing, "I was trying to hang on to the life I thought I had. I didn't understand. I was mentally fighting back, thinking that while I was totally wrong in my actions, my intentions were good. I was thinking I just wanted to make everyone happy and make things work at all costs."[223]

But he wasn't just out partying while his lawyers worked diligently to delay his sentencing hearing. He was back to scamming.

He briefly hired the premier consulting firm, FTI, to defend his reputation as he battled federal fraud charges. Like many a firm that came before, FTI later fired him for nonpayment, though it might well have come if they'd waited long enough. Around the same time they'd signed on, a subsequent FBI report shows, McFarland, out on bail, had begun actively scamming customers from the Fyre mailing list, recruiting a former Magnises employee named Josh Blue and a wannabe rapper's manager named Frank Tribble in his efforts to market event tickets he didn't have.

In September 2017, McFarland hired Tribble to be the face of the new business, NYC VIP Access, and registered everything in his name. And to hide the fact that it was a scam, he continued to pretend to have the only thing that made the business model make sense: access to exclusive events. He just didn't have access to a bank account, which Tribble agreed to sign for.

"McFarland told Employee-1 that his new company was going to be similar to his former company Magnises, which McFarland stated had shut down only due to the bad press surrounding the Fyre Festival that tarnished his reputation," prosecutors later charged. "McFarland said that he still had access to tickets for exclusive high-end events through event sponsors, and offered Employee-1 a job in ticket sales for NYC VIP Access."[224]

According to the feds, McFarland offered Tribble a salary of approximately $300 a week and a 10 percent commission and then handed him a list of the Fyre Festival attendees with the highest salaries and sent him cold-calling. While Tribble did act as the face of the company, talking with and meeting with potential buyers, according to the FBI all the emails under Tribble's name were actually sent by McFarland and the indictment suggests McFarland was actively scamming Tribble at the same time.

Which makes sense. The emails attributed to Tribble had the same used-car salesman vibes that McFarland had been using since the first Spling recruitment emails in 2010. Because I was the reporter who first broke the Fyre story, many of the former victims in receipt of Tribble's communiques began forwarding them to me in real time.

The very first missive from "Tribble" hit the Fyre victims' emails in December 2017, offering a level of luxury even McFarland couldn't have bought his way into: a seat at the coveted Met Gala. But the very first Google result for *Met Gala tickets* reveals a single ticket to the annual *Vogue* dinner goes for about $30,000—and that's if you're even allowed to buy it. According to the *New York Times*, *Vogue* editor-in-chief Anna Wintour has "final say over every invitation and attendee, which means that even if a company buys a table, it cannot choose everyone who sits at its table: it must clear the guest with her and *Vogue*."[225]

And that's just the first page of Google results. You didn't exactly need to be an FBI agent to figure out McFarland's offer was a scam, though the FBI did meet with staffers at the magazine just to be sure. "The vast majority of tickets are sold by invite only, and if a brand purchases a table, all guests must be approved by the magazine. All guests must provide a biography and a photo. All tickets must be paid for and are nontransferable. No third-party brokers were authorized to sell tickets to the Met Gala," Special Agent Brandon Racz affirmed.

Even so, at least fifteen people wired McFarland $2,500 each, based on the following email solicitation: "The 2018 Met Gala is on Monday, April 30, at The Met in NYC. We partnered with the sponsoring brands to get you a chance to buy tickets. Tickets include red carpet, seats for the event/ dinner, and an invitation to the after-party," the email read. "Tickets are extremely limited. Please respond with your brief bio and number of guests you'd like to have attend, and we'll follow up with a call."[226]

When a customer referred to in the indictment as Victim-1 wasn't convinced, McFarland rustled up a fake email purportedly sent from the gala host confirming the ticket sale. His Photoshop skills must have been rusty at that point. The indictment notes that, "According to both Employee-1 and Victim-1, Victim-1 questioned the authenticity of the Gala Host email." Still, she apparently trusted it enough to become Victim-1.

In all, the feds say, McFarland made about $36,000 from that single email.

He was just getting started. A week later, he sent out an email offering Burning Man tickets at a steep discount, especially for tickets that weren't even in presales yet.

"We were going to save this, but the snow in NYC today has us thinking of the playa. We have 2018 Burning Man (8/26–9/3) passes today only for $325 per person," the email read. "Ticket prices go up to $525 tomorrow until we sell our allocation."

One of the recipients of the Burning Man email, a man named Joel Remland, responded asking how that was possible.

"We partner with sponsors to get bulk access," Tribble/McFarland responded, attaching a contract and credit card authorization form to the email.

But Burning Man, which revolves around the practice of decommodification, deliberately does not have sponsors. And Tribble's tickets were at least $100 cheaper than the cheapest official tickets, which wouldn't go on sale for another month.

When Remland didn't respond, Tribble followed up again, asking him to "Please return by end of day Monday so we can keep the discounted price." Remland chose not to take the leap of faith, but at least two other people did.

After getting a tip about the new onslaught of too-good-to-be-true offers, I reached out to ask about the details for the Victoria's Secret Fashion Show. Just like it had with the Fyre Festival, something seemed off.

When I called the number listed in the email, the man who identified himself as Tribble confidently told me that each model got allotted three tickets, located in the fourth of "about ten rows," which the company would sell me for $1,500 apiece. He also offered me "two open seats in the first row, which gives you backstage access to mingle with the models during the show" for $5,000 a seat. Both ticket options, he promised, would come with access to the after-party.

He also offered me tickets to have dinner with LeBron James. I asked how that was even close to possible, and he was quick with an explanation.

"They'll rent out a restaurant, they'll be having a team dinner, and you'll be at this dinner with them, you will be able to take an individual picture with LeBron, and then pictures with the other teammates, and then you have access to go to the club after, so they go out to a club, it will be hosted by a famous artist, and you'll be at the club with them—all VIP access," he said.

He was vague on how he came to acquire the tickets, saying only that the courtside seats were procured through the "player pool" and the dinner access was granted by "the player agents."

"I'm just an agent for the company, but I do know that we're partnered up with ticket organizations for higher-end clients, VIP access. So whoever I reached out to, whoever referred you, they were on a list of people that I was reaching out to, on a list that I received from the company," he said.

"Tribble" said NYC VIP Access was founded by "a couple hip-hop managers and their artists, top artists that have all combined and taken their connections and kind of all came together to see what they could do." The company didn't have much of a digital record, and its website was only created in November 2017, according to Whois records. Tribble wouldn't give names, but he said, "None of the people were involved in the Fyre Festival," when I asked.

"I can't tell you who I work with; I'll lose my job," he said. "There's a major press release on it. So I guess you'll just have to wait until that time."

Asked for a copy of the release, he demurred. "That's going to be in about a month to two months. I'd say half the world's going to know about it. So I mean, it's something that without me even sending you something, you will know about it.

"For the actual tickets, we will send you instructions. You do pick them up at will call. So we give you confirmation stuff before any money is sent. There will be a contract in place, and the reason why you have that contract is because you don't get the tickets upon purchase, you pick them up at will call," he explained, adding that I could pay any way I wanted. "You know, first-time clients feel a little bit more comfortable paying with their American Express credit card, but that's why you do have the contract in place."

When I pressed him for more information about the company and its dealings, he shut the interview down.

"So, before I even give you any more information, it seems like you're just taking out a bunch of information to write articles, which, I mean, I only get on the phone with people who are interested in being clients and purchasing tickets to events and getting access," Tribble said.

"I'm a very busy person, and I don't have time to be interviewed. You're interrogating me, asking me a bunch of questions. None of my clients have ever done this, I have clients all over the world," he added, before hanging up.

In retrospect, it was obvious. NYC VIP Access was just Magnises with another name. But McFarland had even been using the same Magnises mailing list, which tipped off one former member every time he launched a new idea that winter. Because her name had been entered at Magnises with a distinctive typo, she could track every McFarland venture. There was a website called OutEastNY.com, a clear knockoff of the reputable Hamptons real-estate site, OutEast.com. Another offered the use of a multimillion-dollar town house owned by a friend of McFarland's in a Soho House knockoff he called Sousa House. Those emails he signed, *"xx Caroline."*

In early June 2018, with McFarland's sentencing just a week away, I published a final piece on *VICE* News detailing all the schemes he'd been linked to while out on bail. A few hours later, the Southern District of New York put out a press release: McFarland had been indicted and arrested on new charges of wire fraud and money laundering. According to prosecutors, in just six months, he managed to steal at least $100,000 from the same people he'd already scammed with Fyre.[227]

"William McFarland, the defendant, while on pretrial release, perpetrated a scheme to defraud attendees of the Fyre Festival and others by soliciting them to purchase tickets from NYC VIP Access to exclusive events when, in fact, no such tickets existed," the complaint read. "In soliciting ticket sales, McFarland used an email account in the name of a then-employee in order to hide his affiliation with NYC VIP Access. McFarland provided prospective customers with contracts that falsely represented that NYC VIP Access had tickets to exclusive events in fashion, music, and sports."

One detail from the indictment I'll never get out of my mind involved McFarland's logins to accounts related to the NYC VIP Access scheme. According to the FBI records, he spent the last Christmas before he went to jail at home in New Jersey, scamming and catfishing people on his parents' internet.

He was almost Trumpian in his constant lying.

"When he gets caught, even after having done everything he can to conceal his role with NYC VIP Access and have somebody else be the face of the company so that if anybody came asking he wouldn't take the hit for it, after he gets arrested the second time, what does he do?" asked the assistant US attorney Kristy Greenberg.[228] "He asks for a meeting with the government, and he meets with the government for hours and he lies and lies and lies—elaborate stories about how he intended to procure tickets from fake people from fake websites that did not exist. It is just a total blatant disregard for law enforcement."

"When people commit serious crimes which show no respect for the legal system and the law, there must be just punishment, and that punishment must consider individual deterrence and general deterrence," said the judge. "While the defendant has argued that he committed these crimes because he suffers from certain psychological conditions which explain his actions, I reject that evaluation. Rather, it is my conclusion, based on all the submissions which I've carefully considered, that the defendant is a serial fraudster, and that to date his fraud, like a circle, has no end."

I found out a few months later that McFarland had even videotaped himself doing the NYC VIP Access scam, thanks to an artist named Kindo Harper, who had worked with Mc-Farland before on other projects.

Harper had been hired to shoot video of McFarland's attempt to develop his newest business idea, an Instagram awards show. Instead, he accidentally captured part of the NYC VIP Access scam on film.

Harper eventually left the footage in a storage unit, where it remained—that is, until the night McFarland was rearrested. When he heard the news, Harper thought he recognized the name of the sham company, so he raced to the storage unit and started going through the footage, and there it was.

Harper's cameras also captured the return of another Mc-Farland associate: Senator Chuck Schumer's press secretary, Angelo Roefaro.

As it turned out, McFarland wasn't the only former Fyre mastermind to work with a high-ranking member of the New York Democratic Party.

After a dark season in which the publicity brought on by the Fyre Festival documentaries prompted a second look at Jerry Media's less-than-ethical copyright practices, things started to look up in the last quarter of 2019. Mike Bloomberg, the former mayor of New York, was about to spend $1 billion buying the vote of the American people, and he wanted them to help.

The Bloomberg campaign kicked off in February 2020 with a meme- and influencer-based approach that offered anyone who wanted to get involved $2,500 a month to promote

Bloomberg online and directly to friends and family. The organizers did not discriminate in its selection of its "deputy field organizers," according to the *Los Angeles Times*, which noted that the group included among its ranks "a vocal Bernie Sanders supporter," "a Chicagoan with zero followers on Twitter," and "a dozen registered Republicans."[229] Many of the Twitter accounts backing Bloomberg's bid had been opened within the past two months, triggering Twitter's fraud alerts as hundreds of uninspired human users began tweeting like bots by using copied and pasted messages like "A President Is Born: Barbra Streisand sings Mike's praises. Check out her tweet."[230]

"The result has been a stiff outpouring of tweets, Facebook and Instagram posts with little to no engagement and sometimes half-hearted text messages," the *LA Times* reported. "Some organizers were so robotic in their tweeting, Twitter suspended their accounts Friday evening after the *Times* inquired about whether their behavior complied with the platform's rules on spam and manipulation."

The Meme 2020 campaign in particular was so odious even The Fat Jewish, one of the most notorious meme stealers on the platform, felt compelled to speak out against it.

"They asked me to do it, I said no. I grew up in New York City so I can tell you firsthand, Bloomberg is a colossal shitbag. From the subjugation of minorities through stop and frisk policies to his hardline anti-marijuana stance, dude is a total hoe," Josh Ostrovsky, who posts under the handle @thefatjewish, reportedly wrote on Instagram.[231] "I'd encourage any meme account owner to take schmoney from basically any brand… because brands are trash and deserve to have their money taken, but this dystopian black mirror simulation is too much for me I now need to be shot into the fucking sun k bye."

Amol Jethwani, a Florida Democrat who worked as a field

organizer on the Bloomberg campaign from his announcement in November to his dropout in March, said that at first
the meme campaign seemed harmless enough. But Jethwani,
who was born in 1996, making him either a very young millennial or a very old Gen Zer, says he soon realized that the
teens the campaign was targeting weren't laughing.

"As we just saw with the TikTok teens running the [Trump]
Tulsa rally into the ground, you can't outsmart Gen Z on their
own home turf," Jethwani said.[232] "These memes started popping up and everyone was like, 'LOL, this is so funny.' I don't
think he understood that a lot of people were saying, 'LOL,
this is so funny' in a bad way.

"Millennials did not grow up with technology. Millennials
grew up and technology appeared to them. Gen Z has lived
in the tech world since they could remember. And so because
of that, there is a greater skepticism of things that are put out
there. There's a greater understanding of, like, meme value
as something that is not significant and not serious. There is
a greater ease. It's like that *Batman*—Oh, God, I hate to use
this quote—but it's like that *Batman* quote where Bane's like,
'You merely adopted the darkness, I was born in it.' And these
kids were born in it, and so it is their home church. They
know how to smell a fake. They know how people are trying to… It's about cultural competency. Campaigns are all
about cultural competency," Jethwani said. "And so the meme
campaign was a really, really good attempt at it. And I think
that that's something that Democratic campaigns… There's
a lot that Mike did that Democratic campaigns can look at
and say, 'These are good ideas. Mike was a terrible application of them, but we need to seriously start evaluating how
we're reaching voters in an age where no one opens those
emails that are like, *from Barack Obama* that opened with *Dear
friend*. You know?"

But Meme 2020 was ultimately just a small part of a much larger, much more dysfunctional shitshow: the actual campaign.

In just four months, Bloomberg spent close to a billion dollars on a presidential campaign[233]—and the only race he managed to win was in American Samoa. Jethwani wasn't a big fan of Bloomberg's either, but he wanted to learn on a presidential campaign, and Bloomberg's outsize budget meant he'd get firsthand experience on all the fancy tools most campaigns can only hope to access one day.

"I voted for Bernie. But the reality of the situation is you don't always get to work for campaigns that you support. You just kind of have to shoot for what's within the realm of acceptable and just kind of go from there," said Jethwani.

And then there were the salaries.

"I sent in the application for the Mike Bloomberg position, and when I was hired, or when they began the interviewing process, they promised us employment through November, regardless of who the nominee was, and basically that is what did it for me. The promise of having a campaign guarantee employment through November in and of itself is absolutely unheard of. I was sold. That was the first thing," he said. "The second is that Mike Bloomberg was paying three times the going rate for every single position on his campaign."

For a moment, Jethwani said, it felt like everyone in the state was working on the campaign.

"I think he employed maybe three thousand staff total across the country. I know that there were about a hundred fifty in Florida alone. So, like, all of a sudden, all of these down ballot races, like County commission, City commission, House, State, Senate, were scrambling to find staff because all of the people who had any relevant experience are getting called on," Jethwani said. "It was kind of like we sucked the market dry of the supply of experienced political-team staff members, because there aren't really that many of us across the country."

Meanwhile, Bloomberg had poured so much money into advertising that there was barely any airtime left for the other candidates. As a field organizer, Jethwani found himself doing twenty-five interviews a day to fill open campaign slots and opening offices across the state at a rate unlike any he'd ever seen before. Practically overnight, Bloomberg had bought legitimacy.

"I think we totaled out at just fifteen offices in Florida," he said. "Mind you, the entire Hillary campaign in 2016 during the general, when we coordinated all of the resources between the state and national party and the presidential campaign probably had maybe like eight or ten offices total across the state. Maybe fifty or sixty staff across the state. And this is the primary and we have a hundred fifty. There were press people for just the South Florida region, for just the mid Florida region, for just North Florida. It was an absurd amount of resources."

Like McFarland with his Spling campus ambassadors all those years before, Bloomberg also relied on his first wave of hires to put their reputations on the line to recruit the other employees.

"[Bloomberg] guaranteed employment through November, and the company line was *Employment is guaranteed through November; location is not*. And the premise behind that was if you're in a non-battleground state, it's very likely that they'll group you to a battleground state. If you are in a battleground state, it's very likely that they'll move you to a different market within that state based off of data that they get back. The whole thing was centered on data aggregation. We are the smartest campaign, we're the smartest campaign because of the data," Jethwani said. "So at the very beginning, that was what enticed me to join the campaign. I turned down positions with, like, some prominent state house races, and County commission, and County mayoral races that would have done wonders for my career, but also working on a presidential and having that financial security while living in Miami was a huge, huge deal to me. And so when we began that aggressive hiring process, that was not only part of the why we got hired, but also what we used to hire other staff and other team members. That guarantee. It was part of the interview, it was on all of our written paperwork. It's part of what we need to say during the interview, and that was something that we just kind of kept harping on."

But all the money in the world couldn't distract from how ill-suited Bloomberg was for the job.

"Until Mike opened his mouth, he was doing really, really well," Jethwani said. "He was just a terrible candidate. I mean, he was skyrocketing to the top of the polls, and then he qualified for that first debate, and then Elizabeth Warren washed the floor with him. The thing is that he really was just putting out a campaign that was very fabricated, which is very palpable to people the second he started talking. But on paper, Mike looked like the ideal candidate. And when I say *on paper*, that's what carried through in all of his ads. He spent half a billion dollars on ad buys over the course of the campaign to do absolutely nothing."

"[American Samoa], that's what a billion dollars will get you if you aren't doing it for the right reasons," Jethwani said, laughing.

When Bloomberg finally dropped out on March 4, throwing his endorsement to former vice president Joe Biden, he didn't bother to let the staffers inside his own campaign know. But he did let his eponymous news service, which had recused itself from covering the Democratic primary due to Bloomberg's candidacy, break the news. That's how most of his staffers found out it was all over. All their data, including internal campaign communications, was wiped from the Bloomberg platforms soon after.

His former staffers have since bandied some conspiracy theories around about why Bloomberg might have picked that moment, aside from his dismal Super Tuesday showing of course.

"A lot of us have a suspicion that part of the reason that Mike cut all of us off and, like, just kind of cut his losses and ran was because of the impending coronavirus thing that was just starting. He had already started sending to the offices ridiculous amounts, and when I say *ridiculous*, I mean boxes upon boxes of hand sanitizers, sanitary wipes, Lysol, masks, gloves, all kinds of stuff. And this was before masks were recommended," Jethwani said. "So we're pretty sure that this was his like Bloomberg [Limited Partnership], statistical analysis and projections telling them to do that. A lot of us feel like that's part of why he cut his losses and ran: he saw this giant pandemic and just said, 'I don't want to pay for these people.' I honestly wouldn't be surprised. I've met him twice, and he's—ugh. I don't understand how such a tiny man can be so self-centered, but we've all met Chihuahuas."

Needless to say, the campaign's promises of continued employment through November evaporated overnight. The staffers were told by a superior reading off a script that while Bloomberg had appreciated their work, he would not be employing them moving forward. Instead, they were encouraged to apply to the Democratic National Committee via a special pipeline. And the laptops they thought the campaign had given them as signing bonuses turned out to be taxable gifts. On the other hand, Jethwani says, he got two printers out of the deal because the campaign would just buy printers for one-off events instead of transporting them from the campaign offices.

Before it all ended, with so many employees and so little to do, life in the Florida arm of the campaign was still incredibly chaotic, Jethwani said. At least six staffers were put on museum-guard duty after a wealthy donor commissioned a mural for Bloomberg that the campaign was then expected to pick up in a U-Haul and store in Miami. Another had to run to Walmart to secure a bag of Bloomberg's favorite Folgers coffee before his arrival in the Cuban coffee capital of the US. "Mike didn't even drink the coffee," Jethwani said.

Bloomberg's advance team was so ill-equipped for the job that Jethwani was forced at one event to step into a security role.

"In the middle of the press conference, one of [Bloomberg's advance team] aggressively runs up to me and whispers, 'We don't have an exit strategy for Mike,'" Jethwani said. "And so they basically had me run up to Mike, shield him physically with my body, and had our staff create a tunnel for him to escape from."

When the campaign opened a two-suite office space in Little Havana, it became clear to Jethwani that Bloomberg was cursed. While the first office was lovely, the second had an overwhelming stench of dead animal that not even a deep cleaning could eradicate.

"Advance really wanted to use that room for Mike. We're in Little Havana, so they went to a little Santeria shop and bought votive candles and incense," Jethwani said. But the measure failed to hide the smell or break the curse responsible for it. It's the DNC's problem now, though: because he had paid through November, Bloomberg "lovingly bequeathed the space" to the party.

Though all the staffers had signed at-will contracts, meaning they could be fired at any time, a large number say their primary reason for accepting the job was the promise of employment and benefits lasting through November. In the months since Bloomberg dropped out of the race, a number of employees have taken legal action. At least a hundred and eighty former staffers signed on to a class-action suit filed by three field organizers who say they were lured in with a promise of long-term employment and then dumped unceremoniously in the middle of a pandemic with no paycheck and no health care. And a second suit, filed by Jethwani's co-worker in Miami, Donna Wood, also accuses the Bloomberg campaign of breach of contract and failing to pay for employees' overtime.[234] Though Bloomberg's lawyers are asserting that the campaign employees were hired at-will and, as such, lack standing to sue, the campaign did agree to pay for their healthcare through the November election, citing the "difficult and stressful time."[235]

"I think they went in with this approach that Mike Bloomberg is the anti-Trump because he was this rich New Yorker who made his own money rather than resting on the laurels of his father. They just tried to make him this anti-Trump, when in reality, he's just very much the same in a lot of ways, doesn't really care. And that comes through when you open your mouth and haven't lived in the real world," Jethwani said. "It's like that scene in *Arrested Development* where she's like, 'It's a banana, Michael. How much could it cost? $10?' That was exactly the attitude on the campaign."

The experience was enough to dissuade Jethwani from pursuing a future in electoral politics.

"It just made it so obvious to me how much of it is a fuss, how much of it is profiteering. How much of it is just pointless. They kept harping about how if you go out there and you convince people and get them out to vote, and you do, like, strong field work, you'll be able to win an election. When the reality of the situation is Joe Biden really, really won this election on earned media," Jethwani said. "What's the point of doing field work, then?... It was almost scary to watch his rise even from inside the campaign because of how just invasive the size of the campaign enabled it to be," he continued. "I don't think people understand that when you get a call from a campaign...that's there for them to figure out why you are invested in electoral politics. What you care for and things like that. And that information is aggregated in band in the voter-activation network, and then campaigns poll the data again and again, and again, and manipulate their social media strategies, their overall strategies and stuff like that."

It was ultimately a moneymaker for Bloomberg as well.

"It's interesting because Mike committed to spending, I think he said, like, up to a billion or whatever to get Donald Trump out of the Oval Office. But at the same time he's profiting off of what's going on. So he donated $18 million to the DNC after he dropped out, and that's what really got me angry, because I saw all of these leaders of the Florida Democratic Party and the DNC and DNC members who I'm friends with and whatever else celebrating Mike for his $18 million donation, which is a drop in the bucket for a man of his wealth. But he's the sixth-richest man in the world. That's nothing."

But Bloomberg was about to get even richer. While 40 million Americans would soon be filing for unemployment, the nation's billionaires were about to see their net worth increase by about half a trillion dollars.

8

Covidiots

McFarland only stayed at FCI Otisville—the celebrity-studded white-collar prison where fellow inmates included *Jersey Shore*'s Mike "The Situation" Sorrentino and Trump fixer Michael Cohen—for about a year. In September 2019, he was busted with a smuggled recording device, an infraction for which he was placed in solitary confinement for three months and then transferred to a low-security prison in Ohio.

From time to time I'll get an email or a call from someone claiming to be his cellmate offering me information about him, but other than that it's been pretty quiet.

But then his name started popping up again in early April 2020 as the coronavirus pandemic swept across the United States. According to the *New York Post*, McFarland had started a project from behind bars to crowdfund money to cover the fees associated with making phone calls in prison. He was calling it Project-315.

To announce the initiative, McFarland published a twelve-paragraph letter, ten of which were dedicated to a discussion of his own personal growth as a man and as a CEO.[236]

"I'd like you to know that I know how badly I messed up," he wrote. "I lied, deceived, and ultimately hurt many people in pursuit of what I thought would be successful business ventures. What I did was absolutely despicable, and the responsibility for the damages caused starts and ends with me. There's absolutely no excuse for my actions. There's not a day that goes by that my reflection of [sic] these choices doesn't make me sick. Ultimately, my mistakes may prove to be unforgivable, but as I sit here and take all of this in, I think back to the day I was sentenced. I promised to dedicate myself to helping those I hurt through the only way I thought appropriate: by living my apology. After nearly 2 years in jail, I believe in this more than ever. To everyone I hurt, I'm extremely sorry. I'll work for the rest of my life to try and make up, in some small way, for what I did."

The rest of it was like McFarland's greatest-hits album—he mentioned the companies he'd founded, how the Fyre Festival was just his attempt to show people the beauty of the Bahamas—and how much he'd learned.

"The festival was conceived to be the ultimate manifestation of my theme and purpose, in my newfound favorite place in the world," McFarland wrote. "I legitimately tried to execute the festival, but I clearly made wrong, immoral, and terrible decisions along the way. However, while the festival failed, the resulting prison time has matured my mission and only solidified my belief that the good that can be created and shared when different people come together is more than potent; it's my source of inspiration to help those I've wronged."

McFarland closed the letter asking for donations to fund his fellow prisoners' calls by assuring supporters that "I am not touching any of the money. I don't have access to the funds. I'm not getting paid. And I'm not receiving any financial benefit. I'm driven to connect and bring people together while helping everyone I hurt, and most importantly, doing it while operating within the allowed boundaries. Regardless of your stance on my mission, I hope it's obvious that I don't want to come back to jail. I also believe it's imperative that we operate with extreme transparency. Weekly accounting will be published, and any questions regarding the accounting records will be answered publicly."

A week later, the Bureau of Prisons made all phone calls free, and McFarland updated his crowdfunding site to announce all donations would be returned.

At the end of April, McFarland had petitioned for compassionate release, citing preexisting conditions, including asthma since he was a teenager, extreme allergies for issues related to breathing and his cardiovascular system, and heart issues since his early twenties. His attorney also argued that McFarland's only reason for smuggling a recording device into his cell was to pay his victims back faster.

"This incident occurred at the minimum-security camp in Otisville, NY, where Mr. McFarland was cited for the minor offense of having a USB device that he was using to help write a self-reflection book, that he hopes to publish to assist him in fulfilling restitution to those he harmed. Mr. McFarland realizes that he was wrong to have the USB device, for which he served three months in solitary confinement. He thought that it was worthwhile to aid him in writing the book faster to make restitution to the people he hurt. Still, he now realizes, after the worst months of his life, and sincere reflection in the solitary confinement of the Special Housing Unit, how wrong he was to think that way," the motion read.[237]

But the motion was withdrawn after the Southern Dis-

trict came down hard against the request, arguing that Mc-
Farland hadn't gone through the proper channels to request
early release.

"The defendant appears committed to capitalizing on his
infamy to build his own fortune. The defendant's argument
that he should be released so that he can make restitution
should be soundly rejected."

Prosecutors also pointed out that not only had McFarland
never mentioned health problems before, but in a recent medical exam, he indicated he had no allergies or respiratory or
cardiovascular problems.

But Elkton, the Ohio prison to which McFarland had been
transferred, reportedly had an outbreak of COVID-19 so bad
the National Guard had to be called in. On July 4, McFarland tested positive for coronavirus.

"Tested positive for COVID today," McFarland told a *New
York Post* reporter. "Being put in isolation in a big room with
160 other people who have it at this jail."[238]

Like many things after COVID-19, McFarland's status was
no longer funny. But for such a serious ordeal, it would seem
not much was learned. In October, McFarland was sent back
to solitary confinement, this time for launching a podcast from
prison, which had been recorded over the phone.

It doesn't seem like much has changed. Though McFarland
talks about the three months he spent in solitary confinement,
the lessons he says he took away from it are the same lessons
he described after getting arrested, after his sentencing, and
after getting sent to Otisville. When he talks about his goals
for the podcast, he still sounds almost indistinguishable from
Adam Neumann or Elizabeth Holmes ascribing mystical qualities to their mundane business ideas.

"I think that if done properly, this [podcast] can be used
to create and share a lot of good," he said. "So I'm doing the

podcast to bring people together and sharing these connections with anybody who's listening. So I think that if we do
our own little way to recreate this magic through a podcast
that comes at almost, like, the intersection of diverse people
and ideas, with the listeners, that would be really cool."

But there was something slightly different this time around.
This time around, McFarland wasn't the founder, although
he says he owns 50 percent of the podcast (100 percent of his
proceeds are allegedly going straight toward his restitution).
This difference is that this time around, McFarland is the
product. To launch the *Dumpster Fyre* podcast, McFarland had
linked up with Notorious LLC, a "global content studio and
network" that also operates hype houses for internet-popular
teens and young adults in Los Angeles. It was almost a perfect
inception. When the *New York Times* reported that McFarland
had been remanded to solitary confinement for up to thirty
days due to his participation in the podcast, Notorious CEO
Peter Vincer responded by posting on Instagram Stories a
screenshot of the article with the caption "#1 organic Google
news article. Thanks @nytimes." The next day he noted that
it was the "#1 podcast news story IN THE WORLD. Over
Kanye. Rogan and everything else. On Google News and everywhere. Just the beginning…" McFarland, who continues
to maintain that his only reason for living is to make restitution to his victims, was finally getting to see what the influencers he'd hired for Fyre felt like.

It's something I thought about again on March 13, 2020
as fears over the Coronavirus peaked. The virus had spread
around the world, wreaking particular havoc in China and
Italy, and after a month of stalling, New York City was itself
just two days away from shutting down all its schools, bars,
and restaurants. But just off the Bowery in SoHo, in the face
of a global pandemic, dozens of people had crammed together,

collectively risking their lives for something even more viral than COVID-19: a Supreme drop.

As it was, the news of the virus made it a great day to score the elusive skateboarding gear. Justin Marchesani and Roland Carlor, two New York City fans of the brand who I caught leaving the store, said that for an 11 a.m. drop on a Thursday, the line was short and fast-moving. They only had to wait fifteen minutes to get in, and they felt relatively safe, though both said they were concerned about seeing their families after being out in public.

Maybe because it was so short, the people still waiting in line were excited about their chances to score and happy to talk about what brought them there.

"Our boys are fifteen and eighteen," Anne Wilcher, a mother of two visiting New York from the UK told me. "They're into doing the Supreme drops and the Palace drops and things like that."

"We went to the Empire State Building yesterday, and there were no lines. We went straight to the top," her husband, Rob Wilcher, said. But for their kids, they were prepared to wait, COVID-19 be damned. In fact it was actually their second drop of the day, having first stopped at the Palace Skateboard Apparel store to pick up gifts to bring home. They were mildly concerned about the spread of the virus, but more for what it meant for their international travel home than any dangers waiting in the Supreme line.

"You guys are very cool parents," I told them.

"They don't think so," both parents replied in unison.

Jackson Kleinschmidt, who was visiting New York from Florida with his dad, Rick, said he wasn't concerned. "We've just got to live our lives," said Jackson.

"Supreme is worth it?" I asked.

"Oh yeah," said Rick.

"Our lives are worth it," Jackson added.

I asked them what the draw of the brand was.

"He doesn't even know," Jackson said, pointing to his dad. "I just, like, see my friends, kind of, you know, wear it around. The store's in New York, so I was like, 'I want to go!'"

Two days later, citing the pandemic, Supreme temporarily shut down all of its stores outside of Japan.

If any good can even be said to come of something like this pandemic, I think it was that it stripped away a lot of our everyday artifices. And it turned a lot of cynical foregone conclusions into open-ended questions. What do we really need to survive in this world? To thrive? What kind of legacy are we leaving behind? What truly matters when every day is an emergency?

Unfortunately, the celebrities did not get the memo.

It started as a joke, the comments that piled up under Jennifer Lopez's Instagram post showing her son serving drinks to her and her fiancé, Alex Rodriguez, outside in the backyard of her Miami home.

It wasn't something she could have predicted or controlled, really, how much her home looked like the glass-walled home in *Parasite*, the Korean class-warfare film that swept the Oscars with its brutal depiction of a working-class family's attempt to breach the rarified air—and residence—of a wealthy family unable to maintain their home or daily lives without the assistance of a staff.

It's something the *Fifty Shades of Grey* actor Jamie Dornan, however, was conscious of when he was invited by the comedian Kristen Wiig to participate in an ill-advised video featuring a selection of random celebrities singing, in many cases painfully off-key, the lyrics to John Lennon's "Imagine."

"Hollywood A-listers band together to torture the quarantined," the *Washington Examiner* reported, but the celebs' voices weren't the only tone-deaf thing about the video. As Dornan later remarked, most of the famous faces in the "Imagine" video had prominently featured their opulent homes. (I'm told if you play their cover backward, you can hear them whispering "Socialism is dead.")

The timing of the release of the video, as tens of millions of Americans began filing for unemployment and queuing up in miles-long traffic to access food banks, didn't just compound the message that the rich are certainly not like you and me. It also confirmed that they were beyond pretending they weren't.

Except, of course, for Mr. Dornan, who offered as evidence of his community spirit the fact that he had deliberately used the worst room in his home as the backdrop for his segment in the video.

"I'll tell you what the problem was. I literally did mine in the toilet of my house," he remarked later on the podcast *Tea With Me*.[239]

"Quite clearly, people had escaped to their second home. There's too much acreage in the background, too many beautiful trees swinging, clearly by an ocean, that sort of craic. I was quite aware of that whenever I was doing it, to make it normal."

It was a lesson ignored by J.Lo and A-Rod, who were apparently unable to find anywhere to exercise in their ginormous home or expansive backyard and repeatedly departed their compound to work out at a local gym as the virus spread in March and April, supposedly requiring staffers to expose themselves to the virus in order to unlock the front door for their workout—and, of course, keep the general public out while they sweated in private. They did not wear masks. (Nor did they learn from their mistakes—in November, as the United States hit a record 200,000 cases a day and the CDC urged people to skip Thanksgiving trips to avoid Christmas funerals, Rodriguez posted on social media a photograph of them aboard a private jet with a caption about how excited they were to be traveling home to spend time with family. "What are your holiday plans?" he asked his followers.)

Around the same time, Madonna started posting videos of herself waxing poetic about the nature of the disease from her palatial bathtub, earning her instant internet infamy. And then, as if the pandemic had never existed at all, she was soon busted attending parties in the Hamptons.

"It's awesome that you guys are quarantined somewhere nice and whatever. I am still in the Hamptons, but why do you need to flex like that, so hard right now? People are suffering mentally and physically right now, more than ever," said McSweeney, the streetwear designer and *Real Housewives* cast member, on a call from the Hamptons where she'd been holed up with her daughter and sister. "I almost unfollowed Madonna. I love Madonna, but that video was so depressing, and her saying then that, like, it's the 'great equalizer' when it's showing us that it's not the great equalizer, actually. And then, like, there are celebrities singing 'Imagine.' I just can't. I just lost so much respect for Kristen Wiig, and I love her. I'm just, like, what is everybody fucking doing? It's like our phones are making us all idiots."

Conclusion

Like vaccinations, jade eggs, and the value of Elon Musk's companies, COVID-19 quickly turned into an emotional referendum. In this country, at least, how you feel about an issue supersedes any scientific facts, and some people have simply chosen not to believe in the virus, dismissing the advice of epidemiologists as political spin.

At the end of the summer, WeWoreWhat's Danielle Bernstein revealed she had been diagnosed with COVID. She'd been on public lockdown for less than two weeks when anonymous call-out accounts began buzzing that maybe she'd made the whole thing up to cover for her lack of Fashion Week appearances. (She later donated plasma live on her Instagram, firmly proving the haters wrong.) When she finally left her house after testing negative, her first public appearance was a photoshoot for her new swim line. At least two designers have since come forward to point out that her new suits are almost exact copies of their own.

That's also what happened with the independent, woman-of-color–owned brand Second Wind, which Bernstein had messaged on July 2, 2020, just three days after requesting one of their linen face masks with a signature attached gold chain.

"Babe I thought I should let you know I'm also making masks with a detachable chain—similar to the sunglass chains I own—didn't want you to think I'm copying you!" she wrote in a private DM to the company on July 2.[240] (Bernstein claims she started making the masks before ever reaching out to Second Wind.)

As news outlets like E! started to pick up the story, Bernstein went on Instagram Stories to claim she'd been receiving death threats over the allegations, which she followed up with a video of herself getting a manicure from a nail technician who had come to her home mid-pandemic. Then she posted yet another video of herself crying about the things people were saying about her online.

It was all painfully similar to the DM she had sent just two months before to an Italian brand called CB Positano, whose signature Cassiopeia dress Bernstein had also been accused of knocking off.

"So not that I need to constantly explain myself, but I feel like i need to let you guys know, since people get a little crazy about this sort of thing, but the dress that I recently posted was inspired by a dress that I got at a small shop in Italy last summer?" Bernstein said in a video posted after news of the copycat design had started circulating online. "We changed a bunch of aspects of it so that it would be different, but it was inspired by that, so I wanted to give credit where credit is due and let you guys know. I'm not trying to knock off anyone."

She also posted an undated screenshot of her DM to the owner.

"Hi guys!! Your dresses definitely inspired me for my recent dress I posted but we changed many aspects of it to make it our own," she wrote. "I hope you can see that!"

The owner responded by offering to send the dress, saying, "it will help me a lot...but it's okkkk. Take care."

In response, Bernstein promised to "support you and wear your designs!!" (She has not posted any pictures in CB Positano's designs since.)

"It's exhausting the amount I have to explain myself these days, but you guys are crazy!" she said in a follow-up video. "This cancel culture is insane."

She blamed her team for what happened next with a pair of supposedly vintage marigold gym shorts, purchased from an Etsy seller, that she told her followers she was "already remaking for my brand."

"It was quite deflating to see that she will be 'remaking' them for her brand," the Etsy seller wrote. "It states in the listing that I design them and get them made."

A month later, yet another brand, a lingerie company called The Great Eros, stepped forward to accuse Bernstein of copying their tissue paper, which features line drawings of female bodies, to use as a print on a line of WeWoreWhat Onia swimsuits, yoga mats and wallpaper. While the print is clearly inspired by Matisse sketches, The Great Eros has produced documentation showing Bernstein had recently visited their showroom. Bernstein's team and The Great Eros had apparently been privately negotiating, but the allegations exploded into the public domain when Bernstein and Onia preemptively filed a lawsuit asking a court to essentially stop any potential copyright claims by declaring the design infringement-free. In a follow-up post on Instagram, Bernstein seemed to offer in her defense a statement suggesting she'd actually copied someone else's designs for the print. "I personally own several female silhouette decor pieces which served as inspiration," Bernstein admitted.[241]

The next day, she posted an Instagram video of herself crying about the things people had been saying about her online.

(She has also not, to date, addressed the reason why the podcast she initially invited me on, *WeHeardWhat?!*, no longer exists. All of the episodes, mine included, were mysteriously wiped during the summer of 2020 right around the time after early podcast clips of her questioning the value of her college requiring her to study Native American history began circulating on the internet.)

But Bernstein wasn't the only one having a communications crisis as the pandemic swept through the US. The same week Bernstein filmed herself having yet another public breakdown, Musk's company Tesla officially dispensed with its PR team, leaving reporters with no way to reach out to the company for comment—and the company with no one to justify itself to.

"From a societal standpoint, having a PR staff is a form of accountability, allowing for the negotiation of a shared set of facts between the company and the media," technology writer Will Oremus noted. "The absence of PR staff leaves the strategy as one of hype, propaganda, and fostering mistrust of all media reports."[242]

Tesla, of course, did not respond to a request for comment.

Nor did the Fyre Festival end up serving as a kind of cautionary tale to the well-heeled, influential millennials broadcasting their lives on Instagram. Just a few months into the viral spread of COVID—as cases were peaking across the United States—FuckJerry decided to stage another concert, this time in the Hamptons, featuring The Chainsmokers, a DJ group known more for their Instagram presence than their actual music, as headliners. (The Chainsmokers also happen to be investors in FuckJerry's tequila brand, JAJA.)

To really bring things full circle, FuckJerry hired as an opening act David Solomon, who likes to hit the decks as DJ D-Sol when he's not serving as the CEO of Goldman Sachs—a company infamous for pumping and dumping investments with businesses like Uber and WeWork.

And to promote the concert, FuckJerry tapped Danielle Bernstein (also a JAJA investor) as spokesperson. But when it came time to attend the actual festival, I noticed her Instagram Stories didn't quite match the events on the ground. Where her posts showed private tables and just a few other friends, all wearing masks, other attendees' photos posted on social media showed hordes of people, often unmasked, crowded together.

Ticket prices went from $850 all the way up to $25,000 for the show, hilariously titled Safe & Sound, which is neither the name of a Chainsmokers song nor an accurate description of what happened that night. Around two thousand people reportedly attended the drive-in event, though videos reveal them leaving their cars after a short time and forming a crowded pit at the foot of the stage.

"Standing up there and watching the sunset, looking out over this huge field of cars and people on their cars, it was absolutely beautiful," Solomon initially told *Bloomberg*.[243] "The group that put this together did an incredible job in a difficult environment. If we work together and are thoughtful, we can do things that feel more normal and allow us to live with this virus safely."

But authorities disagreed.

"I am appalled," New York governor Andrew Cuomo said in a tweet after the event, linking to a video posted by someone with the handle @firenzemike that showed the large crowds of people, many of whom were unmasked and ignoring social distancing guidelines.[244]

"The Department of Health will conduct an investigation," Cuomo wrote. "We have no tolerance for the illegal & reckless endangerment of public health."

At the time, New York was still in a state of emergency, with gatherings of more than fifty people banned. But not only had Southampton Town Supervisor Jay Schneiderman signed off on the event, he had also performed there with his band. Southampton Villages' thirty-eight-year-old mayor, Jesse Warren, also emceed the event.

"I am at a loss as to how the Town of Southampton could have issued a permit for such an event, how they believed it was legal and not an obvious public health threat," New York health commissioner Howard Zucker wrote in a letter to Schneiderman.[245]

DJ D-Sol, who made $24.7 million at his day job in 2019,[246] quickly dissociated himself from the event. "David agreed to participate in an event for charity in which the organizers worked closely with the local government and put strict health protocols in place. He performed early and left before the show ended. The vast majority of the audience appeared to follow the rules, but he's troubled that some violated them and put themselves and others at risk," Goldman Sachs said in a statement.[247]

And if you need any more evidence that we're living in a simulation, consider the company that FuckJerry partnered with to throw the event: In the Know Experiences, a concierge luxury travel venture that sounds much like a Billy McFarland start-up. In the Know Experiences was formed to "cater to a younger set of savvy travelers who crave insider knowledge and local connections... That means access to coveted restaurant reservations, a shopping day with a personal stylist, and tickets to sold-out events," according to *Travel and Leisure*.[248]

Before the ill-fated event made national headlines and prompted everyone involved to hide their heads, founder Seth Kaplan had threatened to bring his mass gathering to Miami, which had become an epicenter for the disease by that time.

"Our goal is to eventually take this concept to other markets and spread the joy!" he said—as if that were the only thing spreading.[249]

Fortunately, the Safe & Sound tour seems to have gone the same way as McFarland's Fyre tour plans: absolutely nowhere. After the Southampton debacle, planned events for Miami, LA, Nashville, Chicago, and Atlanta appear to have been shelved. Kaplan's company was ultimately fined $20,000, and the town of Southampton is now barred from granting permits for large gatherings without state approval.

But at the White House, the music never stopped. Despite clear warnings from his own government epidemiologists, Trump persisted in defying local orders. He held thousand-person rallies that resulted in the infection of at least eight Trump surrogates (and the death of Herman Cain) and a superspreader event for Supreme Court justice Amy Coney Barrett that saw at least thirty-four White House staffers felled with the illness, according to a leaked FEMA report. Trump himself became so ill he was required to spend several days at Walter Reed hospital, where he was pumped full of experimental drugs and steroids. Still, upon arriving back at the White House—at the height of his infectious period—the president ripped off his mask, potentially exposing dozens of staffers who were in his immediate vicinity, all while filming (and then reshooting parts of) his triumphant return home.

Despite DC's mandatory face mask requirements, White House staffers continued to resist basic health advice, and less than three weeks after Trump's exposure, at least five aides to Vice President Mike Pence—the head of the coronavirus task force—tested positive at the end of October. Despite all the clear advice to the contrary, conservative supporters were still going about life as usual. When Amy Coney Barrett returned to the White House on October 26 for her confirmation, no one—not even the seventy-two-year-old justice who swore her in, Clarence Thomas—was wearing a mask.

"We are always emotional and sometimes rational, it's just human nature," infectious disease expert Dr. William Haseltine told the *Daily Beast* as the United States broke eighty-five thousand cases per day in October. "Belief trumps facts every time."[250]

★ ★ ★ ★ ★

Acknowledgments

First and foremost, I have to thank the people without whom there would be no book—so thank you, thank you, thank you to my editor, Peter Joseph, who guided this from a germ of an idea to something that may yet be worth reading. Your patience is preternatural; your edits, pristine. I am so grateful to you. Similarly, no one would be reading this today without the enduring support of my agents, Ross Harris and David Patterson, who made this whole thing happen, and never gave up on me, no matter how many times I promised the copy was coming…ASAP…very soon…ok, here's the thing…

A hat tip and a thank-you are owed to Chris Smith and Jon Karmen, who, frankly, already told most of this story better than I ever could.

Thanks to Leah McSweeney, Calvin Wells, Marc Weinstein, MDavid Low, Derrick Borte, Dr. Roberto Cavazos, Nick Viall, Nimrod Kamer, Seth Crossno, and Stacy Miller for their expertise and perspective, and to everyone else, on the record and off, for trusting me to tell their stories.

Thanks to Odeon for the steak, but more importantly, the fries.

Thanks to John Cook, whose lessons on rat killing came just in time for me to catch this story and take it out back. And my eternal gratitude to the Plotnicki family—Linda and Steve, Gideon and Chelsea, and Noah and Ashley—in whose perfect kitchen I first had the thought, *Maybe this could be a book?* Thanks to Brad Saveth and Christina Dermond, Hillary Yaffe, Alexis Kaplan, Carly Allen, Rick Sorkin, and Remy Kassimir for all your love and support.

This book was also written across many states, countries, and time zones, and I would be remiss not to thank the following people for their patience, feedback, and restraint whenever I pulled my laptop out at the pool: Greg Richner, Andrew Sacks Hoppenfeld, Brant Talesnick, TJ Ducklo, Brittany Pearl, and, of course, the Number! Five! DJ! In! The! World! *Et enfin mes chères amies parisiennes*, Kendra Kojcsich and Meghan Mitchum.

A VERY enthusiastic thank-you to the boys from Vermont: Trey, Mike, Jon, and Page, whose music brings joy to even the longest, loneliest stretches of writing, and who taught me the most important lesson of all: never miss a Sunday show.

And finally, let it be known… Gawker was a good website.

Endnotes

Introduction

1. Lauren Sanchez, "5 Festivals to Preemptively Fix That Coachella FOMO,"
    Vogue, April 11, 2017, https://web.archive.org/web/20170413205023/
    https://www.vogue.com/article/coachella-fomo-fyre-form-firefly-
    panorama-outside-lands-festival-season.

2. Gabrielle Bluestone, "Rich Millennials Paid Thousands for Ja Rule's Fyre
    Fest and Are Now Stranded on an Island in Disaster-Relief Tents," *VICE*
    News, April 28, 2017, https://www.vice.com/en/article/j5d944/rich-
    millennials-paid-thousands-for-ja-rules-fyre-fest-and-are-now-
    stranded-on-an-island-in-disaster-relief-tents.

3. United States v. McFarland, 1:17-mj-04988, No. 1 (S.D.N.Y. Jun. 30,
    2017), https://www.docketalarm.com/cases/New_York_Southern_
    District_Court/1—17-mj-04988/USA_v._McFarland/1/.

4. IBIS World, *Business Concierge Services Industry in the US*, December 31,
    2019, https://www.ibisworld.com/industry-trends/specialized-mar-
    ket-research-reports/advisory-financial-services/other-outsourced-
    functions/business-concierge-services.html.

5.   Gabrielle Bluestone, "Fyre Festival Founder Charged with Scamming People Out of $100K While Out on Bail," *VICE* News, June 13, 2018, https://www.vice.com/en/article/evkkan/fyre-festival-founder-billy-mcfarland-charged-with-additional-wire-fraud-and-money-laundering.

6.   U.S. Attorney's Office: Southern District of New York, "Manhattan U.S. Attorney Announces Charges Against Individual for Engaging in a Fraudulent Ticket Scam and Laundering Proceeds of the Fraud," press release, June 12, 2018, https://www.justice.gov/usao-sdny/pr/manhattan-us-attorney-announces-charges-against-individual-engaging-fraudulent-ticket.

7.   Colin Moynihan, "Fyre Festival Organizer Sentenced to Six Years in Federal Prison," *New York Times*, October 11, 2018, https://www.ny-times.com/2018/10/11/arts/music/fyre-festival-organizer-sentenced-fraud.html.

8.   United States v. McFarland, 1:17-cr-00600-NRB, No. 69 (S.D.N.Y. Oct. 22, 2018), https://www.courtlistener.com/recap/gov.uscourts.nysd.481447/gov.uscourts.nysd.481447.69.0.pdf.

9.   Chris Smith, *Fyre: The Greatest Party That Never Happened* (New York USA: Netflix, 2019). Documentary Film.

10.   Michael Sheetz, "Secretary DeVos, Walmart Heirs and Other Investors Reportedly Lost Over $600 Million on Theranos," CNBC, May 4, 2018, https://www.cnbc.com/2018/05/04/theranos-devos-other-investors-reportedly-lost-over-600-million.html.

11.   "The Joneses," Box Office Mojo, accessed December 4, 2020, https://www.boxofficemojo.com/release/rl1583187457/.

12.   Vicky McKeever, "This Eight-Year-Old Remains YouTube's Highest-Earner, Taking Home $26 Million in 2019," CNBC, December 20, 2019, https://www.cnbc.com/2019/12/20/ryan-kaji-remains-youtubes-highest-earner-making-26-million-in-2019.html.

13.   Julia Alexander, "Creators Finally Know How Much Money YouTube

Makes, and They Want More of It," The Verge, February 4, 2020, https://www.theverge.com/2020/2/4/21121370/youtube-advertising-revenue-creators-demonetization-earnings-google.

14.   Taylor Lorenz, "Welcome to the Era of Branded Engagements," *The Atlantic*, June 20, 2020, https://www.theatlantic.com/technology/archive/2019/06/was-viral-proposal-staged/592141/.

15.   Koh Ewe, "Influencer Licks Toilet Seat for TikTok Fame in 'Corona virus Challenge,'" *VICE* News, March 18, 2020, https://www.vice.com/en/article/5dm43a/coronavirus-influencer-lick-toilet-seat-tiktok.

16.   Dee LaVigne, "I Buy the Cheapest Thing on Hermes!!!," YouTube video, April 2, 2018, https://www.youtube.com/watch?v=Y1b7j4XnMfc.

17.   Sophie Shohet | Fashion Beauty Lifestyle, "I Looked for the Cheapest Thing Cartier Sold... 6 *Insane* Luxury Items Under £495 | Selfridges AD," YouTube video, June 17, 2020, https://www.youtube.com/watch?v=8ih2_Gq9X58.

18.   Federal Trade Commission, "FTC Staff Reminds Influencers and Brands to Clearly Disclose Relationship," press release, April 19, 2017, https://www.ftc.gov/news-events/press-releases/2017/04/ftc-staff-reminds-influencers-brands-clearly-disclose.

19.   Dan Wheeldon, "AUDI A4—Influencers & One Big Brand," We Are Social, February 9, 2016, https://wearesocial.com/uk/blog/2016/02/audi-a4-influencers-one-big-brand.

20.   Josh Constine, "Snapchat's PR Firm Sues Influencer for Not Promoting Spectacles on Instagram," *Tech Crunch*, October 31, 2018, https://techcrunch.com/2018/10/31/influencer-marketing-lawsuit/.

21.   Katie Roof, "Museum of Ice Cream Valued at $200 Million," *Wall Street Journal*, August 14, 2019, https://www.wsj.com/articles/museum-of-ice-cream-valued-at-200-million-11565782201.

22.   Digital Signage Connection, "Kinetic Makes a Summer Splash with

Launch of Aperol's First Ever OOH Campaign," press release, May 26, 2017, https://www.digitalsignageconnection.com/kinetic-makes-summer-splash-launch-aperols-first-ever-ooh-campaign.

23. Rebekah Peppler, "The Aperol Spritz is Not a Good Drink," *New York Times*, May 9, 2019, https://www.nytimes.com/2019/05/09/dining/drinks/aperol-spritz.html.

24. Nisha Chittal, "Who Cares if Aperol Spritzes are Brand-Engineered? They're Good," *Racked*, July 19, 2018, https://www.racked.com/2018/7/19/17589006/aperol-spritz-campari-brand-marketing-campaign.

25. Bethany Biron, "'Claw is the Law': Why American 'Bros' Suddenly Can't Get Enough of White Claw Hard Seltzer," *Business Insider*, August 1, 2019, https://www.businessinsider.com/white-claw-beloved-by-bros-2019-8.

26. Justin Kendall, "Nielsen: Total Beer Dollar Sales Up 5 Percent During July 4 Holiday Week," Brew Bound, July 17, 2019, https://www.brewbound.com/news/nielsen-total-beer-dollar-sales-up-5-percent-during-july-4-holiday-week.

27. Carmen Reinicke, "Hard-Seltzer Sales are Booming in the US—and UBS Says These 5 Beer Companies are Best Positioned to Profit from the Trend," *Business Insider*, July 30, 2019, https://www.businessinsider.com/beer-companies-stocks-best-for-hard-seltzer-boom-ubs-2019-7.

28. Ibid.

29. Kate Taylor, "Four Loko Teases a Hard Seltzer with Almost Triple the Alcohol Content of White Claw as Booze Makers Battle to Win Over 'Bros,'" *Business Insider*, August 14, 2019, https://markets.businessinsider.com/news/stocks/four-loko-teases-hard-seltzer-2019-8-1028446392.

30. Reuters Staff, "Bloomberg Campaign Pays Social Media Accounts for Memes," Reuters, February 13, 2020, https://fr.reuters.com/article/us-usa-election-bloomberg-meme-idUSKBN2072S9.

31.   Joe Garden, "Area Man Regrets Helping Turn Joe Biden Into a Meme," *VICE* News, May 16, 2019, https://www.vice.com/en/article/xwngb3/area-man-regrets-helping-turn-joe-biden-into-a-meme.

Chapter 1: The Cult of Flounder

32.   Jennifer Furst and Julia Willoughby Nason, *Fyre Fraud* (Santa Monica, CA: Hulu, 2019). Documentary Film.

33.   Eric Rubenstein (friend of Billy McFarland), in discussion with the author, November 2020.

34.   Jennifer Furst and Julia Willoughby Nason, *Fyre Fraud* (Santa Monica, CA: Hulu, 2019). Documentary Film.

35.   Dreamit, "DreamIt Philly Demo Day 2011: Spling," YouTube video, August 5, 2013, https://www.youtube.com/watch?v=EnjUDzt922Q.

36.   Bill McFarland, "Spling.com Announces Successful Launch of New Social Media Website," Cision PRWeb, December 4, 2020, https://www.prweb.com/releases/2011/04/prweb5252764.htm.

37.   Peter Huffman (former intern, Spling), in discussion with the author, April 2020.

38.   "Seed Round—Spling," Crunch Base, accessed December 4, 2020, https://www.crunchbase.com/funding_round/spling-seed—e1e9a870.

39.   Sarah Perez, "New Content Sharing Network Spling Launches, Announces $400K Series A," *Tech Crunch*, December 5, 2011, https://techcrunch.com/2011/12/05/new-content-sharing-network-spling-launches-announces-400k-series-a/.

40.   "List of Spling's 5 Investors," Crunch Base, accessed December 4, 2020, https://www.crunchbase.com/search/principal.investors/field/organizations/num_investors/spling.

41.   Brandon Wenerd (publisher, BroBible), in discussion with author, April 2020.

42.   Sarah Perez, "New Content Sharing Network Spling Launches, Announces $400K Series A," TechCrunch, December 5, 2011, https://techcrunch.com/2011/12/05/new-content-sharing-network-spling-launches-announces-400k-series-a/.

43.   Alexis C. Madrigal, "The Uber IPO is a Landmark," *The Atlantic*, April 11, 2019, https://www.theatlantic.com/technology/archive/2019/04/ubers-ipo-historic-despite-its-10-billion-loss/586999/.

44.   Lydia Ramsey Pflanzer, "The Rise and Fall of Theranos, The Blood-Testing Startup That Went from Silicon Valley Darling to Facing Fraud Charges," *Business Insider*, April 11, 2019, https://www.businessinsider.com/the-history-of-silicon-valley-unicorn-theranos-and-ceo-elizabeth-holmes-2018-5.

45.   Erik Larson, "Festival Fraudster Who Targeted Status Seekers Gets 6 Years," *Bloomberg*, October 11, 2018, https://www.bloomberg.com/news/articles/2018-10-11/festival-fraudster-who-targeted-status-seekers-gets-six-years.

46.   U.S. Marshals Service, *U.S. Marshals Selling Items From Fyre Festival Fraud Scheme:* by the U.S. Department of Justice, July 30, 2020, https://www.usmarshals.gov/news/chron/2020/073020.htm.

47.   Calvin Wells (venture capitalist), in discussion with the author, 2017–2020.

48.   Rick Claypool and R. Weissman, "Disrupting Democracy: How Uber Deploys Corporate Power to Overwhelm and Undermine Local Government." Washington, DC: Public Citizen, 2016, https://www.citizen.org/wp-content/uploads/uber-disrupting-democracy-corporate-power-report.pdf.

49.   Rob Stumpf, "Tesla Had 3 Times as Many OSHA Violations as the 10 Largest US Plants Combined, The Drive, March 3, 2019, https://www.thedrive.com/news/26727/tesla-had-3-times-as-many-osha-violations-as-the-10-largest-us-plants-combined.

50.   Russ Mitchell, "Tesla Had Worse Safety Records than Slaughterhouses and Sawmills, but Says it's Improving," *Los Angeles Times*, May 24,

2017, https://www.latimes.com/business/autos/la-fi-hy-tesla-work-place-safety-20170524-story.html.

51. Taylor Telford, "Elon Musk: Tweet that Cost $20 Million was 'Worth It,'" *Washington Post*, October 29, 2019, https://www.washington-post.com/business/2018/10/29/musk-tweet-that-cost-million-was-worth-it/.

52. Tom Krisher, "3 Crashes, 3 Deaths Raise Questions About Tesla's Autopilot," AP News, January 3, 2020, https://apnews.com/article/ca5e62255bb87bf1b151f9bf075aaadf.

53. Shane Parrish and Josh Wolfe, "50: Inventing the Future," January 22, 2019, in *The Knowledge Project*, produced by Farnam Street, podcast, mp3 audio, 1:37:25, https://fs.blog/knowledge-project/josh-wolfe/.

54. Elaine Low, "As Quibi Shutters, So Goes Nearly $2 Billion in Major Hollywood Investments," Variety, October 21, 2020, https://variety.com/2020/tv/news/quibi-shuts-down-hollywood-in-vestoes-1234812522/.

55. Elon Musk (@elonmusk), "Based on current trends, proba-bly close to zero new cases in US too by end of April," Twit-ter, March 19, 2020, 11:38 p.m., https://twitter.com/elonmusk/status/1240754657263144960.

56. Elon Musk (@elonmusk), "Tesla is filing a lawsuit against Alam-eda County immediately. The unelected & ignorant 'Interim Health Officer' of Alameda is acting contrary to the Governor, the Pres-ident, our Constitutional freedoms & just plain common sense!," Twitter, May 9, 2020, 6:34 p.m., https://twitter.com/elonmusk/sta-tus/1259159878427267072.

57. Ryan Mac, Mark Di Stefano, and John Paczkowski, "In a New Email, Elon Musk Accused a Cave Rescuer of Being a 'Child Rapist' and Said He 'Hopes' There's a Lawsuit," BuzzFeed News, September 4, 2018, https://www.buzzfeednews.com/article/ryanmac/elon-musk-thai-cave-rescuer-accusations-buzzfeed-email.

58. Jon Passantino, "Elon Musk Says He Sent Ventilators To California

Hospitals, They Say They Got Something Else Instead," CNN Business, April 17, 2020, https://www.cnn.com/2020/04/17/tech/elon-musk-ventilators-california/index.html.

59. Avery Hartmans, "Elon Musk Lashed Out at Reports That He Never Delivered Ventilators to California Hospitals. Here's What's Going On, and Why Musk's Ventilator Efforts Have Become Controversial," *Business Insider*, April 17, 2020, https://www.businessinsider.com/elon-musk-tesla-ventilator-controversy-explained-2020-4#april-2-musk-defends-the-ventilators-he-delivered-after-facing-criticism-for-sending-non-invasive-bipap-machines-instead-of-traditional-ventilators-6.

60. Tyler Sonnemaker, "The Hackers Who Took Over the Twitter Accounts of Joe Biden and Elon Musk May Have Made Off With as Much as $120,000 Worth of Bitcoin—But We May Never Know for Sure," *Business Insider*, July 16, 2020, https://www.businessinsider.com/twitter-hackers-joe-biden-elon-musk-received-120000-bitcoin-payments-2020-7.

61. Bill Ruthhart and John Byrne, "Chicago Taps Elon Musk's Boring Company to Build High-Speed Transit Tunnels That Would Tie Loop with O'Hare," *Chicago Tribune*, June 14, 2018, https://www.chicago-tribune.com/politics/ct-met-ohare-high-speed-transit-elon-musk-boring-company-20180613-story.html.

62. Jack Holmes, "A Trump Surrogate Drops the Mic: 'There's No Such Thing as Facts,'" *Esquire*, December 1, 2016, https://www.esquire.com/news-politics/videos/a51152/trump-surrogate-no-such-thing-as-facts/.

63. Donald J. Trump (@realDonaldTrump), "In addition to winning the Electoral College in a landslide, I won the popular vote if you deduct the millions of people who voted illegally," Twitter, November 27, 2016, 10:30 p.m., https://twitter.com/realdonaldtrump/status/802972944532209664?lang=en.

64. Steven Shepard, "Poll: Half of Trump Voters Say Trump Won Popular Vote," Politico, July 26, 2017, https://www.politico.com/story/2017/07/26/trump-clinton-popular-vote-240966.

65. Lee McIntyre, *Post-Truth* (The MIT Press Essential Knowledge series, February 16, 2018), Page: 175. Book.

66. Tom Huddleston Jr., "Fyre Festival: How a 25-Year-Old Scammed Investors out of $26 Million," CNBC, August 18, 2019, https://www.cnbc.com/2019/08/18/how-fyre-festivals-organizer-scammed-investors-out-of-26-million.html.

67. Securities and Exchange Commission v. William Z. ("Billy") McFarland et al., Civil Action No. 1:18-cv-6634 (S.D.N.Y. filed July 24, 2018), https://www.sec.gov/litigation/complaints/2018/comp-pr2018-141.pdf

68. Robert Frank, Scott Zamost, Hannah Kliot, and Jasmine Wu. "Tailspin: JetSmarter Tried to Be the Uber of Private Jets, Now it Faces Lawsuits, Losses and Security Questions," CNBC, January 10, 2019, https://www.cnbc.com/2019/01/08/jetsmarter-faces-lawsuits-losses-and-security-questions.html/.

69. Richard Morgan, "JetSmarter may be sold for a fraction of its targeted value," *New York Post*, February 10, 2019, https://nypost.com/2019/02/10/jetsmarter-may-be-sold-for-a-fraction-of-its-targeted-value/.

70. Jeffrey Atkins, (aka Ja Rule), "Through the Fyre: A Fireside Chat with Ja Rule," Speech, Internet Summit, Raleigh, NC. November 14, 2019.

71. "Stacy Miller Wins Case Against Fyre Festival," Miller Law Group, PLLC, accessed December 4, 2020, https://millerlawgroupnc.com/fyre-fest/.

72. Cheryl Paradis, "Forensic Psychological Report; William McFarland; S2 17 Cr. 600 (NRB)," letter submitted to court, August 26, 2018.

73. Andrew P. Levin, "Re: William McFarland; United States District Court, Southern District of New York, 17-CR-00600-NRB and 18-CR-00446-JMF," letter submitted to court, August 20, 2018.

74. Alex Sherman, "WeWork's $47 Billion Valuation Was Always a Fiction

Created by SoftBank," CNBC, October 22, 2019, https://www.cnbc. com/2019/10/22/wework-47-billion-valuation-softbank-fiction.html.

75. Adam Neumann, Baruch College Commencement 2017. Speech, Baruch College, New York, NY, June 12, 2017.

76. Kevin Roose, "Do Not Disturb: How I Ditched My Phone and Unbroke My Brain," *New York Times,* February 23, 2019, https://www. nytimes.com/2019/02/23/business/cell-phone-addiction.html.

77. Ben Gilbert, "WeWork Paid Its Own CEO $5.9 Million to Use the Name 'We,' But Now He's Giving It Back After the Deal was Criticized," *Business Insider,* September 4, 2019, https://www. businessinsider.com/wework-ceo-gives-back-millions-from-we-trademark-after-criticism-2019-9.

78. Amy Chozick, "Adam Neumann and the Art of Failing Up," *New York Times,* November 2, 2019, https://www.nytimes.com/2019/11/02/ business/adam-neumann-wework-exit-package.html.

Chapter 2: Fake It Till You Make It

79. Jennifer Furst and Julia Willoughby Nason, *Fyre Fraud* (Santa Monica, CA: Hulu, 2019). Documentary Film.

80. Mara Siegler, "Wannabe Socialite Swindler May Have Bilked Fyre Festival Fraudster," Page Six, July 23, 2018, https://pagesix. com/2018/07/23/socialite-swindler-may-have-bilked-fyre-festival-fraudster/.

81. Jack Crosbie, "Elon Musk Made Me a Socialist," Discourseblog, Substack.com, May 2, 2020, https://discourseblog.substack.com/p/elon-musk-made-me-a-socialist.

82. Kim Bhasin and Polly Mosendz, "How a Black-Card Wannabe Went Down in Flames," *Bloomberg,* August 31, 2017, https://www.bloomberg. com/news/articles/2017-08-30/how-a-black-card-wannabe-went-down-in-flames.

83. Securities and Exchange Commission v. William Z. ("Billy") Mc-

Farland et al., Civil Action No. 1:18-cv-6634 (S.D.N.Y. filed July 24, 2018), https://www.sec.gov/litigation/complaints/2018/comp-pr2018-141.pdf.

84. Doree Lewak, "The College Dropout Behind NYC's Most Exclusive Credit Card," *New York Post*, July 5, 2014, https://nypost.com/2014/07/05/the-22-year-old-dropout-who-created-nycs-most-exclusive-credit-card/.

85. Gregory E. Miller, "Ja Rule Steals Rick Ross' Fashion Week Show," *New York Post*, September 6, 2014, https://nypost.com/2014/09/06/ja-rule-steals-rick-ross-fashion-week-show/.

86. Kathianne Boniello, "Tech Bro Sued for Trashing $13K-a-Month West Village Pad," *New York Post*, June 28, 2015, https://nypost.com/2015/06/28/tech-bro-sued-for-trashing-13k-a-month-west-village-pad/.

87. Rachel Kurzius, "Guess What Happened When Fyre Festival Organizer Promised D.C. A Ja Rule Concert," *DCist*, May 3, 2017, https://dcist.com/story/17/05/03/fyre-festival-ja-rule-magnises-wale/.

88. Confidential Staff, "Fyre Festival Debacle No Surprise to New York Jet-Setters," *New York Daily News*, May 2, 2017, https://www.nydailynews.com/entertainment/gossip/confidential/new-york-jet-setters-surprised-fyre-festival-chaos-article-1.3130499.

89. "Update: Earn a Free Apple Watch by Referring Members to Magnises," Wefunder, accessed December 4, 2020, https://wefunder.com/updates/10950.

90. Author interview with former Magnesis employee, 2017.

91. Gabrielle Bluestone, "Exclusive Documents Reveal Fyre Festival's 'Shitshow' Ticket Scheme," *VICE* News, September 8, 2017, https://www.vice.com/en/article/j5dae8/fyre-fest-concert-tickets-billy-macfarland.

92. Edward Helmore, "Anna Sorokin: Fake German Heiress Sentenced To Up To 12 Years in Prison," The Guardian, May 9, 2019, https://

www.theguardian.com/us-news/2019/may/09/anna-sorokin-sentence-fake-heiress-scammer-delvey-jail-time-latest-news-new-york-trial.

93. Jessica Pressler, "How Anna Delvey Tricked New York's Party People," The Cut, May 28, 2018, https://www.thecut.com/2018/05/how-anna-delvey-tricked-new-york.html.

94. Nimrod Kamer, "Trump Lawyer Offered to Buy My Fake Obama Birth Video," Nimrod Kamer, October 14, 2020, https://nnimrodd.medium.com/trump-lawyer-offered-to-buy-my-fake-obama-birth-video-e1600c377173.

95. Timothy Noah, "The Trump You've Yet to Meet," The Atlantic, November 30, 2020, https://www.theatlantic.com/ideas/archive/2020/11/trump-youve-yet-meet/617200/.

96. Graham Isador, "These Artists Scammed a '$36K Film Shoot' by Faking an Engagement," VICE News, January 21, 2020, https://www.vice.com/en/article/884gw5/these-artists-scammed-a-dollar36k-film-shoot-by-faking-an-engagement.

97. Jessica Rach, "Youtuber Natalia Taylor Fakes Holiday to Bali in Ikea," Daily Mail, February 19, 2020, https://www.dailymail.co.uk/femail/article-8015663/Youtuber-Natalia-Taylor-fakes-holiday-Bali-Ikea.html.

98. Taryn Ryder, "Billionaire Socialite Bought Kim Kardashian's House and Now They're Partying Together," Yahoo Finance, March 6, 2018, https://finance.yahoo.com/news/billionaire-socialite-bought-kim-kardashians-house-now-theyre-partying-together-165335068.html.

99. The Blast Staff, "Kim Kardashian's House Sale Obligated Fame Promotion for Rich Buyer," The Blast, July 6, 2018, https://theblast.com/kim-kardashian-kanye-west-marina-acton-mansion-sale-singing-career/.

100. Marina Acton v. Deeona Capital, Case No. SC 129047 (Cal. 2018), https://trellis.law/ruling/SC129047/MARINA-ACTON-VS-NOVEIL-CAPITAL/20180511abab4b.

101. Vanna Le, "Gisele Audited by IRS, Blames Forbes: 'I Earn Plenty, but

Not as Much as They Say,'" *Forbes*, April 11, 2014, https://www.forbes.com/sites/vannale/2014/04/11/gisele-audited-by-irs-says-its-forbes-fault-i-earn-plenty-but-not-as-much-as-they-say/?sh=62679d83302a.

102. Chase Peterson Withorn and Madeline Berg, "Inside Kylie Jenner's Web of Lies—And Why She's No Longer a Billionaire," *Forbes*, June 1, 2020, https://www.forbes.com/sites/chasewithorn/2020/05/29/inside-kylie-jennerss-web-of-lies-and-why-shes-no-longer-a-billionaire/?sh=3488492c25f7.

103. Sarah Hansen, "Kylie Jenner, Responding To Forbes Report, Says She Never 'Tried To Lie,'" *Forbes*, May 29, 2020, https://www.forbes.com/sites/sarahhansen/2020/05/29/kylie-jenner-responding-forbes-report-says-she-never-tried-to-lie/?sh=41a9f9792bc4.

104. TFL, "Coty is Being Sued for Allegedly Overpaying for 'Inflated' Kylie Cosmetics, Deceiving Shareholders," The Fashion Law, September 14, 2020, https://www.thefashionlaw.com/coty-is-being-sued-for-allegedly-overpaying-for-inflated-kylie-cosmetics.

105. Jonathan Greenberg, "Perspective | Trump Lied to Me About His Wealth to Get onto the *Forbes* 400. Here are the Tapes," *Washington Post*, April 20, 2018, https://www.washingtonpost.com/outlook/trump-lied-to-me-about-his-wealth-to-get-onto-the-forbes-400-here-are-the-tapes/2018/04/20/ac762b08-4287-11e8-8569-26fd-a6b404c7_story.html.

106. Dan Alexander, "The Case of Wilbur Ross' Phantom $2 Billion," *Forbes*, December 12, 2017, https://www.forbes.com/sites/danalexander/2017/11/07/the-case-of-wilbur-ross-phantom2-billion/?sh=19d6303b7515.

107. Ibid.

108. Dan Alexander, "New Details About Wilbur Ross' Business Point To Pattern of Grifting," *Forbes*, August 7 2018, https://www.forbes.com/sites/danalexander/2018/08/06/new-details-about-wilbur-rosss-businesses-point-to-pattern-of-grifting/?sh=1a1f2bc81c33

109. Ibid.

110. Scott Simon, "How a Fake Restaurant Became London's Top Spot on TripAdvisor," NPR, December 9, 2017, https://www.npr.org/sections/thesalt/2017/12/09/569601017/opening-the-hottest-fake-restaurant-in-town.

111. Ranjan Roy, "Doordash and Pizza Arbitrage," TheMargins.Substack.com, May 18, 2020, https://themargins.substack.com/p/doordash-and-pizza-arbitrage.

112. Deanna Pai, "When (and How and Why) Sunday Riley Got So Effing Buzzy So Damn Fast," *Allure*, March 17, 2017, https://www.allure.com/story/sunday-riley-skin-care-facts.

113. Leah Prinzivalli, "Sunday Riley Responds to Allegations of Fake, Employee-Written Sephora Reviews [Updated]," *Allure*, October 18, 2018, https://www.allure.com/story/sunday-riley-admits-asking-employees-post-fake-reviews.

114. FTC, "Sunday Riley Modern Skincare, LLC; In the Matter Of," Federal Trade Commission, October 4, 2019, https://www.ftc.gov/enforcement/cases-proceedings/192-3008/sunday-riley-modern-skincare-llc-matter.

Chapter 3: Under the Influencer

115.   Chris Smith, *Fyre: The Greatest Party That Never Happened* (New York USA: Netflix, 2019). Documentary Film.

116. Private internal emails reviewed by author, November 2016.

117. Chris Smith, *Fyre: The Greatest Party That Never Happened* (New York USA: Netflix, 2019). Documentary Film.

118. Jennifer Furst and Julia Willoughby Nason, *Fyre Fraud* (Santa Monica, CA: Hulu, 2019). Documentary Film.

119. Robert Prentice, "Under Fyre," Ethics Unwrapped, March 28, 2019, https://ethicsunwrapped.utexas.edu/under-fyre.

120. Private internal emails reviewed by author, December 2016.

121. Chris Smith, *Fyre: The Greatest Party That Never Happened* (New York USA: Netflix, 2019). Documentary Film.

122. Emma Brockes, "It's Not Just the Fyre Festival—This is the Golden Age of the Social Media Con | Emma Brockes," The Guardian, January 17, 2019, https://www.theguardian.com/commentisfree/2019/jan/17/fyre-festival-social-media-con-documentaries.

123. Kaya Yurieff, "Snapchat Stock Loses $1.3 Billion after Kylie Jenner Tweet," CNNMoney, February 23, 2018, https://money.cnn.com/2018/02/22/technology/snapchat-update-kylie-jenner/index.html.

124. Brian Feldman, BNet.Substack.com.

125. Alexandra Sternlicht, "Instagram Influencer Danielle Bernstein (WeWoreWhat) Launches Tech Suite For Influencers," *Forbes*, October 2, 2019, https://www.forbes.com/sites/alexandrasternlicht/2019/10/02/instagram-influencer-danielle-bernstein-weworewhat-launches-tech-suite-for-influencers/.

126. Rachel Strugatz, "How WeWoreWhat's Danielle Bernstein Sold Nearly $2 Million in Swimwear in 12 Hours," The Business of Fashion, May 3, 2019, https://www.businessoffashion.com/articles/retail/how-weworewhats-danielle-bernstein-sold-nearly-2-million-in-swimwear-in-12-hours.

127. Tanya Chen, "A Poshmark Reseller Somehow Got Her Hands on a Major Fashion Influencer's Unreleased Clothing. Drama Ensued," BuzzFeed News, January 22, 2020, https://www.buzzfeednews.com/article/tanyachen/dramatic-saga-between-fashion-influencer-weworewhat-and.

128. Layla Ilchi, "The Biggest Influencer Controversies of 2020—So Far," *Women's Wear Daily*, August 18, 2020, https://wwd.com/fashion-news/fashion-scoops/the-biggest-influencer-controversies-of-2020-arielle-charnas-danielle-bernstein-jeffree-star-1203690408/.

129. Dara Prant, "We Wore What is in Hot Water over Allegedly Copying Jewelry Designs [Updated]," Fashionista, July 11, 2018,

https://fashionista.com/2018/05/danielle-bernstein-we-wore-what-jewelry-copy-diet-prada-allegations.

130. Lia Eustachewich, "Influencer Squats at Hamptons House After Not Paying $14K Back Rent: Suit," *New York Post*, October 28, 2020, https://nypost.com/2020/10/28/influencer-squats-at-hamptons-house-after-not-paying-rent-suit/.

131. Taylor Lorenz, "The Original Renegade," *New York Times*, February 13, 2020, sec. Style, https://www.nytimes.com/2020/02/13/style/the-original-renegade.html.

132. Michael Wittner, "Beverly Hill Investigates TikTok Party Mansion," Patch, August 28 2020, https://patch.com/california/beverlyhills/beverly-hills-investigates-tiktok-party-mansion

133. Silke M. Müller et al., "Maximizing Social Outcomes? Social Zapping and Fear of Missing Out Mediate the Effects of Maximization and Procrastination on Problematic Social Networks Use," *Computers in Human Behavior* 107: 106296, June 2020, https://doi.org/10.1016/j.chb.2020.106296.

134. Daria Kuss and Mark Griffiths, "Social Networking Sites and Addiction: Ten Lessons Learned," *International Journal of Environmental Research and Public Health* 14, no. 3: 311, March 17, 2017, https://doi.org/10.3390/ijerph14030311.

135. Oriana Schwindt, "TV Ratings: 'The Bachelor' Wins Big, 'Celebrity Apprentice' Grows," Variety, January 17, 2017, https://variety.com/2017/tv/news/tv-ratings-the-bachelor-celebrity-apprentice-1201961492/.

136. Influencer Marketing, "The State of Influencer Marketing 2019: Benchmark Report [+Infographic]," Influencer Marketing Hub, March 15, 2019, https://influencermarketinghub.com/influencer-marketing-2019-benchmark-report/.

137. Jacob Dirnhuber, "Children Turn Backs on Traditional Careers in Favour of Internet Fame, Study Finds," *The Sun*, May 22, 2017, http://

www.thesun.co.uk/news/3617062/children-turn-backs-on-traditional-careers-in-favour-of-internet-fame-study-finds.

138. Josef Adalian, "CBS Took a Big Gamble on Love Island this Summer. Did it Pay Off?" Vulture, August 7, 2019, https://www.vulture.com/2019/08/cbs-love-island-ratings-renewed.html.

139. Sarah Manavis, "The Love Island Contestants Ranked by the Best Sponsorship Deals," New Statesman, July 30, 2018, https://www.newstatesman.com/culture/tv-radio/2018/07/love-island-contestants-ranked-best-sponsorship-deals.

Chapter 4: The Allegory of the Fave

140. GumGum, "The Man Who Stopped the Internet with a Single Color," Medium, August 18, 2020, https://medium.com/gumgum-advertising/the-man-who-stopped-the-internet-with-a-single-color-44a8272b41a1.

141. Katharine Schwab, "Fyre Festival's Lead Designer Talks About Branding a Scam," Fast Company, March 26, 2019, https://www.fastcompany.com/90324689/fyre-festivals-lead-designer-on-branding-a-scam.

142. Jeffrey Atkins (aka Ja Rule). "Through the Fyre: A Fireside Chat with Ja Rule." Speech, Internet Summit, Raleigh, NC. November 14, 2019.

143. Hannah Karp, "At Up to $250,000 a Ticket, Island Music Festival Woos Wealthy to Stay Afloat," Wall Street Journal, April 2, 2017, https://www.wsj.com/articles/fyre-festival-organizers-push-to-keep-it-from-fizzling-1491130804.

144. Ben Kaye, "Kendall Jenner Settles Fyre Festival Lawsuit, Ordered to Pay $90K," Consequence of Sound, May 20, 2020, https://consequenceofsound.net/2020/05/kendall-jenner-fyre-festival-lawsuit-settlement/.

145. Case No: 06634, July 24, 2018, Pages: 25, Court: UNITED STATES DISTRICT COURT, PDF, www.sec.gov/litigation/complaints/2018/comp-pr2018-141.pdf.

146. Kenzie Bryant, "Can a Critical Mass of Victoria's Secret Models and a Hadid Give Bahamas Tourism an Insta-Boost?'" *Vanity Fair*, April 26, 2017, https://www.vanityfair.com/style/2017/04/bella-hadid-emily-ratajkowski-fyre-festival-exumas-bahamas.

147. Nir Eyal, *Hooked: How to Build Habit-Forming Products*. Editor: Ryan Hoover. (New York: Portfolio/Penguin, 2014). Book.

148. Kevin Roose, "Do Not Disturb: How I Ditched My Phone and Unbroke My Brain," *New York Times*, February 23, 2019, www.nytimes.com/2019/02/23/business/cell-phone-addiction.html.

149. Chris Lindahl, "Facebook Slams the Social Dilemma as Sensationalist, Says Netflix Doc Unfairly Scapegoats Platform," IndieWire, October 3, 2020, www.indiewire.com/2020/10/facebook-response-the-social-dilemma-1234590361/.

150. Russell Brand, "Stop Being Your Phone's Slave!" YouTube video, September 19, 2019, www.youtube.com/watch?v=Yjixt4eKSas.

151. Nir Eyal, *Hooked: How to Build Habit-Forming Products*. Editor: Ryan Hoover. (New York: Portfolio/Penguin, 2014). Book.

152. Ibid.

153. Ibid.

154. Ibid.

155. Albert Bandura, *Social Learning Theory* (New York: General Learning Press, 1977). Book.

156. Thomas Gültzow, Jeanine P.D. Guidry, Francine Schneider, and Ciska Hoving, "Male Body Image Portrayals on Instagram," *Cyberpsychology, Behavior, and Social Networking*, Volume: 23, No: 5, May 6, 2020, www.liebertpub.com/doi/10.1089/cyber.2019.0368.

157. Brenda K. Wiederhold, "Instagram and the Male Body Image," *Cyberpsychology, Behavior, and Social Networking*, press release, 2020, https://www.eurekalert.org/pub_releases/2020-04/mali-iat042720.php.

158. Raghavendra Katikalapudi, Sriram Chellappan, Frances Montgomery, Donald Wunsch, and Karl Lutzen, "Associating Internet Usage with Depressive Behavior Among College Students," *JIEEE Technology and Society Magazine*, Volume: 31, No: 4, December 24 2012, https://ieeexplore.ieee.org/document/6387969.

159. Nir Eyal, *Hooked: How to Build Habit-Forming Products. Editor: Ryan Hoover* (New York: Portfolio/Penguin, 2014). Book.

160. BJ Fogg, "BJ Fogg's Video Guide to How Behavior Works," https://community.virginpulse.com/bjfogg-how-behavior-works-301.

161. Morten L. Kringelbach and Kent C. Berridge, "The Functional Neuroanatomy of Pleasure and Happiness," *NIH PublicAccess*, Volume: 9, No: 49 (December 22, 2010), Pages: 579–587, www.ncbi.nlm.nih.gov/pmc/articles/PMC3008353/#::text=Just%20over%20fifty%20years%20ago,their%20brains%20(Olds%20and%20Milner.

162. Charles E. Moan and Robert G. Heath,, "Septal Stimulation for the Initiation of Heterosexual Behavior in a Homosexual Male," *Journal of Behavior Therapy and Experimental Psychiatry*, Volume: 3, No: 1, March 1972, Pages: 23-26, www.sciencedirect.com/science/article/abs/pii/0005791672900298.

163. Nir Eyal, *Hooked: How to Build Habit-Forming Products. Editor: Ryan Hoover* (New York: Portfolio/Penguin, 2014). Book.

164. David J. Linden, "The Neuroscience of Pleasure," HuffPost, July 7, 2011, www.huffpost.com/entry/compass-pleasure_b_890342.

165. Louis Bergeron, "The Influence of the Irrelevant: Researchers Show Stimuli Unrelated to a Decision Can Still Influence the Choice We Make," Stanford, April 2, 2008, https://news.stanford.edu/pr/2008/riskybiz-040208.html.

166. Nir Eyal, *Hooked: How to Build Habit-Forming Products. Editor: Ryan Hoover* (New York: Portfolio/Penguin, 2014). Book.

167. Andrew K. Przybylski, Kou Murayama, Cody R. DeHaan, and Valerie Gladwell; "Motivational, Emotional, and Behavioral Correlates

of Fear of Missing Out," *Computers in Human Behavior*, Volume: 29, No: 4, July 2013, Pages: 1841-1848, www.sciencedirect.com/science/article/abs/pii/S0747563213000800?via%3Dihub.

168. Ibid.

169. Silke M. Müller et al., "Maximizing Social Outcomes? Social Zapping and Fear of Missing Out Mediate the Effects of Maximization and Procrastination on Problematic Social Networks Use," *Computers in Human Behavior* 107 (June 2020): 106296, https://doi.org/10.1016/j.chb.2020.106296.

170. Janice T.S. Ho, C.E. Ang, Joanne Loh, and Irene Ng; "A Preliminary Study of Kiasu Behaviour - Is It Unique to Singapore?" *Journal of Managerial Psychology*, Volume: 13, No: 5/6, Pages: 359-370, August 1, 1998, https://pdfs.semanticscholar.org/1ac2/5041da336e61a2c243 d81b304422cbaf1808.pdf.

171. Aleks Eror, "Why Are Supreme Fanboys Hating on 'Game of Thrones' Star Maisie Williams?" Highsnobiety , June 21, 2016, https://www.highsnobiety.com/p/supreme-maisie-williams/.

172. Lara Chan-Baker, 'Interview: Shawn Stussy,' *Acclaim*, n.d., https://acclaimmag.com/style/interview-shawn-stussy/.

173. Noah Johnson, "Supreme Leader: The Extended James Jebbia Interview," *GQ*, July 26, 2019, www.gq.com/story/supreme-james-jebbia-extended-interview.

174. Foster Kamer, "The Battle of Supreme vs. Married to the Mob is Over, and This is Why," Complex, July 01, 2013, www.complex.com/style/2013/07/the-war-of-supreme-vs-married-to-the-mob-has-ended-with-a-settlement.

175. Foster Kamer, "Barbara Kruger Responds to Supremes' Lawsuit," Complex, May 02, 2013, www.complex.com/style/2013/05/barbara-kruger-responds-to-supremes-lawsuit-a-ridiculous-clusterfk-of-totally-uncool-jokers.

176. Jake Flanagin, "Supreme x Carlyle Group: The Hype-Fueled Partner-

ship with Ties to the War in Yemen," *Esquire*, January 16, 2019, www.esquire.com/style/mens-fashion/a25736933/supreme-carlyle-group-yemen-saudi-arabia/.

177. Alex Leach, "Has Supreme Lost its Edge?"; Highsnobiety, n.d., www.highsnobiety.com/p/supreme-debate/.

178. David Shapiro, July 5, 2016, *Supremacist*, Pages: 200. (New York: Tyrant Books, 2016).

179. Nadia Khomami, "Red Clay Brick On Sale for Up to $1,000 On eBay," The Guardian, September 30, 2016, www.theguardian.com/technology/2016/sep/30/red-clay-brick-selling-for-up-to-1000-on-ebay.

180. Stewart Perrie, "Supreme is Now Selling Packets of Oreos For $12," LADbible, February 19, 2020, www.ladbible.com/news/food-supreme-is-now-selling-individual-oreos-for-12-20200219.

181. Harald Dutzler, Laura Leeb, and Willibald Kofler, "Streetwear: The New Exclusivity: Five Ways Fashion Brands Can Win in a Growing Market," Strategy&, n.d., www.strategyand.pwc.com/gx/en/insights/2019/streetwear.html.

182. Yiannis Gabriel, "Psychoanalysis-and-Identity-1," YiannisGabriel.com, March 2015, www.yiannisgabriel.com/2015/03/psychoanalysis-and-identity-1.html?q=%22%E2%80%9CIf+the+therapeutic+function+of+freedom%22.

183. Terry Carter Jr., "Here are All the Celebrities Who Were Lucky Enough to Get an Ivy Park x Adidas Box From Beyoncé," BuzzFeed, January 17, 2020, www.buzzfeed.com/terrycarter/beyonce-sent-celebrities-ivy-park-x-adidas-boxes.

184. Joan Summers, "Kim Kardashian Swears She Didn't Mail Herself a Giant Orange Ivy Park Gift Box," Jezebel, January 29, 2020, https://jezebel.com/kim-kardashian-swears-she-didnt-mail-herself-a-giant-or-1841326278.

185. Meagan Fredette, "Kim Kardashian Finally Received Her Orange Ivy

Park Box," Revelist, January 29, 2020, www.revelist.com/style-news/
kim-kardashian-ivy-park/17162.

186. Jessica Jacolbe, "On Brands' Bad Social Media," JSTOR, July 27, 2019,
https://daily.jstor.org/on-brands-bad-social media/.

187. Naomi Klein, "No Logo at 10," *The Baffler*, Vol. 2, No. 1 [18], pp. 30–
39, 2010, https://www.jstor.org/stable/43307610?seq=1.

188. Emily Gosling, "Fyre Festival Designer Oren Aks Opens Up, Reveals Unused Designs + Bizarre Text Convos," AIGA, April 2, 2019,
https://eyeondesign.aiga.org/fyre-festival-designer-oren-aks-opens-
up-reveals-unused-designs-bizarre-text-convos/.

189. Aleks Eror, "What David Shapiro's 'Supremacist' Teaches Us About
Supreme Fuccbois," Highsnobiety, June 16, 2016, https://www.high-
snobiety.com/p/david-shapiro-supremacist/.

190. Tom Peters, "The Brand Called You, Fast Company," *Fast Company*,
August, 31, 1997, www.fastcompany.com/28905/brand-called-you.

191. Lee McIntyre, *Post-Truth* (The MIT Press Essential Knowledge series,
February 16, 2018), Page: 175. Book.

192. Harry Markopolos, *No One Would Listen : A True Financial Thriller*
(Hoboken, N.J.: Wiley; Chichester, 2011). Book.

193. Onur Varol et al., "Online Human-Bot Interactions: Detection,
Estimation, and Characterization," International AAAI Conference on Web and Social Media, March 27, 2017, https://arxiv.org/
pdf/1703.03107.pdf.

194. Michael Newberg, "As Many as 48 Million Twitter Accounts Aren't
People, Says Study," CNBC, March 10, 2017, http://www.cnbc.
com/2017/03/10/nearly-48-million-twitter-accounts-could-be-bots-
says-study.html.

195. Seung-A Annie Jin and Joe Phua, "Following Celebrities' Tweets
About Brands: The Impact of Twitter-Based Electronic Word-
of-Mouth on Consumers' Source Credibility Perception, Buying

Intention, and Social Identification With Celebrities," *Journal of Advertising* 43, no. 2 (April 3, 2014): 181–95, https://doi.org/10.1080/00 913367.2013.827606.

196. BBC, "How Much Does Kylie Jenner Earn on Instagram? CBBC Newsround," BBC, July 26, 2019, https://www.bbc.co.uk/news-round/49124484.

197. Nicholas Confessore et al., "The Follower Factory," *New York Times*, January 27, 2018, https://www.nytimes.com/interactive/2018/01/27/technology/social media-bots.html.

198. Rand Fishkin, "We Analyzed Every Twitter Account Following Donald Trump: 61% Are Bots, Spam, Inactive, or Propaganda," SparkToro, October 9, 2018, https://sparktoro.com/blog/we-analyzed-every-twitter-account-following-donald-trump-61-are-bots-spam-inactive-or-propaganda/.

199. Beatrice Dupuy, "Are Donald Trump's Followers Real? Almost Half Could Be Fake, a Report Found," *Newsweek*, October 26, 2017, http://www.newsweek.com/donald-trumps-twitter-following-could-be-fake-694231.

200. SparkToro, "The Problem with Follower Count," sparktoro.com, accessed December 3, 2020, https://sparktoro.com/tools/fake-followers-audit.

201. Maria Tenor, "Ariana Renee, Influencer with More than 2mill. Followers Fails in the Sale of 36 Shirts," Highxtar, May 29, 2019, https://highxtar.com/ariana-renee-influencer-with-more-than-2mill-followers-fails-in-the-sale-of-36-shirts/?lang=en.

202. Martinne Geller, "Unilever Takes Stand against Digital Media's Fake Followers," Yahoo Sports, June 18, 2018, https://sports.yahoo.com/unilever-takes-stand-against-digital-220100095.html.

Chapter 5: Fyre in the Hole

203. Case No: 06634, 24 July, 2018, Pages: 25, Court: UNITED STATES

DISTRICT COURT, Source file: PDF, URL: www.sec.gov/litigation/complaints/2018/comp-pr2018-141.pdf.

204. Author interview with MDavid Low, the product designer of Fyre, May 2017.

205. Case No: 06634, 24 July, 2018, Pages: 25, Court: UNITED STATES DISTRICT COURT, Source file: PDF, URL: www.sec.gov/litigation/complaints/2018/comp-pr2018-141.pdf.

206. Gabrielle Bluestone, "Fyre Festival Fraudster Billy McFarland Said He Scammed Everyone Because He's Bipolar. Prosecutors Say He's a Liar," VICE News, October 4, 2018, https://www.vice.com/en/article/vbkpxd/fyre-festival-fraudster-billy-mcfarland-said-he-scammed-everyone-because-hes-bipolar-prosecutors-say-hes-a-liar.

207. Case No: 06634, 24 July, 2018, Pages: 25, Court: UNITED STATES DISTRICT COURT, Source file: PDF, URL: www.sec.gov/litigation/complaints/2018/comp-pr2018-141.pdf.

208. Dennis Green, "The Organizers of the Doomed Fyre Festival are Now Facing a Lawsuit from Lenders Who Allege They're Missing Millions," Business Insider, May 15, 2017, https://www.businessinsider.com/fyre-festival-organizers-sued-by-lender-2017-5.

209. Mara Siegler and Emily Smith, "A-Listers Told to Avoid Ja Rule Music Fest before Disaster Hit," Page Six, April 28, 2017, https://pagesix.com/2017/04/28/a-listers-told-to-avoid-disastrous-fyre-festival-before-it-began/.

210. Laura Italiano, "Medics: We Got Burned by Fyre Festival Too," Page Six, May 6, 2017, https://pagesix.com/2017/05/05/medics-we-got-burned-by-fyre-festival-too/.

Chapter 6: On the Internet No One Knows You're a Fraud

211. Andrea Park, "Caroline Calloway's 'Creativity Workshop' Taught Me Nothing About Creativity, But a Lot About Scamming," W Magazine

News, January 14, 2019, https://www.wmagazine.com/story/caroline-calloway-creativity-workshop/.

212. Katherine Rosman, "Everyone Writes. But is Everyone a Writer?" *New York Times*, September 18, 2019, sec. Style,https://www.nytimes.com/2019/09/18/style/all-the-writers-workshops.html.

213. Sophie Lewis, "How Instagram Influencer Caroline Calloway's World Tour Fell Apart," CBS News, January 19, 2019, http://www.cbsnews.com/news/how-instagram-influencer-caroline-calloways-world-tour-fell-apart/.

214. Kayleigh Donaldson (@Ceilidhann), "Further update: The 'influencer' sold out her seminars! So she's netting a gross profit of like $15k (more than my annual wage), so pardon me if I spend today feeling like hard work and talent are a tad pointless." Twitter, December 21, 2018, https://twitter.com/Ceilidhann/status/1076056280601636864.

215. Ibid.

216. Kayleigh Donaldson, "The Empty Mason Jar of the Influencer Economy: The Case of Caroline Calloway and Her Creativity Workshop Tour," Pajiba, January 18, 2019, https://www.pajiba.com/web_culture/the-case-of-caroline-calloway-and-her-creativity-workshop-tour.php.

217. Ibid.

218. Kaitlyn Tiffany, "'Close Friends,' for a Monthly Fee," *The Atlantic*, September 17, 2019, http://www.theatlantic.com/technology/archive/2019/09/close-friends-instagram-subscription-charge-influencers/598171/.

219. Caroline Calloway (@carolinecaloway), "I fucked up. I said Part One would be 15,000 words, but it's actually 6,000. I wrote it in a Word doc with a bunch of other notes and I must not have selected the text properly when I checked the word count. My bad! Please accept this uncensored nude along with my humble apology", Twitter, April, 1, 2020, https://twitter.com/carolinecaloway/status/1245558978685407234?lang=en.

220. Author interview with Dr. Garth Fisher, a Beverly Hills plastic surgeon, February 2020.

221. Author interview with Dana Omari, a registered dietician, April 2020.

Chapter 7: The Fyre Next Time

222. Case No: 18 MAG. 5026, n.d, 'US .v. William McFarland,' Court: UNITED STATES DISTRICT COURT.

223. Andrew Gowdy, "Fyre Festival Founder Billy McFarland Wants Out of Prison," *5 Magazine*, April 16, 2020, https://5mag.net/news/fyre-festival-founder-prison-coronavirus/.

224. Case No: 18 MAG. 5026, n.d., 'US v. William McFarland,' Court: UNITED STATES DISTRICT COURT, Source file: PDF, URL: www.justice.gov/usao-sdny/press-release/file/1071186/download.

225. Vanessa Friedman, "Everything You Need to Know About the Met Gala 2017," *New York Times*, April 30, 2017, sec. Fashion, https://www.nytimes.com/2017/04/30/fashion/everything-you-need-to-know-about-the-met-gala.html.

226. Case No: 18 MAG. 5026, n.d., 'US .v. William McFarland,' Court: UNITED STATES DISTRICT COURT, Source file: PDF, URL: www.justice.gov/usao-sdny/press-release/file/1071186/download.

227. Geoffrey S. Berman, "Manhattan U.S. Attorney Announces Charges Against Individual For Engaging in a Fraudulent Ticket Scam and Laundering Proceeds of the Fraud," www.justice.gov, June 12, 2018, https://www.justice.gov/usao-sdny/pr/manhattan-us-attorney-announces-charges-against-individual-engaging-fraudulent-ticket.

228. Geoffrey S. Berman, "Manhattan U.S. Attorney Announces Charges Against Individual For Engaging in a Fraudulent Ticket Scam and Laundering Proceeds if the Fraud," www.justice.gov, June 12, 2018, https://www.justice.gov/usao-sdny/pr/manhattan-us-attorney-announces-charges-against-individual-engaging-fraudulent-ticket.

229. Suhauna Hussain, "'Please Disregard, Vote for Bernie': Inside Bloom-

berg's Paid Social Media Army," *Los Angeles Times*, February 23, 2020, http://www.latimes.com/business/technology/story/2020-02-23/mike-bloomberg-paid-twitter-social media.

230. Makena Kelly, "Twitter Suspends 70 Pro–Michael Bloomberg Accounts for 'Platform Manipulation,'" The Verge, February 22, 2020, https://www.theverge.com/2020/2/22/21148516/twitter-suspends-mike-bloomberg-facebook-google-platform-manipulation.

231. Isabelle Lichtenstein, "Observational Comedy: We're Just Kind of Riffing Now," ObservationalComedy.Substack.com, February 24, 2020, https://observationalcomedy.substack.com/p/observational-comedy-were-just-kind.

232. Author interview with Amol Jethwani, a Florida Democrat who worked as a field organizer on the Bloomberg campaign, July 2020.

233. Tarini Parti and Lukas I. Alpert, "The Bloomberg Effect: Huge Spending Transforms 2020 Campaign Dynamics," *Wall Street Journal*, January 16, 2020, https://www.wsj.com/articles/the-bloomberg-effect-huge-spending-transforms-2020-campaign-dynamics-11579191368.

234. Rebecca R. Ruiz, "Ex-Field Organizers Sue Bloomberg Campaign, Claiming They Were Misled," *New York Times*, March 23, 2020, sec. US, https://www.nytimes.com/2020/03/23/us/politics/bloomberg-employee-lawsuit.html.

235. Maura Barrett and Josh Lederman, "Bloomberg to pay laid-off staffers' health care through November amid lawsuits, public pressure," NBC News, December 16 2019, https://www.nbcnews.com/politics/meet-the-press/blog/meet-press-blog-latest-news-analysis-data-driving-political-discussion-n988541/ncrd1193551#blogHeader

Chapter 8: Covidiots

236. Teresa Roca, "Billy McFarland Apologizes for Fyre Festival Fraud and Begs Followers for Money for New Prison Project," *The Sun*, April 3, 2020, http://www.the-sun.com/entertainment/633254/billy-mcfarland-apologizes-fyre-festival-fraud-begs-money/.

237. Rebecca Rosenberg, "Fyre Fest's Billy McFarland Shouldn't Be Freed Amid Outbreak: Prosecutors," Page Six, April 28, 2020, https://pagesix.com/2020/04/28/billy-mcfarland-shouldnt-be-freed-amid-coronavirus-prosecutors/.

238. Doree Lewak, "Fyre Fest Fraudster Billy McFarland Contracts COVID-19 in Prison," *New York Post*, July 4, 2020, https://nypost.com/2020/07/04/fyre-fest-fraudster-billy-mcfarland-contracts-covid-19-in-prison.

239. Sarah Tulloch, "Jamie Dornan Addresses Backlash Over 'Cringeworthy' Celebrity Cover of John Lennon's Imagine," *Belfast Telegraph*, April 8, 2020, https://www.belfasttelegraph.co.uk/entertainment/news/jamie-dornan-addresses-backlash-over-cringeworthy-celebrity-cover-of-john-lennons-imagine-39113711.html.

Conclusion

240. Samantha Schnurr, "WeWoreWhat's Danielle Bernstein Addresses Claim She Copied Design From Mask Brand," E! Online, 2020, https://www.eonline.com/news/1172444/weworewhats-danielle-bernstein-addresses-claim-she-copied-design-from-mask-brand.

241. Maria Sherman, "WeWoreWhat's Danielle Bernstein is Suing a Small Business After Allegedly Stealing Yet Another Design," Jezebel, October 19, 2020, https://jezebel.com/weworewhats-danielle-bernstein-is-suing-a-small-busines-1845411916.

242. Will Oremus (@WillOremus), "From a societal standpoint, having PR staff is a form of accountability, allowing for the negotiation of a shared set of facts between the company and the media. The absence of PR staff leaves the strategy as one of hype, propaganda, and fostering mistrust of all media reports," Twitter, October 6, 2020, https://twitter.com/willoremus/status/1313491326265155585.

243. Sridhar Natarajan and Amanda L Gordon, "Hamptons Concert Turns Into Lightning Rod After Cuomo Vows Probe," *Bloomberg*, July 28, 2020, https://www.bloomberg.com/news/articles/2020-07-28/hamptons-concert-with-goldman-ceo-chainsmokers-faces-n-y-probe.

244. Marina Villeneuve, Associated Press, "'Appalled' Cuomo to Investigate Crowded Chainsmokers Concert," ABC News, July 29, 2020, https://abcnews.go.com/Entertainment/wireStory/appalled-cuomo-investigate-crowded-chainsmokers-concert-72030374.

245. Jem Aswad, "Chainsmokers Promoter Fined $20,000 for Non-Socially-Distanced Hamptons Concert," Reuters, October 14, 2020, https://www.reuters.com/article/variety/chainsmokers-promoter-fined-20000-for-non-socially-distanced-hamptons-concert-idUSL4N2H53MQ.

246. Reuters, "Goldman Sachs CEO's 2019 Compensation Rises 19%," Reuters, March 21, 2020, https://www.reuters.com/article/us-goldman-sachs-compensation-ceo/goldman-sachs-ceos-2019-compensation-rises-19-idUSKBN2173L5.

247. AFP-Agence France Presse, "NY Governor Pans Concert Where Goldman Sachs CEO Performed," *Barrons*, July 28, 2020, https://www.barrons.com/news/ny-governor-pans-concert-where-goldman-sachs-ceo-performed-01595962805.

248. *Travel + Leisure*, n.d., https://www.travelandleisure.com/a-list/lia-batkin.

249. Nicole Barylski, "INTERVIEW: In the Know Experiences Co-Founder Seth Kaplan on the Hamptons 'Safe & Sound' Benefit Concert Featuring The Chainsmokers and More," *Hamptons.Com*, accessed December 4, 2020, https://www.hamptons.com/mobile/Community/Community-News/26727/Out-And-About/For-The-Cause/26695/INTERVIEW-In-The-Know-Experiences-Co-Founder.html#.X8lfgTozbDd.

250. Olivia Messer, "Americans Should Brace for 100,000 New COVID Cases a Day, Experts Say," *The Daily Beast*, October 25, 2020, https://www.thedailybeast.com/americans-should-brace-for-100000-new-covid-cases-a-day-experts-say.